Justice in a Time of War

JUSTICE
in a Time of War

THE TRUE STORY
BEHIND THE
INTERNATIONAL
CRIMINAL TRIBUNAL
FOR THE FORMER
YUGOSLAVIA

By Pierre Hazan

Translated from the French by
James Thomas Snyder

Foreword by
M. Cherif Bassiouni

Texas A&M University Press
College Station

Eugenia and Hugh M. Stewart '26
Series on Eastern Europe
Stjepan Meštrović, General Editor

The paper used in this book meets the minimum requirements
of the American National Standard for Permanence
of Paper for Printed Library Materials, Z39.48-1984.
Binding materials have been chosen for durability.
∞

Hazan, Pierre
    [Justice face à la guerre. English]
    Justice in a time of war : the true story behind the International
    Criminal Tribunal for the Former Yugoslavia / by Pierre Hazan ;
    translated from the French by James Thomas Snyder ; foreword
    by M. Cherif Bassiouni.—1st ed.
        p.   cm. — (Eugenia and Hugh M. Stewart '26 series on
        Eastern Europe)
    Includes bibliographical references and index.
    ISBN 1-58544-377-8 (cloth : alk. paper)—
    ISBN 1-58544-411-1 (pbk. : alk. paper)
    1. International Tribunal for the Prosecution of Persons
Responsible for Serious Violations of International Humanitarian
Law Committed in the Territory of the Former Yugoslavia since
1919—History. 2. International criminal courts—History.
3. Yugoslav War Crime Trials, Hague, Netherlands, 1994–
I. Title. II. Series.
KZ1203.A2H39 2004
341.6'9'0268—dc22
                          2004007211

Originally published as *La Justice face à la guerre: de Nuremberg à La
Haye* (Paris: Stock, 2000)

For my children

CONTENTS

FOREWORD

M. Cherif Bassiouni

The tension between *realpolitik* and justice has existed in every society since time immemorial, and it also manifested itself in the context of the conflict in the former Yugoslavia. Unlike earlier historic conflicts in which realpolitik ultimately prevailed, in this conflict justice prevailed. Admittedly, it was not so at all times throughout the conflict, nor can it be said that the cup of justice overflowed. But it is by all means a cup more than half full. To understand the significance of this accomplishment as well as the obstacles conquered along the way, it is necessary to assess it in light of modern efforts at establishing international criminal justice.

The first efforts followed World War I, when the pursuit of post-conflict justice was sacrificed to political considerations. The German kaiser was not prosecuted, notwithstanding a Treaty of Versailles provision that required it. Most European governments were not willing to have a precedent established that their heads of states, especially monarchs, would be held criminally accountable. The United States and Japan strongly dissented from the recommendations of a report released in 1919 by a commission investigating responsibility for the war and crimes committed during its course. Among those recommendations was prosecuting Turkish officials for crimes against the "laws of humanity." The prosecution of Turkish officials for the Armenian massacre of 1915 had been specified in the Treaty of Sèvres of 1920, but that effort was abandoned when it became obvious to the European allies that Turkey was an essential bulwark against the new bolshevik government of Russia. As a result, the Treaty of Lausanne of 1922 was signed, and it contained an unpublished appendix giving amnesty to all Turkish officials. As a result of these and other political machinations, there were no international prosecutions for war crimes. Instead, a few Germans were tried before the supreme court of Germany in 1922–23. The Leipzig trials, named for the city where the supreme court sat, tried only 12 persons, of whom 6 were convicted. Considering that the 1919 Commission had recommended the prosecution of 20,000 and that when the allies had agreed to defer to the German supreme court they had presented a list of 895 persons to be prosecuted, the limited number of those actually prosecuted demonstrates how seriously justice was compromised.

The next stage for post-conflict justice was after World War II, when the cause of international criminal justice was significantly advanced, albeit evidencing one-sidedness and many flaws. The International Military Tribunal at Nuremberg, the International Military Tribunal for the Far East in Tokyo, and Allied prosecutions in their respective German-occupied areas as well as throughout the Pacific reveal that no member of the victorious Allied forces was prosecuted for war crimes. This situation led many to call the prosecutions that were carried out "victor's justice." While no one can doubt the responsibility of those brought to trial at Nuremberg and the relative fairness of those proceedings, there is ample doubt as to whether a number of those brought to trial at Tokyo indeed merited such a fate. Moreover, the Tokyo tribunal left much to be desired in terms of procedural fairness, even by comparison to its Nuremberg counterpart, which was far from flawless. But it was particularly the subsequent proceedings in Japan that lacked substantive and procedural fairness. One case in particular, that of General Tomoyuki Yamashita, who was tried by an American military commission, was a miscarriage of justice. General Douglas MacArthur wanted to make an example of a Japanese general, and he used all his influence to achieve a result that was both substantively and procedurally wrong. In this case, justice was clearly abused for political reasons.

During the period between World War II and 1991, when the war in the former Yugoslavia began, international criminal justice was put on hold. This was due to the cold war, which left little room for East and West to agree on something as laden with moral and ethical significance as international criminal justice.

During the half century that followed World War II, the world experienced more than 250 conflicts of all types, taking place on almost every continent. These conflicts produced twice as many casualties as World Wars I and II combined. The low estimates of these conflicts put figures at 70 million persons killed, yet the international community was unable or unwilling to respond with any justice initiative. As a result, most of the perpetrators, in particular the senior decision-makers, benefited from impunity.

But during that same half century, as government officials accommodated themselves to the ongoing practice of impunity and the continued exercise of realpolitik to the exclusion of international criminal justice, international civil society increased its opposition to violent *raison d'état*. But the ability of international civil society to influence governments was limited. However, the emergence of globalization gave international civil society greater influence over governments' realpolitik practices in connection with international criminal justice.

The conflict in the former Yugoslavia and the efforts to assign international criminal responsibility to its senior leaders and worst perpetrators of "crimes against humanity" and "war crimes" reflect the classic historic tensions between realpolitik and justice. At first the Europeans, especially the British and the French, wanted to find a diplomatic solution to the disintegration of the Federal Republic of Yugoslavia. More particularly, the United Kingdom saw the problem in terms of a popular English tale about an egg-shaped personage called Humpty Dumpty who was sitting on a wall but fell and broke into several pieces. The tale goes on about trying to put Humpty Dumpty back together and upon the wall once again. But the former Yugoslavia, like the egg-shaped Humpty Dumpty, could not be put together again, and thus another outcome was needed. But the major powers, the United States in particular, preferred to look the other way in the hope that the conflict would either go away or end faster than world public opinion could react to it.

In the meantime, however, ethnic cleansing, unconscionable conditions in prison camps, systematic rape, and other serious crimes were taking place and could not be covered up. One of the consequences of globalization is instant communication and worldwide dissemination of information. Consequently, the world became a witness to daily atrocities that Europe had thought it would never see again. Something had to be done. The United States under President Bill Clinton had at first shown a willingness to be involved militarily, but under the influence of then–Secretary of State Warren Christopher and General Colin Powell, who was chairman of the Joint Chiefs of Staff, the Clinton administration backed away from any military involvement. The British and French troops on the ground were split up into small units hardly capable of defending themselves, let alone constituting a threat to the dominant Serb forces. Both Britain and France could have but were unwilling to commit their total military forces to what would become another European war.

In the midst of this political maelstrom the United States, mostly through the efforts of its United Nations ambassador at the time, Madeleine Albright, came up with an idea reminiscent of Nuremberg. A Security Council commission would be established to record the crimes committed by all sides and also to refocus world public attention on that aspect of the conflict, as opposed to the major powers' inability to solve it. Albright and the leadership of the United Nations' nonaligned states forged ahead with this idealistic plan, and they succeeded: In October, 1992, the Security Council established the Commission of Experts to investigate "crimes against humanity" and "war crimes" committed during the conflict. But even in naming the commission, realpolitik played its role. The commission could have been called a war crimes commission or something of that sort to convey the moral significance of its mandate. Instead, it was called the Commission of Experts Established Pursuant to Security Council Resolution 780 of 1992. Even though its name was innocuous, the commission's mandate gave it the broadest international investigative authority since the United Nations War Crimes Commission, which was established during World War II.

No sooner was the commission established than it became evident that no resources would be allocated to it. At that time, on behalf of the European Union (EU) and the United Nations, Lord David Owen and Cyrus Vance, a former U.S. secretary of state, were conducting negotiations to bring about an end to the conflict. Owen and Vance had for all practical purposes no carrot and no stick to produce the desired diplomatic result. Certainly the negotiators could dangle before Serbia and Croatia the distant carrot of future membership in the EU and brandish the stick of making the two combatants (particularly Serbia) world-class pariahs. But that was hardly enough. The diplomats could, however, offer legitimacy to Serbia by annexing parts of Bosnia, which would become merely a loose conglomeration of enclaves without much hope for economic or political viability. To accomplish this and other aspects of the Owen-Vance plan, it was necessary to show that all sides were morally equivalent. Thus, no side should appear as having committed "crimes against humanity" and "war crimes" against the other. An investigative commission would certainly not make things easier, particularly if it highlighted the victimization of the Bosnians at the hands of the Serbs, since the victims would pay the price of a political settlement. Surely it would have been impossible for Owen and Vance to negotiate with Slobodan Milosevic, Radovan Karadzic, Ratko Mladic, and Franjo Tudjman, if some or all would have been the subject of an international criminal investigation, let alone if such an investigation produced evidence of their criminality. Nevertheless, while Owen and Vance advanced the proposition of "equal moral blameworthiness," Secretary of State Lawrence Eagleburger of the United States denounced Milosevic and the Serbs for crimes against the Bosnians.

For the realpolitik exponents, the Commission of Experts was intended to serve the purpose of appeasing world public opinion. Its existence suggested that something was being done to seek justice, but at the same time the commission had to be on a short leash to prevent it from having any detrimental effect on the Owen-Vance negotiations. Little did the planners of this scenario anticipate that I, as chairman of the commission, would manage to work around it by finding the necessary resources and conducting the proper investigations, which later led to the establishment of the International Criminal Tribunal for the Former Yugoslavia (ICTY), and now the prosecution of Milosevic. Surprisingly, it had never occurred to those who feared that the commission could become a "loose cannon on deck" that it might prove to be quite responsible. In fact, at no time during the commission's two years of existence, nor up to now, has a single item of evidence collected during its investigations been leaked to the public or made public in any other way. This international criminal investigation was one that was conducted and concluded with absolute confidentiality and utmost professionalism. But at the time, the *realpoliticiens* feared it.

The work of the commission led to the establishment of the ICTY. The evidence collected by the commission was turned over to the ICTY's first prosecutor, Richard Goldstone. But that action too has its own little story, revealing how the realpolitik exponents' resistance to justice can be reduced to the pettiest levels. That story began in August, 1993, when U.N. Secretary-General Boutros Boutros-Ghali nominated me to be the prosecutor of the ICTY. The United Kingdom led the opposition, and an informal vote of the Security Council revealed a division of 7 to 7, with one abstention. Presumably, a 9-to-6 vote on the second round could have been obtained, but the United States, which had voted in my favor on the first round, preferred to accommodate the United Kingdom and agreed that instead of an election by vote, the candidate would be elected by consensus. The reason given by a high UK source and published in the *New York Times* was that I was too victim-oriented (presumably favoring the Bosnians) and thus biased because I was a Muslim. Any comment I might make on such a position would be superfluous. After that, however, it took fourteen months from the date of my nomination's rejection to the time when Richard Goldstone took office in The Hague. After he was appointed, no efforts were made to connect both of us so that he could benefit from my work, experience, and members of my staff who were willing to work on his staff. Once again, I bypassed official channels and reached out to him directly, and he was most receptive. He arrived in The Hague on a Friday, and I arrived on Sunday, when we had our first meeting. On Monday he went to his spotless, antiseptic new office, only to find out that he did not even have a map of the former Yugoslavia. Fortunately, I had brought maps, as well as the necessary information for him and his staff to get started with. Our relationship was friendly and cordial, as it remains today.

Goldstone soon had to face the same problems I encountered with some in the United Nations bureaucracy who were more attuned to the call of realpolitik than to the cause of justice. Goldstone overcame it more adroitly than

I did, and he deserves much credit for giving credibility to his office and for re-inforcing world public opinion's belief in justice. But if the commission's documents had not been made available to him in a timely fashion, his work would have been delayed and the progress of justice slowed.

Realpolitik was still, however, the prevailing practice, and the 1995 Dayton Accords reflect it, though only for those who know the background of the accords more intimately. Inasmuch as one can criticize these accords, they nonetheless must be lauded for bringing about a settlement to the war, notwithstanding General Ratko Mladic's unexpected butchery in Srebrenica in July, 1995, when he ordered the slaughter of seven thousand Bosnians who had surrendered or who were civilians. Their deaths were blamed on the failure of the Dutch battalion assigned to the protection of this United Nations "safe haven." The battalion had only four hundred men carrying light sidearms, and their request for reinforcement by the area commander, General Bernard Janvier of France, had been denied, as had air support from the North Atlantic Treaty Organization (NATO), which the beleaguered Dutch had requested. The inside story has it that General Janvier was ordered to act that way by one of the highest authorities in his government because the pre-signing of the Dayton Accords secretly allowed the Serbs to enlarge the territorial corridor between Srebrenica and Brcko on the Bosnian side of the Drina River. This was to be the payback for letting the Croatians remove the Serbs from the Krajina without Milosevic renewing hostilities with the Croatians. That was the deal. The Croatians, with U.S. help, played their part flawlessly, but Mladic did not.

The Dayton Accords had, among others, two components relevant to this book. The first is that they tacitly condoned the ethnic cleansing of Serbs in Croatia and of Bosnians in certain parts of Bosnia. The carefully orchestrated military-political maneuvers, of which the most significant was the Croatian army's removal of some 200,000 Serbs in the Krajina after the United States had trained and re-equipped the Croatian army, were probably the most extraordinary feat, but they were hardly just.

Had it not been for the Srebrenica massacre, the Dayton Accords would have been heralded as one of the post–World War II era's most successful political negotiations to end a civil conflict.

The second component relevant to this book was that the Dayton Accords preserved the appearance that no deal was made with any of the protagonists to interfere with the justice processes of the ICTY. That, too, was an extraordinary accomplishment, considering the circumstances. Radovan Karadzic, the former president of the rump Bosnian Serb republic, was under indictment and in hiding, as was General Ratko Mladic, the head of that republic's army, who was also officially on the rolls of Serbia's army and who was a trusted and loyal supporter of Milosevic, the president of Serbia, who was after all the architect of the wars in Croatia and Bosnia.

Presumably Milosevic was promised some sort of de facto impunity and was also assured that his cronies, Karadzic and Mladic, would not be arrested. All the facts lead to that conclusion, though nothing so far has turned up to prove that assumption. Certainly neither Karadzic nor Mladic has been arrested to date, but presumably their time will come. Milosevic himself was safe until he made the mistake of trying to repeat in Kosovo what he had failed to accomplish in Bosnia, namely, ethnic cleansing. On his instructions, the Serb army and security forces engaged in a rapid and massive ethnic cleansing of Albanian Kosovars and briefly succeeded in expelling some 800,000 people in less than a month. But this time he did not count on President Clinton's resolve or that of NATO to stop him before he could reignite war in the Balkans. Having crossed the line, Milosevic was beyond the pale of whatever undisclosed protection the Dayton Accords may have included for him. As his days of political viability dwindled, with opposing Serb political forces gaining ground against him, he was ousted from power.

After Milosevic's Kosovo invasion and the loss of whatever tacit immunity he may have gotten as a result of agreeing to the Dayton Accords, he was indicted by the ICTY's second prosecutor, Louise Arbour, but only for crimes committed in Kosovo. Many were surprised that the Arbour indictment was so narrow and so limited, and many started to ask why it did not include crimes committed in Bosnia or Croatia. Those questions led to another: Why had Goldstone not returned earlier on an indictment against Milosevic for crimes committed during the conflict in Croatia and Bosnia? All these questions remained unanswered until shortly after the Serb government turned Milosevic over to ICTY custody. The ICTY's third prosecutor, Carla Del Ponte, then returned two additional indictments against him: one pertaining to crimes committed in Croatia and the other, to crimes committed in Bosnia. It took her six months to produce these indictments because, as she mentioned to me and presumably to others, her predecessors had not prepared files containing such evidence, even though the report, annexes, and evidence of the Commission of Experts contained enough material to show that Milosevic was responsible for many crimes in Croatia and Bosnia under the theory of command responsibility. If nothing else, the siege and bombardment of the city of Sarajevo for three years offered a prime case for command responsibility. Interestingly, since the beginning of Milosevic's trial, he has asked to have former U.N. ambassador Richard Holbrooke, the architect of the Dayton Accords, testify in his case. The latter has so far managed to avoid being called as a witness in that trial.

Pierre Hazan was one of the journalists who followed the war and devastation in the former Yugoslavia with intense intellectual and emotional commitment. He wrote many articles in Swiss and French newspapers. He also watched, from close proximity in Geneva, the Owen-Vance negotiations that brought to his town the entire cast of characters of the time, including Milosevic, Karadzic, Tudjman, Alija Izetbegovic, and the infamous General Mladic. Of these, Tudjman is dead, Izetbegovic retired, Milosevic is on trial, and Karadzic and Mladic are indicted fugitives. This intense involvement with the events that convulsed the former Yugoslavia is what led to this book.

During the conflict, Hazan interviewed many of those involved in the negotiations and others, including myself as chairman of the Commission on Experts. He was among those journalists in Europe and the United States who consistently sought to peel from tragic events the deceiving layers of stories placed there by politicians, including the lack of commitment by major governments to do what needed to be done to bring that conflict to an end. Like other journalists who covered these events, Hazan sought to draw clearly the lessons of that story, and that is what this book is all about. It is not a detailed description of the conflict in the former Yugoslavia, nor a blow-by-blow account of all its parts. Instead, it is intended to capture the essential facts of how realpolitik suffused the major events that marked this conflict. It is in some respects a bird's-eye view of realpolitik's road map, described in straightforward and simple terms. In the style of many contemporary political historians, Hazan describes history through specific facts and events, which the reader should find easy to relate to and understand.

Such works are indispensable supplements to our records of human tragedies and more valuable still because they show why such tragedies occurred and why they were allowed to become what they were. There should be no doubt in anyone's mind that "genocide," "crimes against humanity," "war crimes," and the unseen tragedy of modern slavery in the form of trafficking in women and children for commercial sexual exploitation are not only the product of those who commit these crimes but also of those whose indifference allows these crimes to be committed.

Books like this one are intended to shake our complacency and to shock our conscience so as to make indifference impossible, if that is possible, but at least a little more difficult the next time we are faced with a tragedy like the war in the former Yugoslavia, Rwanda, Sierra Leone, Liberia, or Cambodia. I could go on and on to name the 250 conflicts since World War II that have brought about immense human tragedies while we watched impassively. Indeed, as I write this foreword, the tragedy of the Great Lakes region of southern Africa and the Congo goes on unnoticed and seldom reported, while Charles Taylor of Liberia lives comfortably in Nigeria because the United States refused to send troops there to end the civil war in Liberia and apprehend him. For the same reason, Raoul Cedras of Haiti now lives happily in Panama. If Haiti and Liberia, or for that matter Sierra Leone, Congo, East Timor, and Cambodia, had as much oil as Iraq, the United States would have been the champion of regime change in these countries, heralding to the world its commitment to bring criminal leaders to justice. But realpolitik is still stronger than the commitment of governments to international criminal justice. This situation is still evident in Iraq, where a number of major offenders have yet to face justice.

When Pierre Hazan says in his introduction that he wrote this book because he wanted to "understand," what he is trying to do is to make others understand what paradoxically can never be understood. Politics compromises justice, and the interests of state trump those of justice. But the struggle for justice goes on because there are some who will not give up the fight for justice.

It is therefore my great personal pleasure to contribute this foreword to Pierre Hazan's book and to express to him and through him, to the journalists of the world whose consciences, like his, have caused the world to be more aware of the tragedies that *realpoliticiens* would rather we forget about. Regrettably, these politicians fail to see that without justice, there can be no lasting peace after bloody and violent conflicts. Great tragedies like the Holocaust and other lesser ones cannot be forgiven or forgotten. Only retributive and restorative justice can bring some form of closure to these tragedies. That is why we owe it to the victims, as well as to humanity itself, to remember and to keep on calling for justice, while simultaneously rejecting the political deals that give impunity to the perpetrators of these massive crimes.

The struggle for justice continues with the International Criminal Court, but it still has a long way to go, and we need more journalists like Pierre Hazan to record and to remind us, so that to paraphrase George Santayana, we may learn the lessons of our past in order not to repeat our mistakes in the future.

PREFACE

This book was born of my need to understand. In Rwanda, in Bosnia, in Kosovo and elsewhere, I, like many others, witnessed the horror in the wake of appalling crimes. I remember the old man, decapitated, and the women crying beside a pile of bodies whose faces had been shot off. I remember the aftermath of a massacre one bright Friday in mid-January, 1999, in Kosovo, the resigned faces of relatives, only fear holding back their anger. Such memories are born out of violence and hate, ineluctable horror, the spreading culture of the Kalashnikov, and traumas bestowed by one generation upon another.

Then I remembered the words of a Rwandan priest, Abbé Modeste Mungwareba. During the genocide in his country, Abbé Modeste hid for nine days in his church's sacristy. "I read and reread the Book of Jeremiah, the chapter 'Lamentations,'" he told me. "All around me, I heard cries, death roaming. I said to myself, 'If they find me, I will keep talking to them until they kill me. I will ask them, "Have you gone insane? Have you lost all reason?"'"[1]

"I was very frightened. So frightened I could not breathe. I was all knotted up. I lay down so that I could breathe. But it is not then that you lose faith. It is after, thinking of the hardness of hearts, of the resistance to truth, the forgetting of crimes, that you begin to doubt man and God both. But if someday I come across a killer who says to me, 'Listen, Modeste, I was the one who killed your father,' I will break down and cry: I will say to myself, 'This man has returned to humanity. He has come back to the surface.'"[2]

How does one "come back to the surface" after the abyss of a genocide? Of a civil war? How does one confront the Other? How does one live with the mutilated and amputated pieces of one's being? How does one accept this "gray zone" evoked by Primo Levi, the blurred frontier between victim and executioner inside a man, reminding us of the barbarism that we all, undoubtedly, carry within ourselves? Above all, how do we live together in the aftermath?

As described by Abbé Modeste, the idea of humanity itself is attacked and rent. Yet the hope remains, after all, that the executioner will recognize his crime, that this recognition will bring him back into the human community. Even independent of differing religions, the great majority of victims agree on one thing: that they must speak out for truth and justice before any reconstruction is possible. Only through witnessing can they, perhaps, recover their wounded dignity in their own eyes. Only by exposing the truth can they one day occupy the same geographic space as the killers without being constantly tormented by hate and the thirst for vengeance.

From this tragedy comes not only hope but also profound questions about the emerging international court discussed here. I remember the widows of Srebrenica who, reversing our roles, asked me, "Do you yourself believe in it, in The Hague tribunal?" Their hope and their questions sent me to examine the work of the International Criminal Tribunal for the Former Yugoslavia (ICTY). The international community was presenting the tribunal as a tool to help break the cycle of violence, vengeance, and hate. As an instrument of dissuasion and to prevent conflicts. As impartial justice, abetting reconciliation among peoples. In short, the dawn, at last, of an international judiciary so long desired.

I wanted to understand the impact of this instrument, so essential for the victims and at the same time such an innovation in the field of international relations. As a journalist, I had followed the interminable diplomatic negotiations on the former Yugoslavia and traveled several times to the different republics during the war. So I was present at the birth of The Hague tribunal. This experience, no doubt, helped me to observe close up the unprecedented dialectic mingling war and justice, morality and politics. How, in a world of realpolitik, would the hope for justice and truth be shaped by the international community? What ulterior motives, calculations, and state policies lay behind the speeches, to create history's first truly international tribunal? To what degree did the states intend to give free rein to the Office of the Prosecutor? Can a tribunal, created at the will of the United Nations Security Council, become truly autonomous, truly independent of all political pressure, and even turn on its own founding fathers? Can international justice be transplanted into a culture where it is a truly foreign concept and be expected to engender national reconciliation?

These questions appear to me all the more important now that The Hague tribunal today stands as the most advanced entity in the emerging reality of international criminal jurisprudence. Some fifty years after the Allied military tribunals at Nuremberg, The Hague tribunal has sparked a revolution in international criminal law, most notably in the prosecution of General Augusto Pinochet and the establishment of the International Criminal Court, charged now with redressing the most abominable crimes.

But as dominant as it is, The Hague model is not the only one. South Africa explored the idea of "amnesty without amnesia" through its Truth and Reconciliation Commission. The equivalent of national psychoanalysis, this commission, no doubt, aided the birth of that new nation. Twenty thousand victims of the apartheid regime testified, as did hundreds of killers and other faithful executors of orders.

Certainly for Bosnia and South Africa, neither the history nor the context is the same. But beyond the singularity of the situations, what paths are best taken so that shattered societies may find their way back to a life together? Obviously, the stakes are not insignificant today. The question goes far beyond morality, although morality is important in itself. Civil war is our contemporary form of war, and no thinking on regional security can now exclude any social engineering that holds this violence in check, to whatever small degree. For this reason, it appears to me essential to learn from the work of the International Criminal Tribunal for the Former Yugoslavia. Did it achieve its objectives? Was it able to free itself of political influence? Did it succeed in grafting a "transplanted" justice onto a society where it was foreign? These are the questions I wanted answers to, and answering them is the goal of this book.

ACKNOWLEDGMENTS

I cannot mention all those—they are too numerous—who helped me, whether it was by their personal experience or by their reflection, to better understand and explore the different themes dealt with in this book.

I would like, however, to name some people who by their remarks and suggestions enriched the manuscript.

In particular I must thank Emmanuelle Michel and Yaël Reinharz Hazan for their collaboration.

Similarly, I must express my gratitude for their precious aid to Yolanda Jacquemet, Yves Laplace, Luis Lema, Nicolas Levrat, Marc Semo, and Valérie Frey, without forgetting, of course, Dzevad Osmanovic, translator and friend, with whom I crisscrossed Bosnia-Herzegovina. I would also like to express my thanks to James Thomas Snyder and Sarah Veal, without whom this book would not have crossed the Atlantic Ocean.

—Pierre Hazan

My greatest thanks go to Pierre Hazan for accepting an unsolicited letter from an American law student who proposed to translate this book for an English-language audience.

My family and friends, especially my wife Lorelei and brother Jason, were wonderful as always and more than tolerated my preoccupation with this project. Paul R. Williams supported the book from the start. Karen Smyth of the United Nations Information Agency and Amanda Williamson of the International Committee of the Red Cross, both in Washington, D.C., assisted me with document research. And Sarah Veal in Geneva provided invaluable aid by agreeing to review my translation and offering encouragement along the way. I cannot thank her enough. That said, of course, any errors in translation are mine alone.

—James Thomas Snyder

Justice in a Time of War

Introduction

Fiat Justitia ne pereat mundus.
[Let Justice be done so the world may not perish.]
— Georg W. F. Hegel, 1821

The Theater of Truth

66 "The Court will please rise." The bailiff repeats the phrase in French: "La Cour, veuillez-vous lever." The ritual is invariable. The three judges enter by a side door. They sit on a small platform framed by two flags of the United Nations. At an equal distance from the bench are the representatives of the prosecutor's office and the lawyers for the defense.

The International Criminal Tribunal for the Former Yugoslavia appears to be a trial under siege; a sheet of glass separates the public gallery from the court. The glass is not only a security screen but also a supplementary distance from the reality of Yugoslavia. It is not there just for looks, a symbolic reference to the trial of Otto Adolf Eichmann, one of the engineers of the Final Solution, famously locked in his glass cage during his 1963 trial in Jerusalem. For here at The Hague, in this old insurance company building become theater of truth, everyone is a potential target: the judges, the prosecutor, the defense attorneys, and the accused, of course. It is the price to pay for international justice *en vivo*.

The power and passions of the Balkans are far from appeased by this court. Here, the search for truth is a dangerous exercise. The Dutch secret service worries about "attempts to infiltrate the tribunal" by spies from the various Balkan states. One lawyer for the defense is held in contempt of court and barred from the tribunal for seeking to introduce false evidence and manipulating witnesses.[1] Close to the regime in Belgrade, this lawyer had worked in

3

effect against his own client's interests. Several attempted arrests have ended in bloodshed. Other accused men have been cut down by unknown assassins. NATO soldiers, still in Bosnia, are potential targets, as are the witnesses of the tribunal and their families. But these are not the only ones risking their lives. On March 12, 2003, Prime Minister Zoran Djindjic of Serbia was assassinated in Belgrade. The crime later proved to have been organized by members of the Serb police's Special Operations Unit (JSO), better known as the Red Berets, backed by a mafiosi clan. The determination of Zoran Djindjic to cooperate with the tribunal, and notably the key role that he played in the decision to arrest former Yugoslav president Slobodan Milosevic and transfer him to The Hague in 2001, was one of the triggers of his assassination by extremist elements within the Red Berets who opposed the arrest of Serbs sought by the tribunal.[2]

Certain sessions are closed. Many witnesses are "protected," testifying behind a screen that renders them anonymous to the public. If they feel threatened, they may be allowed to change their identities and immigrate to Great Britain, the United States, or elsewhere. Even some former members of the U.N. peacekeeping force, the Blue Helmets, some of whom are French, prefer discretion when bearing witness, both to avoid exposing their comrades in the Balkans to eventual reprisals and, no doubt, to avoid embarrassing their governments by revealing compromises reached with the belligerents during the war as well.

Security requirements are sometimes difficult to harmonize with the transparency demanded of such high-profile justice. Tiny video cameras are installed in each of the three hearing rooms to document and broadcast the trial. Sometimes they focus only on the hands of the protected witnesses, nothing more. Rugged peasant hands, hands of rape victims, smooth hands in white cuffs. Often these hands belong to victims of atrocities who are being heard here as witnesses for the prosecution at the risk of their lives.

The lighting, the decoration of the courtroom, even the choice of colors have been savvily chosen for media impact. The three trial chambers—an old cafeteria, the insurance company safe, and a meeting room—have become television studios. In each, six remote-controlled cameras record the deliberations. The rules are strict. The cameras focus first on the judges, then on the accused or on the lawyers. The photographer is forbidden to film public demonstrations, a judge or lawyer whispering in the ear of another, or a close-up of any document. The president of the court has a control screen and may interrupt the broadcast at any moment. He has never used this prerogative, but he retains the power of censorship nonetheless. By constructing the image of a tribunal marked by solemnity, emphasis is placed on the conscience and responsibility with which the international community has undertaken this work of memory and justice.

The images are public, broadcast almost live. The delay in transmission is hardly detectable: a lapse of twenty minutes is required to ensure that no confidential identity is divulged. Any television channel in the world may broadcast the unfolding trial. Private individuals, thanks to the Internet, can do the same in their own homes. In the translating booths, the interpreters translate the proceedings into the two official working languages, English and French, as well as Serbo-Croatian, now renamed with the politically correct term Bosnico-Croato-Serbe, or "BCS," as it is called here.

Such minutiae and extreme care given to the smallest details are explained by the ambition of the task. This international court, equipped with a budget of $100 million and eight hundred employees to judge a mere handful of individuals, aims to be a lesson to the world: the serene justice of The Hague set against the tumult of the Balkans, civilization founded on law juxtaposed against hatred and barbarity. But the stakes of the tribunal surpass even Yugoslavia, even the legitimate aspirations of the victims and of public opinion, for, ever since Auschwitz and Hiroshima, humanity has glimpsed its own extinction. In this world haunted by vulnerability, liberated from a cold war that had paradoxically checked its own demons, justice appears as both a hope and a barrier against the chaos unleashed by ideologies of hatred and destruction.

This book recounts the history of such a utopia—the dream of containing "the barbarity of the world in a hearing room," incarnated as The Hague tribunal.[3] This utopia would be marked by a gesture of rare daring: sealing the cracks of a world fissured after the explosion of nationalist and ethnic violence. But how? Through symbolic reparation: by offering to the victims the right to invoke before a tribunal the magnitude of the crimes committed against them and to punish those actions. As one witness put it, "to provide at last a coffin for the dead."[4]

But beyond the hopes of the victims and the high political rhetoric, what is this International Criminal Tribunal for the Former Yugoslavia? An instrument that allows Western governments to cleanse their bad consciences? A curtain to cover the hypocrisy of the U.N. Security Council? Or perhaps the first awkward steps toward a truly independent international court? These are the questions that this book tries to answer. Since its creation, the ICTY has been an antilogy, the bearer of all hopes and contradictions. For better or for worse, an extraordinary laboratory of international law is being born, the judicial side of globalism. Object of all pressures and desires, the tribunal is a mine field, for its work consists not only in judging the past but also in molding the present and the future. Among the objectives explicitly assigned to it by the U.N. Security Council is to contribute to the reestablishment of international peace and security. This objective is a first: justice before peace, in the service of peace, and not the other way around. "It is as if the tribunal of Nuremberg had begun its deliberations in 1944, when Hitler was in power and the war still raged," explains one investigator.[5]

This utopia will continue to be challenged by Western governments and their complicated agendas. These governments created this international court but have also cynically tried to use all means at their disposal to influence it: bureaucratic maneuvering, financial asphyxiation, political recruitment of personnel, pressures of all sorts, media manipulation, and so on. This paradox, too, is the subject of this book: the confrontation between two concurrent and contradictory logics of international relations, the relation of force buttressed by the principle of national sovereignty, now confronted by universal values of humanity intended to moralize international public life. In other words, the world ruled by *raison d'état* versus the rule of law.

To plunge into the political history of the tribunal is to plunge into the most elaborate laboratory of this transformation in international relations.

All we know is that we can neither punish nor forgive such
offenses and that they therefore transcend the realm of human
affairs and the potentialities of human power, both of which they
radically destroy where they make their appearance.
—Hannah Arendt, *The Human Condition*

A Time of Alibis

New York, February 22, 1993. Unanimously, the fifteen representatives of the United Nations Security Council affirm Resolution
808. They have come here to create the International Criminal
Tribunal for the Former Yugoslavia. This is a historic moment:
For the first time, a truly international tribunal will pursue war criminals. In a
spirit of self-satisfaction, the diplomats rival one another in grandiloquent
proclamations. To judge by their words, the engineers of ethnic cleansing and
their zealous servants can only tremble before the power of the law.

"For the first time since the Nuremberg Tribunal, war criminals will thus
know the sanction of international law," proclaims U.N. Secretary-General
Boutros Boutros-Ghali.[1]

"From today, criminals know that they will be punished," affirms Ahmed
Snoussi, president of the Security Council.[2]

"To pursue those responsible, is to respond to a demand of justice for the
victims and by the international community. To pursue those responsible also
sends a clear message to those who continue to tolerate these crimes: they will
account for their acts," reiterates Jean-Bernard Mérimée, France's ambassador
to the United Nations.[3]

In Bosnia, however, far from the muffled salons of the U.N., reality has a
taste of ash and horror. While the diplomats celebrate the establishment of an

international court for the former Yugoslavia, Serb forces are floating another smokescreen before the international community. Military forces block relief convoys in the direction of the Muslim enclave at Gorazde. It is an illegal act that surprises no one; who cares about one more violated promise?

Since April 6, 1992—the date of the recognition of Bosnia-Herzegovina by the European Community—the country has burned and bled. Aspiring to construct a Greater Serbia on the ruins of the multinational Yugoslavia, nationalist Serbs have launched a massive offensive and quite literally executed their ethnic cleansing policy against the Muslim and Croat populations. The shelling of civilians, starvation sieges, selective destruction of villages, arbitrary detentions, massacres, torture and rape, summary executions, forced deportation, and the resettlement of hundreds of thousands of people—such are the instruments of this terrorist policy. Divided and preoccupied with the dismemberment of the Soviet Union, the Western governments procrastinate. Entangled in political and diplomatic impasses, they dispatch U.N. peacekeeping troops alone. But the mission has failure written into its mandate, for in Bosnia-Herzegovina, there is no more peace to maintain.

By the time the U.N. Security Council adopts Resolution 808 on this February 22, Serb forces have already conquered 70 percent of Bosnian territory. The dead join the dead. Hundreds of thousands of men, women, and children have been chased from their homes, and more continue to be forced to flee. But the international community is incapable of responding to this extortion.

So what is this U.N. court being born, even as blood, death, devastation, and persecution continue to escalate? What is this sudden brandishing of the sword of justice? Is it merely demagoguery, or the moral reaction so long awaited from the international community? Is it eyewash or real determination to combat the intolerable?

In Sarajevo, under constant bombardment, the editorial writer for the daily newspaper *Oslobodjene*, Zlatko Dizdarevic, has lost all faith in the United Nations, as have many of his compatriots. "We, the people of Bosnia-Herzegovina," he writes, "we know that the proud glass house on the banks of the East River [the United Nations], far from being the fortress of brave horsemen quick to defend the rights of nations, houses only mediocre bureaucrats, blind, greedy and cowardly. [They] who gargle grand words while genocide goes on." [4]

The Western media, observing the first tentative steps of the international court, waver between hope and skepticism. They worry that the future tribunal will serve only to wash away the bad conscience of the international community, that the Western public's desire for justice will be merely manipulated. The people of the West, confronted by images saturated in horror, are demanding action from their governments. For months, they have been the impotent spectators of ethnic cleansing via their television screens—accounts of atrocities, murder, rape, and pillage following one upon the other, images of women and children crammed onto buses and forcibly deported from Serb territory, the shelling of civilians, the terror of sniper fire—set against the United Nations' making a show of its impotence and easing its conscience by sending humanitarian aid and U.N. peacekeepers.

The news media, however, are not duped by the Security Council's strategy regarding the future tribunal. As one commentator writes, "Justice held up to ridicule and laws that are unapplied damage the morale and the law itself by authorizing their own derision. It is, however, necessary to applaud the will of the Security Council to set a deadline, to move 'humanitarian law' forward and to engage a mechanism that may, despite everything, some day achieve effective results. Let us hope that it will suffice to make those responsible muzzle their dogs of war, instead of encouraging their ethnic cleansing." [5]

Early Hostility by Western Governments

The Security Council's idea was not born on February 22, 1993. In its modern form, the will to chastise powerful "aggressors" and war criminals dates back to World War I. The allies had then briefly considered indicting Kaiser Wilhelm II of Germany, but their determination quickly frayed. Thereafter, the League of Nations, followed by the United Nations, tried without success to set up a court that could punish mass crimes.[6] Only the tribunals of Nuremberg and Tokyo gave impetus to a justice without borders, but it was a justice stained with original sin: that of its birth at the will of conquerors.

It was only in 1991 that the idea of punishing a head of state again surfaced. After the invasion of Kuwait by Iraq, Prime Minister Margaret Thatcher of Great Britain and President George H. W. Bush of the United States publicly evoked the necessity of trying Saddam Hussein. This public effort was an attempt, among other things, to criminalize the master of Baghdad and thereby legitimize in the name of universal morality—and not just of geostrategic and petroleum interests—the validity of the Gulf War campaign against this tyrant. Condemning Hussein was not difficult, of course, so heavy is his "past"; he did not hesitate to gas his own Kurdish population, whose martyred village Halabja became a tragic symbol of his reign.

With the Iraqi leader's notoriety in mind, Germany's foreign minister, Hans-Dietrich Genscher, submitted to the twelve European Community states the idea of an international court destined to judge Saddam Hussein. During the European Community's Intergovernmental Conference summit in Luxembourg on April 15, 1991, Genscher proposed that the European Community hold Saddam Hussein "personally responsible for genocide and war crimes."[7] His colleagues supported Genscher's proposal for a "Nuremberg-type procedure" to judge Hussein, without being more precise. In the name of the twelve, Foreign Minister Jacques Poos of Luxembourg wrote in his capacity as EC president on April 16, 1991, to the U.N. secretary-general, Javier Perez de Cuellar, "The brutality of repression and the unprecedented scale of the movement of refugees demand of us that we not content ourselves with mere words in our condemnation of the Iraqi regime. My twelve Community colleagues have asked me to address myself to you, so that you examine the question of personal responsibility of the Iraqi leaders in the tragedy that is unfolding, in particular on the basis notably of the Convention to Prevent Genocide, and the possibility of trying them before an international court."[8]

But very quickly the political will of Europe and the United Nations to move forward slackened. Undoubtedly, the Western nations calculated the dangers of such an operation; for years they had given massive aid, including chemical technology, to Saddam Hussein, who had served conveniently as a counterweight to the Islamic Republic of Iran—all without being offended at the time by his contempt for human rights. Would a tribunal worthy of its name that was set up to judge Saddam Hussein, even *in absentia,* stay quiet about the political and military support he had received? The West abandoned the idea, granting de facto impunity to a man responsible for war crimes and genocide.

One year later, in the context of the war in the former Yugoslavia, the Americans remain hostile to the idea of an ad hoc tribunal. How can they justify indicting the Serb leadership when they have so recently renounced judging Saddam Hussein, the archenemy of the United States? This policy would appear to create a double standard, a contradiction difficult to justify. In addition, the Americans remain opposed even to the principle of a permanent international court, fearing that foreign judges could one day condemn American soldiers for operations in Panama, Grenada, or elsewhere. They dread having their unilateral military interventions scrutinized by just such an international court.

As the cold war ends, what remains of Yugoslavia has lost all strategic interest for the Americans, to the point that U.S. Secretary of State James Baker affirms colloquially, "We don't have a dog in that fight."[9] Washington is preoccupied instead with Iraq and the consequences of the Soviet Union's disintegration.

The Europeans, on the other hand, boast of settling this "internal" problem without recourse to outside assistance. "This is the hour of Europe, not the Americans," trumpets Jacques Poos of Luxembourg.[10] Creating an additional obstacle on the road to a diplomatic solution, which remains their absolute priority, is not an option. The Europeans want to keep quiet anything that, by its nature, would "complicate" a negotiated settlement, because Europe, as well as the United Nations and the Americans, knows about the atrocities committed by Serb forces in the spring of 1992 but keeps that knowledge secret. Policymakers fear public reaction in the face of crimes of a rare cruelty. A confidential report by U.N. peacekeepers dated July 3, 1992, presumes the existence of concentration camps. The U.N. High Commission for Refugees also has information about massive internment of civilians, torture, deportation, and summary executions.[11] But the European governments do not want a "risky" military intervention.

This shocking silence of Western governments coincides with the most murderous period of ethnic cleansing, excepting the massacres at Srebrenica in July, 1995. Since World War II, Europe has not known an equivalent scale of death. Ethnic and religious clichés about the Balkans are used to explain away the atrocities as "inevitable," and each Western government encourages this prejudice. By minimizing the weight of the crimes or by explaining to their constituents that ethnic cleansing is a civil war resulting from age-old hatreds, they eliminate the fundamental culpability of Serb aggression. Certainly, the great Western nations do not know everything. But they do know the broad strokes of the unraveling tragedy, which makes their silence all the more deafening.

They know, for example, that tens of thousands of non-Serb men, women, and children have been forced out of northern Bosnia and that thousands of men have been imprisoned, of whom many have perished.

On April 17, 1992, Bosnian Serb paramilitary forces and those from other parts of the former Yugoslavia take control of Bosanski Samac, a town in northern Bosnia, and launch a campaign of terror to force the majority of the Muslims and Croats of Bosnia to flee the region: arrests, torture and sexual violence, deportation of civilian populations, pillage of goods. In the street, civilians are forced to wear white bands to identify themselves as non-Serbs. From May 7 to May 21, 1992, Serbian guards in the camp of Luka near Brcko kill hundreds of Muslim and Croat prisoners with a bullet in the head or back. Often the camp guards force the prisoners about to be slaughtered to put their heads on a metal grate so that their blood will flow directly into the Sava River, thereby reducing the cleanup required after the executions.[12]

Omarska, a mining complex not far from Prijedor, is one of the most sinister camps. Between April and autumn of 1992, thousands of Croats and Muslims are detained in vast warehouses close to an iron mine. Dozens among them perish in the "White House," a two-room villa transformed into an interrogation center. Years later, the tribunal will comment on the affair during the trial of Dusko Tadic: "Cruel and degrading treatment, humiliation, sexual servicing, rapes, assassinations." A prisoner named Hase Icic has his ribs broken during torture in the White House, which he describes in these terms before the tribunal: "a very messy slaughterhouse, stench and blood, urine, and beaten-up people, blood sprayed on the walls, horror." [13]

The Press and Civil Society React

In July, 1992, the truth about the Bosnian Serb camps begins to break into the international press. It acts as a veritable bomb, returning the West to the trauma of World War II. The West, cemented by its victory against Nazi barbarity, is suddenly horrified by the resurgence of nationalist hatred it thought had been vanquished. In an article published by the New York daily *Newsday* on August 2, 1992, "Bosnia's Camps of Death," Roy Gutman gives voice to two survivors held in "concentration camps in which more than a thousand civilians have been executed or starved and thousands more are being held until they die." [14] That same day he publishes "A Witness' Tale of Death and Torture," in which Alija Lujinovic, a fifty-three-year-old traffic engineer from the village of Brcko, describes "nearly every form of humiliation the Serb captors inflicted on Muslim prisoners, from desecration of his local mosque to witnessing the murder and mutilation of male prisoners and gang rape of Muslim women." [15]

Around the same time, the British television network ITN broadcasts images of starving prisoners—eyes bulging from their sockets, paralyzed with fear—detained in the Omarska camp. These images have been filmed with the consent of Serb forces who apparently have no idea of their potential impact on international public opinion.

Without a mandate to stop these persecutions, U.N. agencies are reduced to the role of statisticians and humanitarian accomplices to ethnic cleansing. The numbers they assemble send a chill up the spine. The U.N. High Commission for Refugees estimates that in Bosnia-Herzegovina one inhabitant in three is homeless due to the war. The odious mechanism of ethnic cleansing continues inexorably: Each day, ten thousand refugees are forced out of the country; the great majority are Muslims fleeing toward neighboring Croatia. By July 29, 1992, 2.3 million people have been displaced by combat, a third from Bosnia alone. Two hundred thousand of these people have found refuge in Germany, 60,000 in Hungary, 50,000 in Austria, 44,000 in Sweden, and 12,000 in Switzerland. Through this forced exodus, the war of the former Yugoslavia has crossed the Balkan frontier.

On July 7, the day after the ITN footage is shown worldwide, President George H. W. Bush of the United States says in a press conference, "We know that there is horror in these detention camps. I cannot confirm on hard evidence the—some of the charges that have been made. It is absolutely essential—whatever is going on there—that there be open inspection, and that humane treatment of the people in these concentration camps be guaranteed. But in all honesty, I can't confirm to you some of the claims that there is indeed a genocidal process going on there."[16]

Bush worries that using the word "genocide" will oblige him to intervene, and American diplomats are told to proscribe the word from their vocabularies when discussing events in Bosnia to avoid triggering implementation of the United Nations Convention on Genocide, which obligates states to prevent and punish acts of genocide.[17]

As much as President Bush might wish to banish the word "genocide" and to play down the role of legal prosecutions, the facts are stubborn. The American public is appalled by the images of emaciated prisoners that evoke the brutality of World War II. On July 31, the principal U.S. human rights organization, Human Rights Watch, publishes a report entitled *War Crimes in Bosnia-Herzegovina,* which, supported by testimony, meticulously documents the ethnic cleansing. It is a cry of alarm "at the proof of genocide." The report states, "The indiscriminate use of force by Serbian troops has caused excessive collateral damage and loss of civilian life. A policy of 'ethnic cleansing' has resulted in the summary execution, disappearance, arbitrary detention, deportation, and forcible displacement of hundreds of thousands of people on the basis of their religion or nationality." The report cites, by name, ten culpable Serb and Bosnian Serb military officials and politicians—including President Slobodan Milosevic of the Serb Republic; the Serbian president of Bosnia, Radovan Karadzic; Bosnian Serb forces commander Ratko Mladic; Zeljko Raznatovic (known as "Arkan"), the leader of the Bosnian Serb paramilitary Tigers; and *tchetnik* Serb paramilitary leader Vojislav Seselj—judging "that sufficient evidence is available to warrant the investigations [of] . . . war crimes." The report notes as well that "the Croat and Muslim armies are guilty of holding Serb civilians as hostages, of having mistreated prisoners detained and more generally for having harassed Serbs in certain zones that they control," but that "the most egregious and overwhelming number of violations of the rules of war have been committed by Serbian forces."[18]

Criticism follows the international community's failed reaction to this horror. Helsinki Watch notes,

[The] United States' policy toward the former Yugoslavia has been inert, inconsistent and misguided. . . . The European Community [EC] has been slow and divided in its response to the war in Bosnia-Herzegovina. Germany is the only EC country that has supported an activist policy in Bosnia-Herzegovina.

France has supplied much humanitarian aid to Bosnia-Herzegovina but has been restrained in its criticism of Serbian forces in that country. Greece has sought to deflect criticism of Serbia because it views that state as an ally in its effort to deny international recognition to the former Yugoslav republic of Macedonia. Britain has been ambivalent about criticizing human rights abuses in Bosnia-Herzegovina and it generally has been passive about the conflict.[19]

This context of extreme emotion gives a new impetus to the idea of a tribunal. In contrast to the Iraqi precedent, the idea for this tribunal comes from below, from civil society. In its report at the end of July, 1992, Human Rights Watch calls for an international tribunal charged with investigating, pursuing, judging and punishing without distinction those responsible for war crimes on the territory of the former Yugoslavia: "We believe that this [investigation] should have been coupled with the establishment of an international tribunal to prosecute, adjudicate and punish war crimes."[20] From then on, the question of punishing the authors of war crimes and crimes against humanity in Bosnia overflows into the public domain. The shock provoked by the reporting of Roy Gutman and the ITN footage of prisoners gives a decisive new impulse to the idea of an international court for the former Yugoslavia. The American and French governments, which "played" with this idea in the preceding months only to reject it, can no longer oppose it. Their need to act is now motivated even more by the fact that they, like the other Western governments, are being called on to justify their wait-and-see policy.

Mitterrand Gives His "Yellow Light"

From the spring of 1992, Robert Badinter is one of the first to evoke the necessity of pursuing war criminals, but his voice goes unheard. Badinter, the former justice minister under President François Mitterrand and the man who abolished the death penalty in France in October, 1981, was also the president of the Constitutional Council, France's supreme judicial body. He presided over the Commission of Arbitrage for the former Yugoslavia that was created in the summer of 1991 and charged with finding an institutional arrangement capable of defusing the conflict. During an informal dinner at the Constitutional Council that spring, Badinter pleads for the creation of a tribunal to judge war criminals. Badinter's conviction to act is, above all, a moral reaction to transgressions of the fundamental rules of humanity: "We were a mere handful who could not allow that, in Europe at the end of the century, fifty years after the Second World War, genocide could be committed before our very eyes. Nor could we bear the idea that the instigators could, after a cease-fire and peace terms that would assure them a convenient amnesty, return peacefully to their homes, surrounded by the affection of friends and loved ones . . . and go fishing. This, our consciences would not permit."[21]

At the same table, Jean-Pierre Puissochet, the French Foreign Ministry's judicial affairs director, is hostile to the idea. He explains that "to elaborate a treaty to create a tribunal would take years" and that it would appear unlikely for "the Security Council to take such an initiative."[22] Technically, he is correct. For close to a half century, jurists have found themselves each year at the United Nations in Geneva lobbying for the creation of an international criminal court, without advancing their proposal one inch. As for the Security Council, it has never launched an equivalent venture. Nothing indicates that it even has the jurisdiction to do so. Nothing suggests, either, that China or Russia would not veto such an initiative. For the French authorities, the core of the discussion is less legal than political. The reluctance of the Quai d'Orsay (the French Foreign Ministry) and the presidency is the same; the priority is to search for a diplomatic solution. Creating institutions that would, by their nature, retard that primary goal is not part of the plan.

Robert Badinter speaks of his project to Lord Peter Carrington and Cyrus Vance, mediators for the European Community and United Nations, respectively, who have hurried to the bedside of the former Yugoslavia. The two men hardly react. Badinter also discusses it with President Mitterrand, who shows little interest. Badinter finally approaches Roland Dumas, at the time the French foreign minister. Dumas quickly understands the political use that he can make of the proposal. Some of Badinter's arguments, he thinks, could be valuable for defusing criticism against the government for not coming to the aid of the Bosnian Muslims: "The pressure of public opinion was very strong in reaction to the bombardment of Sarajevo, the snipers, the stories of atrocities." Dumas's concern is not to modify presidential policy but to confront criticism against the government: "Badinter's point of departure was legal. My point of departure was different. It was political. I was convinced of the necessity for a political solution, but given the grave nature of the crimes that were being committed, I could not let us give the public the impression that these criminals were absolved from the moment that they accepted peace."[23]

Dumas explains the necessity of protecting oneself against public criticism, including long-term criticism: "I did not want to find myself in the situation of post–World War II, when the world discovers the death camps, and nothing was available for punishing those responsible. I wanted that at least, in one way or another, they would answer to justice, since we already did not want to intervene militarily in Bosnia. I did not want us to appear as accomplices to crimes that were still being committed."[24]

So the French foreign affairs minister goes to see the president: "I proposed to Mitterrand the creation of an ad hoc tribunal for the former Yugoslavia. Mitterrand was very reluctant. 'That will not succeed,' he told me. 'What is needed is a political solution.'" Mitterrand does not favor an instrument that would complicate a negotiated settlement, already difficult to attain. In June, 1992, Mitterrand goes to Sarajevo, accompanied by Bernard Kouchner, his minister of humanitarian action. President Alija Izetbegovic of Bosnia has sent him a list of ninety-four places of detention, including several possible concentration camps, asking Mitterrand to do everything possible to get a human rights mission to come and direct an investigation. Mitterrand gives him no response.

In the following weeks, with the accounts of horror coming one after another, the mobilization of public opinion is such that President Mitterrand finally concedes to Roland Dumas. "Finally, he said to me, 'Since you seem so taken with this idea for a tribunal, pursue it.' It was his manner of being nice, when he didn't want to say no," Dumas notes. "I thus continued with the 'yellow light' Mitterrand gave me."[25]

In the spirit of Roland Dumas, the future tribunal is conceived at the time as a salve for French public opinion and as political insurance against eventual postwar accusations of complicity. Only marginally is it envisaged as a dissuasive weapon against the belligerents, without which this idea cannot go beyond the stage of pious vows. But at the base, Dumas does not truly believe that justice can be served while the former Yugoslavia is still at war.

Two years earlier, journalist Mirko Klarin was without a doubt the first to suggest the idea of an international tribunal charged with pursuing crimes committed in the former Yugoslavia. In an article entitled "Nuremberg Now," published in the Belgrade daily *Borba* on May 16, 1991, he proposed that a new Nuremberg tribunal be established without delay, to judge crimes against peace and crimes against humanity in Yugoslavia. He insisted on the preventive nature such a tribunal would have. Klarin believed in the effectiveness of law as a political weapon. Justice, he pleaded, could be, must be, the substitute for war:

> At present . . . the most our . . . leaders will agree to are make-believe negotiations, promptly followed by the invalidation, denial or diametrically opposed interpretation. . . . [W]ould it not be better if our leaders were made to sit in the dock instead of at the negotiating table? And if, with the help of world-famous experts in international laws of war, we had a Nuremberg Trial of our own, no matter how small and modest? . . . If someone here is planning and preparing war, calling for mass atrocities, and fomenting ethnic, religious and

FRANÇOIS MITTERRAND and ROLAND DUMAS—The wily French President (at center during a 1991 NATO meeting) opposed the Tribunal as a threat to a negotiated settlement—until it became politically useful to him. He then gave his Foreign Minister (right) the "yellow light" that was crucial to its establishment. (NATO)

racial hatred . . . there is no reason to leave the Yugoslav mini-Nuremberg for when 'it is all over.' It would be much more cost-effective to 'anticipate,' or rather, 'avoid.' Huge savings could thus be made in terms of both human life and material goods.[26]

This prophetic article made hardly an echo outside of Yugoslavia. Fifteen months and thousands of dead later, the idea of an international tribunal is reborn.

London's Turning

On August 26, 1992, three weeks after the shocking discovery of the camps, a conference is held in London to discuss ending the war. Emotion is still intense, public opinion haunted by the memory of the Nazi genocide. It is a critical moment. The meeting aims to re-launch the peace negotiations and close the appalling detention camps. Western diplomats use the entire range of "pressure": They threaten those responsible for ethnic cleansing by naming a special investigator to probe the crimes, they impose economic sanctions, and they raise the idea of military intervention. The words are strong, but no one is fooled. Behind the rhetoric and spectacle of politicians outraged by the policy of ethnic cleansing, this conference is, above all, an attempt to intimidate the belligerents into compliance and to calm an indignant public. It is not about sending soldiers to die for Sarajevo. The threat to criminalize the authors of ethnic cleansing is only brandished because the idea of a tribunal is, at this particular moment, more an idea than a concrete project.

The Europeans are divided. They have neither a foreign policy nor a common defense, and they carry the scars of their dissension on the subject of recognition for Croatia—a critical decision that, in part, sparked the Balkans wars. The Germans express the hardest line, but, ironically, the atrocities committed by the Nazis during World War II preclude them from intervening militarily in the Balkans. The French and British furnish the main part of the U.N. Blue Helmet peacekeepers, but they do not want to provoke reprisals against their troops. As for the Americans, they are careful to stay out of what appears to be a quagmire. In the glow of their success in the Gulf War, the Pentagon is persuaded that the GIs are more comfortable in sand dunes than in wooded mountains.[27] Lacking a strategy beyond imposing a *cordon sanitaire* aimed at containing the Balkan blaze, Europe and the Security Council exhaust themselves in an incoherent flight forward, soon to be undone on the principles they seek to uphold.

The London Conference is the theater of this flight forward. All of the players of the Yugoslav tragedy are present. Yugoslav president Dobrica Cosic, Serb president Slobodan Milosevic, Bosnian Serb leader Radovan Karadzic, Croatian president Franjo Tudjman, his Bosnia counterpart Alija Izetbegovic—all are there to see what position Europe will take. But the Europeans, divided, continue to procrastinate.

White-hot public opinion demands words without concessions. It gets satisfaction on the form, but not on the foundation. Klaus Kinkel, the German foreign affairs minister, proposes the creation of a criminal tribunal and warns,

This conference must send a clear message: "Enough of the killings and expulsions!" We cannot and will not allow ourselves to be put off any longer with empty promises while heavy artillery continue to reduce one town after another in Bosnia and Herzegovina to ruins. There must now be unequivocal commitments, and we expect them to be honored as innocent people are killed. I appeal to the Serbian leadership: realize that you stand at the crossroads. One of the roads leads back into the community of nations, to peace and prosperity. The other leads to absolute isolation and impoverishment.

And make no mistake: The community of nations will never countenance acquisitions of territory or drawing of new borders resulting from the use of force or terror. Those responsible for the devastation will be held accountable for what has been senselessly destroyed.[28]

Does he believe this himself? Roland Dumas, who wants to isolate the Serb nationalists in order to escape any accusation of complicity, thunders, "It is not just a matter of denouncing these crimes; their perpetrators must know that such acts will not go unpunished and that they will be prosecuted."[29]

These strong words are above all to appease public opinion, for whom the ethnic cleansing, the persecutions, the frantic flight of civilian populations, and the camps evoke the darkest days of World War II. The public relations campaign launched by the humanitarian aid organization Doctors of the World pushes the comparison even further, comparing Milosevic to Hitler.

The Serb leadership is not the least intimidated by the Western threat of armed intervention or the inculpation for war crimes. They know that behind the verbal force, there has been no commitment to stop the bloodbath. The very idea of a tribunal to judge war criminals is not concrete. It is, once again, merely a bluff.

Backed against the wall by the press and public opinion, the Western governments in London use strong words to mask their own disarray. They find themselves entangled in a network of contradictions: On the one hand, they cannot tolerate the nature and magnitude of the crimes committed without denying their own fundamental morality and policy; on the other, they do not want to intervene militarily. They hope to judge the executioners, but they dread postponing or sabotaging a negotiated settlement. They are hard-pressed to separate the ideology of human rights they profess from the *raison d'état* that forces them to deal with any interlocutor.

How to take on such a bitter case? Europe had persuaded itself through conventions and treaties that barbarism on its soil was a thing of the past, justly consigned to the museum of the century's horrors and to the history books. Was not the United Nations created after the victory against Nazism and its compulsion toward destructive hate? But the war in the former Yugoslavia has swept away such comfortable certainties. Against all reality, the Western governments refuse to recognize the collapse of their own system of values.

They go so far as to search out a survivor of the Nazi genocide, Elie Wiesel, to set up a "dialogue" with Cosic, Milosevic, and Karadzic on the closing of the death camps. "[T]hat look, as of a Lazarus risen from the dead, yet still a prisoner within the grim confines where he had strayed, stumbling among the shameful corpses," wrote François Mauriac of Wiesel in the preface to *Night*,

Wiesel's autobiographical account of his concentration camp hell.[30] For the politicians, the symbolism is perfect: This living dead man returned from the Nazi camps meets the organizers of "ethnic cleansing."

Under criticism, the politicians take shelter behind Wiesel, this incarnation of Western moral conscience. In calling one genocide survivor to the negotiation table, they are trying to conjure the past, to demonstrate to a critical public the moral commitment of Western governments. Wiesel's presence is "proof" that history does not repeat itself. Roland Dumas proposes that "Elie Wiesel, winner of the Nobel Peace Prize for his work as a living memory of the Holocaust, outstanding figure in ethics and history whose life is the witness before our conscience as a whole," is charged with "the mission of being a witness of the prison camps that must be closed or placed under the control of international organizations."[31] The only hitch: The French minister fails to explain exactly how he plans to get the camps closed.

At the London Conference, Wiesel meets Cosic, Milosevic, Izetbegovic, and Karadzic. The famous writer does not immediately realize that the Western politicians hope to extract from his presence in London proof of their own morality and that the Serbian negotiators hope to gain a veneer of legitimacy. "Cosic invited me to come to his tormented country, promising me free movement and the possibility of access throughout. At my request, he ordered Karadzic to close all the camps on his territory. To my surprise, Karadzic accepted. The two went as far as signing an agreement," Wiesel recounts.[32] This document would be one of innumerable "paper" agreements that would never take effect.

Throughout the Yugoslav conflict, the fact that the West has not finished with World War II is clear. In calling for the creation of a "mini-Nuremberg," Mirko Klarin puts his finger on the problem. The heritage of the Nuremberg tribunals is at the same time the foundation and the spearhead of the Western democracies that now find themselves torn between their own ideals and *raison d'état*. In effect, the Nuremberg tribunals cannot be reduced to the punishment of Nazi dignitaries alone. They were actually the crucible of the culture of law in human rights and played a major role in the formation of a universal conscience of humanity, incarnating the antithesis of the racist ideologies at work in the former Yugoslavia. In decreeing that there is a limit to the intolerable, Nuremberg pressed its will to construct a legal order that transcends national borders. This transgression of national sovereignty is the "lesson" of the camps: Never again must respect for national borders serve as an excuse for persecution. This new restriction on the intolerable is the essence of the new charge raised against the Nazis, that is, "crimes against humanity." The invocation of "humanity" for the first time signified that this crime is beyond all permissible parameters, not only in war, but also in politics.

In the wake of Nuremberg, Western countries undertook a movement toward the moralization of international life, drafting treaty after treaty. In 1948 the Universal Declaration of Human Rights and the United Nations Convention on Genocide are adopted; in 1949 the Geneva Conventions are completed to protect civilians in wartime; in 1950 the European Convention on Human Rights is signed. These texts are not always consistent with one another. Many lack, among other things, mechanisms for their application and enforcement. But the essential remains: The universality of human rights, contested here and there, progressively imposes itself over time, even if the work toward an international court hardly advances. The war of the former Yugoslavia tests this collective experience of civilization and imperils it.

In brandishing the threat of an international court, Western diplomats hope to hide their own impotence. All the high-flung rhetoric of "never again" after the discovery of the Nazi camps reveals itself inoperative. "After the humanitarian bone, the judiciary bone," says the French philosopher Alain Finkielkraut, making bitter irony of the alibis used by Western governments for not intervening.[33] For humanitarian aid, the cushion of good Western conscience has lost its credibility. Ill-adapted by its nature to treat the cause of conflict, humanitarian assistance has itself become the target of the belligerents. The assassination near Sarajevo of Frederic Maurice, mission chief of the International Committee of the Red Cross, on May 18, 1992—which provoked the withdrawal of the most senior members of the humanitarian organizations in Bosnia for nine months—is the symbol of this crisis. The refusal of the French section of Doctors without Borders/Médecins sans Frontières (MSF) to play the role of "humanitarian alibi" puts it bluntly: Aid is no substitute for military intervention. In an article entitled "Humanitarian Aid, the Modern Name of Cowardice," published by the Paris daily *Libération,* MSF president Rony Brauman writes, "Transformed by the states into an ambulance service, humanitarian aid has become the smokescreen behind which one modestly hides one's impotence or renunciation. . . . Behind our piles of medicines and our humanitarian convoys is emerging the first racial state in Europe since the fall of the Third Reich, which we find quasi-achieved based on an 'ethnic cleansing' program announced in advance and then realized with no real opposition from the European Community which was, however, built on the repudiation of such practices."[34]

On the ground, representatives of the U.N. High Commission for Refugees and the International Committee of the Red Cross are authorized to evacuate persecuted populations based on extreme criteria developed so they will not be accused of promoting ethnic cleansing. On condition of anonymity, a humanitarian aid worker in the Serb Republic confides his uneasiness: "At what moment must we authorize the evacuation of a Muslim or a Croat? That the façade of his house is pocked with bullets, that he is injured or assaulted in the street, that he trembles in fear is not enough. No, he must be in danger of death: A grenade must explode in his kitchen; he must be explicitly threatened with murder, his wife must be raped. Excellent criteria. Only, sometimes, we get there too late."[35]

The measures decided upon in London and New York by the international community are iniquitous and ineffective. The imposition of an arms embargo essentially harms only the weakest, the Bosnians. It violates a state's right to defend itself, to fight an aggressor, as recognized by Article 51 of the United Nations Charter. The mediators and permanent members of the U.N. Security Council (with the exception of the Americans) consider this arms embargo necessary because they fear a widening of the conflict. This situation reflects an absolute cynicism: The international community threatens to hold the aggressor accountable to history but at the same time denies the victims the right to defend themselves.

As for the economic sanctions and U.N. resolutions, they remain largely ineffective. Resolution 770, passed on August 13, 1992, authorizes "all measures necessary" to close the Serb camps that have so shocked the world. The resolution remains a dead letter. The decision made in London by the Europeans and the United Nations to undertake mediation (by Cyrus Vance and Lord David Owen) in effect provides Serb negotiators a chance to win some time to continue ethnic cleansing, indeed, to obtain a ruling that secures their territorial gains. Under pressure, the Omarska camp is eventually closed. But the survivors of this mining complex are transferred to other camps at Manjaca and Trnopolje. At the end of August, 1992, the number of detainees at Manjaca has doubled, approaching forty-five hundred. Milosevic and Karadzic agree to trade the closure of the camps for an evacuation sanctioned by the United Nations; tens of thousands of prisoners are taken to Croatia or, more often, to a third country such as Germany, Switzerland, the United States, Canada, or Australia. At the end of 1992, fifty-three thousand of fifty-six thousand non-Serbs in the region of Prijedor have been chased from their homes and the others submitted to permanent harassment and to such dangerous tasks as digging trenches on the front lines. Between August and November, forty thousand Muslims and Croats are forced from the region of Banja Luka and required to give up all their belongings and to accept deportation, often organized by the local Red Cross as directed by extremist Serbs.

One of the rare concrete measures taken in London is the naming of a U.N.

special *rapporteur* charged with investigating crimes committed in the former Yugoslavia: former Polish prime minister Tadeusz Mazowiecki. His mandate is closer to that which Roland Dumas would have conferred on Elie Wiesel: to document the crimes. He acquits himself of his mission until July 27, 1995, the day he writes his letter of resignation to "His Excellency Boutros Boutros-Ghali," refusing to be the mere "stenographer of horror": "The character of my mandate permits me only to describe the crimes and violations of human rights. But the critical moment that we are in the process of living obligates us to realize the true nature of these crimes and the responsibility of Europe and the international community and their impotence in responding to it. . . . How can we believe in the Europe of tomorrow that will be built by the children of those who have been abandoned today?" [36]

After the London conference in 1992, ethnic cleansing continues. The meeting has been an absolute fiasco.

"Money Talks"

On September 23, 1992, before the U.N. General Assembly, Klaus Kinkel re-submits an agenda item on the idea of a tribunal. The preparatory stage occurs on October 6, when the Security Council adopts Resolution 780, calling on the U.N. secretary-general to establish a commission of experts on war crimes. The resolution proposes documenting the crimes committed and investigating the most odious among them as an attempt to limit the atrocities. (The resolution also menaces the belligerents by threatening to unleash this commission on a tribunal.) This slow graduation demonstrates one more time the West's desperate caution. We discover this reluctance in, for example, the unenforced resolutions of the Security Council: 713, 721, 743, 752, 776, 781, 798, 807, 836, 837. Resolution 781, for example, which prohibits aerial surveillance of Bosnia, is violated five hundred times before a subsequent resolution (816) authorizes flights of NATO aircraft to enforce compliance.

The Americans launch the idea of a war crimes commission. This move amounts merely to a change of tactics, not a reorientation of objectives. Ever hostile to intervention, the United States seeks from then on to take the moral high ground to respond to the pressing demands of American public opinion. Still a marginal actor in the Balkans, the United States shapes this commission according to its needs. It should be neither too weak—because it would have no credibility and could not threaten Bosnian Serb leaders—nor as strong as a tribunal, which the White House and especially the Pentagon do not want. As seen from Washington, a commission is judged to be, in effect, less dangerous because it is controllable and easily dismantled, in contrast to a tribunal,

which is autonomous and whose indictments, once launched, cannot be annulled. In short, the Americans want an instrument that can serve as their lever
of political influence while they remain firm in their decision not to shed the
blood of a single soldier to save civilians.

Among the five permanent Security Council members (China, the United
States, France, Great Britain, and Russia), the discussion stalls on the name
of this future organ, an absurd quarrel that speaks volumes about the Security Council's lack of ambition. The Americans want a "Commission on War
Crimes," but the other permanent members insist on the less ambitious
term "Committee." A compromise is found; the "Commission of Experts" is
established. Quarreling about the name is only a prelude to the confrontation
(more and more virulent among the Americans, the British, and the French)
between the Americans, who watch the conflict from afar, and the Europeans,
who are sending thousands of Blue Helmets into the Balkans.

Pushed by public opinion and by the fact that they esteem themselves the
birthplace of human rights and democracy, France and Great Britain are prisoners of their own contradictions. They want to hasten peace without exposing their Blue Helmets, all the while asserting themselves in favor of a court
that they still believe will constitute a hindrance to the negotiated settlement
that is their primary objective. They surmount this contradiction by emptying
its content of juridical force. The Western governments now begin an elaborate dance: The Americans speak of justice to mask their unwillingness to deploy troops, while the French and British, who have dispatched soldiers, fear
this justice even as they solemnly declare it to be of paramount importance.

An American diplomat who wished to remain anonymous recalls, "We
wanted to give the power of investigation to the new commission. The British
and the French thought that the pursuit of war criminals would place the political solution in danger. Their preference was to create a passive committee
that would collect and analyze information that would be transmitted to it.
Under the force of American pressure, [the Europeans] accepted, but they
reached it by torpedoing its financing, in obligating this commission to take its
resources out of the regular U.N. budget and not from a specific budget."[37]

With no money, the new organ will have a reduced capacity for action.
London and Paris have shown great political finesse; Washington, which owes
the United Nations hundreds of millions of dollars in arrears and champions
zero growth in the U.N. budget, can with difficulty object to its allies' refusal
to create supplementary charges for the new organization.

The Americans stress another point as well. They insist on including in the
resolution a clause requiring that, first within thirty days, then at regular inter-
vals, the governments transmit to the future commission any information they

hold concerning human rights violations in the former Yugoslavia. The clause is intended to make the commission a media forum to pressure the Serb leadership. The Americans believe that other governments will transmit information, but, in fact, they will be the only ones to transmit such information.

Resolution 780 is adopted unanimously on October 6, 1992. Roland Dumas congratulates the Security Council for it: "The vote on Resolution 780 deciding on an international investigation on crimes against humanity in the former Yugoslavia is a considerable step in the evolution of international law. This decision, unprecedented since the creation of the United Nations Organization, opens the way for the establishment of a Permanent International Criminal Tribunal." Then, adding a hymn to the grandeur of his country: "If one adds to this measure the resolutions concerning the right to intervene on humanitarian grounds and the forthcoming ban on flights over Bosnia by aircraft of all nationalities other than those of the U.N., three French initiatives and suggestions have been adopted. They will transform the life of peoples and states. . . . They also attest to the authority France enjoys on the international scene, in particular in the United Nations."[38]

Nevertheless, the lives of the people most concerned will hardly change at all.

If it is true that politics is nothing more than an unfortunate
necessity to conserve life and humanity, then it has effectively
begun to make itself disappear. That is to say, that its meaning
was thrown out in absence of meaning.
—Hannah Arendt, *Was ist Politik?*

Guerrilla Diplomacy

America versus Europe

ehind the diplomatic smiles and the public expressions of consensus, European and American allies at the United Nations in New
York are at odds, a still-buried but no less real conflict setting them
apart. At stake is domination of the instruments of the United Nations. Who will determine what kind of profile and power and how much force
to give the Commission of Experts in its investigation of the war crimes committed in Bosnia? The traditional fault line prevails. The Americans want the
commission to become ultimately an instrument of accusation. The British
and French, on the other hand, want to show that they are not insensitive to
the human tragedy in the former Yugoslavia, but they want to do so without
adding another party to complicate their search for peace.

The Europeans win the first round: The British manage to eliminate the
likely president-designate for the Commission of Experts, Cherif Bassiouni.
Born in Egypt, a naturalized U.S. citizen, and a specialist in the law of
war, Bassiouni is alleged to be an "activist," which worries London. Willful,
a man of action, fluent in Arabic, French, and English, the fifty-year-old
Bassiouni has an impressive number of contacts, but London considers him
"uncontrollable."

Bassiouni also does not possess the correct "pedigree." As Bassiouni himself puts it, the U.N. legal division has quickly warned Boutros-Ghali that an Arab Muslim like himself would not be an appropriate choice, because Belgrade would consider him to be pro–Bosnian Muslim and anti-Serb. "I must say that this argument almost convinced me," Bassiouni later recalls.[1] A man more reassuring in the eyes of London and Paris is chosen: Frits Kahlsoven, a venerable Dutch law professor, aged seventy. Relegated to the number-two position, Cherif Bassiouni becomes the commission rapporteur. (Despite these obstacles, it is Bassiouni who will carry the commission, elected to the presidency by other members such as William Fenrick, a Canadian army lawyer; Keba M'Baye, former president of the Senegalese Supreme Court; and Torkel Opsahl, a Scandinavian professor.)

Almost immediately, practical problems arise. The members of the commission are astonished at their Spartan working conditions in Geneva. They accost the U.N. Secretariat and demand to know why they have no office to work in, no personnel, no translators, and no funds to begin investigations.

"It is true that in the beginning, the Commission of Experts had no offices, no personnel, and no budget," recalls Ralph Zacklin, who held the number-two slot in the U.N. legal division. "Neither the U.N. General Assembly nor the Security Council had given them anything. We found a little bit of money that was in principle reserved for the Law of the Sea to give to the Commission, but it was insufficient," Zacklin says.[2]

Are we to believe that no funds could be allocated for such an important mission? Rather, there seems to have been a deliberate will to asphyxiate the Commission of Experts even before it could begin its work. This will to failure is all too easy to accomplish; leave it to the U.N. bureaucracy, which is already on the verge of bankruptcy.

"In short," Bassiouni observes, "we had zero resources to lead an investigation into war crimes that the U.N. Security Council, the most powerful organ in the international community, had entrusted to us. We had no computers. Conference Services at the Palace of Nations in Geneva was in the process of acquiring new IBM 386 computers and almost threw out the older 286 machines before we were able to save three. The whole affair was crazy."[3]

Searching for alternate financial resources, in January, 1993, the commission members ask to set up a separate fund to which member countries can make voluntary contributions. Incredibly, the U.N. Office of Legal Affairs tries to block this independent funding, ruling that Resolution 780 makes no provision for such a fund and that voluntary contributions to the United Nations cannot be allocated to any specific department.

M. CHERIF BASSIOUNI—Deprived of funding when charged to investigate Balkan war crimes in 1992, the distinguished law professor infuriated his U.N. superiors by moving the operation to DePaul University and enlisting the Chicago Police Department to protect it. (UN)

Under these conditions, Cherif Bassiouni decides to begin work at his law school office at DePaul University in Chicago. The U.N. Office of Legal Affairs reminds him that he is now working for the United Nations. Bassiouni retorts, "No problem. Give me an office, personnel, and money, and I will work wherever you want me to. Zacklin and [U.N. Under-Secretary General for Legal Affairs Carl-August] Fleischhauer want me to follow the rules, but they furnish no resources to do the work."[4]

Indeed, the objectives of the United Nations are in parts contradictory: make peace and dispatch humanitarian aid (which implies, in both cases, collaborating with the belligerents), all the while hunting down war criminals, a process that risks derailing humanitarian aid operations and the search for a political solution. For the United Nations, the top priority remains a peace accord—to be signed by war criminals. Asked about this tension between peace and justice, Ralph Zacklin obliquely concedes, "Our job was to make a judicial institution function, first the Commission of Experts, then the Tribunal, but it is true that the situation was a little bizarre with the mediators who were trying to find a political solution." Cherif Bassiouni is more blunt. "Anything that could by its nature slow the diplomatic objective, like the work of the commission, had to be kept under tight control," he says.[5]

The guerrilla war between Bassiouni and the Office of Legal Affairs intensifies when, with a staff of fifty students and volunteer lawyers and $800,000 donated by the Soros Foundation and the MacArthur Foundation, Bassiouni installs at his law school in Chicago a computerized documentation center on war crimes committed in Yugoslavia, "without a dime from the United Nations," he emphasizes. The U.N. legal affairs bureau is furious, insisting that it is not the role of a private institution, equipped with its own resources, to pursue a mandate handed down by the U.N. Security Council. "What posed a problem," according to Ralph Zacklin, a member of the U.N. Secretariat, "is that Bassiouni's database was established in a private university over which the United Nations had no control, containing highly sensitive material that should never be found outside United Nations auspices. But Bassiouni always responded, 'Do you have the resources?' And no, we did not have them. So, it was very difficult to refuse what Bassiouni was doing, because in the last resort money talks."[6]

To each practical objection of the United Nations, Bassiouni finds an answer. For example, he puts the research center in a room guarded by a security system, imposes oaths of confidentiality on his staff, and obtains protection from the Federal Bureau of Investigation and the Chicago police. The U.N. legal division likes none of it. In truth, the situation is curious: The U.N. Security Council has created a commission with a crucial task, without providing it with the means to function. And the commission's members, with private money provided by American foundations, are working outside U.N. control. But the affair is doubly shocking because it demonstrates both the hypocrisy of the Security Council and the vast capacity of certain rich states—and even of private groups—to "buy justice."

Boutros-Ghali lets it go. He is more concerned with stemming a growing confrontation between Washington on one side and Paris and London on the other. "Boutros-Ghali never tried to impede our work," Bassiouni notes. "At some times, he suggested that I 'be more calm.' He asked me, 'Why do you take such risks?' For example, I was going to go to the former Yugoslavia, which didn't please the Secretariat. Zacklin told Boutros-Ghali that if I were taken hostage, it would put the United Nations in a difficult position; that it was not going to help ameliorate relations with the Serbs, nor keep them from continuing their dirty business."[7] Another consideration: France and Britain have thousands of lightly armed soldiers in the Balkans who are also hostage risks, and the two countries want to avoid anything that would appear to be a supplementary provocation.

"A Suddenly Useful Truth"

The feared "provocation," however, comes from the Americans, who want to play the primary role at this stage of international justice.

The action unfolds in Geneva, at the Palace of Nations. The Commission of Experts on War Crimes meets for the first time on December 12, 1992, in a room next door to the negotiating chamber for the International Conference on the Former Yugoslavia. There the American secretary of state, Lawrence Eagleburger, unexpectedly delivers a bombshell of a speech: He accuses Serbian president Slobodan Milosevic and Bosnian Serb leaders Radovan Karadzic and Ratko Mladic of war crimes. The negotiators and the diplomats in attendance are speechless. "The reaction in the room was dead silence from America's closest allies," one journalist writes.[8] The same man who, in August, 1992, had played down the reality of the concentration camps has suddenly made himself the denunciator of those barbaric crimes.

It is pure opportunism; the truth has become politically useful. Eagleburger has no intention of doing anything whatsoever about his denunciations. No change in American foreign policy is implied, which is, in any case, to pass into Democratic hands on January 26, 1993. On the contrary, this "truth-speaking" allows Eagleburger to make a magnificent exit while torpedoing the mediation plan prepared by the joint negotiating team of former U.S. secretary of state Cyrus Vance and Lord David Owen, which is supported by the French and the British. No doubt the Americans are not sorry to make things a bit more difficult for their European allies, with whom relations have not been as tense since the Suez Crisis in 1956, while taking a moral tone to help heal its wounded relationship with Arab states in the wake of Operation Desert Storm.

Lawrence Eagleburger—nicknamed "Lawrence of the Balkans" for his knowledge of Yugoslavia—declaims:

> My government believes it is time for the international community to begin identifying individuals who have to answer for crimes against humanity. We have, on the one hand, a moral and historical obligation not to stand back a second time in this century while a people faces obliteration. But we have also, I believe, a political obligation to the people of Serbia to signal clearly the risk they run of sharing the inevitable fate of those who practice ethnic cleansing in their name. We know that crimes against humanity have occurred, and we know when and where they occurred. We know, moreover, which forces committed those crimes, and under whose command they operated. And we know, finally, who the political leaders are to whom those military commanders were—and still are—responsible. Let me begin with the crimes themselves, the facts of which are indisputable.[9]

LAWRENCE EAGLEBURGER—As U.S. Secretary of State, Eagleburger (here with Dumas in 1992) stunned a Geneva conference by naming Slobodan Milosevic, among others, as a war criminal. (NATO)

Eagleburger then lists the siege of Sarajevo, which is creating dozens of victims nearly every day; the blockades and harassment of humanitarian aid; the destruction of Vukovar in the autumn of 1991 and the forced deportation of the majority of its population; the terrorizing of thirty thousand Muslims in Banja Luka by bombing, beatings, and murder; forcible detention, inhumane treatment, and the willful murder of civilians in the internment camps at Manjaca, Omarska, and Trnopolje; the August 21, 1992, murder of more than two hundred Muslim men and boys by Bosnian Serb police in the Vlasic mountains close to Varjanta; the massacre in May and June of two thousand to three thousand Muslim men, women, and children by Serb irregulars in a brick factory and a pig farm near Brcko; the mass execution in June of one hundred Muslim men at Brod; and the mass murder on May 18 of at least sixty-six members of a Muslim family at Grbavel, near Zvornik. He mentions, too, the fact that at the end of October, Croat combatants killed or wounded more than eight hundred Muslims at Probor and that, between September 24 and 26, the Muslims of Kamenica killed more than sixty Serb soldiers and civilians.

"We can do more than enumerate crimes," he then adds. "We can also identify individuals who committed them." [10] He cites Borislav Herak, a Bosnian Serb who confessed to killing 230 civilians; "Adil and Arfi," two Bosnian

Croats accused of killing about 50 Serb civilians traveling by bus; Arkan, whose real name is Zeljko Raznatovic, the leader of the sadistic Tigers paramilitaries, accused of murdering 3,000 Muslims close to the village of Brcko; Vojislav Seselj, whose White Eagles militia committed atrocities in several Bosnian towns, notably Brcko; Drago Prcac, commander of the internment camp at Omarska, a factory of mass killing and torture; and Adem Delic, commander of the Bosnian camp at Celebici, where at least 15 Serbs were beaten to death in August, 1992.

Eagleburger then turns to their nationalist leaders. "Leaders such as Slobodan Milosevic, the President of Serbia, Radovan Karadzic, self-declared President of the Serbian Bosnian Republic, and General Ratko Mladic, commander of the Bosnia Serb military forces, must eventually explain whether they sought to ensure, as international law requires, that their forces comply with international law and, if so, by what means," he says. The U.S. secretary of state concludes, nevertheless, with this caveat: "They ought, if charged, to have the opportunity of defending themselves by demonstrating whether and how they took responsible action to prevent and punish the atrocities I have described which were undertaken by their subordinates." [11]

It is an understatement to say that the mediators Vance and Owen, as well as the French and British, are angry about Lawrence Eagleburger's fiery speech. They are enraged. They have come to Geneva to seize a decisive moment in the peace process. They had believed that, with Cyrus Vance and Lord David Owen sponsoring a peace accord that they prepared to present to the belligerents a few days later, they could count on Washington's support. At the very least, they thought they would be protected from a sabotage attempt like this.

Now, in calling the Serb leaders war criminals, the entire delicate architecture of negotiation put in place by Vance and Owen is threatened with collapse. Paris and London want an accord based on the cooperation of Milosevic, Karadzic, and Mladic—the same men now accused of responsibility for war crimes and crimes against humanity. Eagleburger expresses impossibly naïve astonishment at the reaction his speech provokes. "David Owen made it clear that he considered my remarks unhelpful," he remembers. [12]

That is an understatement. British and French diplomats are seething with anger. According to one informed source, "While the Americans herald moralism in the Balkans and torpedo any chance for peace—without being prepared to send a single GI there for fear he will get scratched—our soldiers are dying in the mud of Bosnia, vulnerable to snipers, land mines, and reprisals." [13]

Daggers are drawn between the allies on both sides of the Atlantic. Prime Minister John Major of Britain even forbids his ministers from using the term "special relationship," the traditional description for the close ties that unite their country with the United States. London and Paris are fed up. "We, the British and French, were playing the *harkis* for the Germans and Austrians who told us, 'Go ahead, the Serbs are the villains here,' while they hid behind their World War II past to avoid intervening," one exasperated diplomat explains. "Meanwhile, the Americans stake out the moral high ground to avoid getting wet, while we take all the hits in Bosnia."[14]

Even at the U.S. State Department some are stupefied by their boss's speech. "What's happened to Eagleburger?" John Fox, an Eastern Europe expert on the high-level policy planning staff at Foggy Bottom, asks himself. "Has he suddenly become a partisan for this legal weapon? Or is it merely cynicism?" The answer is soon apparent. Eagleburger's remark comes to nothing. "On his return, Eagleburger does not do what all secretaries of state usually do after publicly launching such an initiative, that is, create a working group to study how to enact such a proposition," says Fox, who soon quits his job at the State Department.[15]

Lawrence Eagleburger has perfectly assimilated the political playbook of Roland Dumas. He takes shelter behind the figure of Elie Wiesel to explain the reasons for his denunciation. "It was a meeting between Elie Wiesel and myself in the closing months of the Bush Administration that convinced me that the United States could no longer remain silent on the issue of war crimes," Eagleburger later explains. "Mr. Wiesel—victim of the holocaust and eloquent defender of human rights—personifies the principle that crimes against humanity cannot and will not be ignored. His example led me, in Geneva, to call for action against the perpetrators of the horrors that have marked the Bosnian/Yugoslav conflict."[16] Recourse to Elie Wiesel helps Eagleburger emphasize the ethical dimension of American policy. Telling the truth about the authors of these crimes, or at least a part of the truth, has become simply good politics. Eagleburger has not spoken out in a moment of passion. His speech, in fact, had been cleared by the White House, and Department of State lawyers had read it carefully to ensure that "the statement contained the requisite legal caveats and qualifiers," according to American diplomat Michael Scharf. It is significant to note that Eagleburger has not used the term "war criminals" for the ten people he names, as some in the press reported it, but says that they are "suspected" of war crimes.[17]

For his part, Elie Wiesel believes that he has been instrumental in bringing Eagleburger around to this position. "In December, I had a long discussion with my friend Larry Eagleburger on the possible means for stopping the butchery in the former Yugoslavia," Wiesel says. "It was about the true atrocities, crimes against humanity. It was in discussing them that the idea of an international tribunal came to us. We agreed that not to judge the criminals would be to acquiesce to their crimes. In extreme situations, silence is culpability. So the first list of names [of presumed war criminals] was drawn up." [18]

Unfortunately, the lack of follow-up that Eagleburger gives to his own proposal shows that it is more a public relations exercise than a true will to criminalize the butchers.

The Race between the French and the Americans

Events speed up in January, 1993. It is out of the question now for the French to leave the moral monopoly to the Americans alone. On January 3, mediators Cyrus Vance and David Owen present their peace plan in Geneva.[19] The Americans are hostile to it. On January 8, the Paris daily *Libération* publishes a confidential report from the European Commission's investigation into the treatment of Muslim women; it details systematic rapes in Bosnia by Bosnian Serb forces. The investigation is led by Simone Veil, an Auschwitz survivor who became the first president of the European Parliament after holding important ministries in the French government. Veil directly accuses Bosnian Serb forces.

According to this report, the rapes in Bosnia are not a secondary effect of the conflict but part of the systematic policy of ethnic cleansing, "perpetuated with the conscious intention of demoralizing and terrorizing communities, driving them from their home regions and demonstrating the power of the invading forces." The commission estimates that at least twenty thousand Muslims have been raped.[20] At the same time, Richard Boucher, the State Department spokesman, confirms that seventy thousand people remain in detention in Serb concentration camps, facing death in the harsh winter. Media pressure continues to build on the European governments.

The idea of a tribunal is advanced and accelerated when Roland Dumas discovers that "the Italians had the same idea as we did. We were in competition." [21] On January 16, 1993, Dumas asks French prosecutor general Pierre Truche, who in 1987 prosecuted Klaus Barbie, the former chief of the Gestapo in Lyon, to preside over a committee of jurists charged with examining the creation of an international criminal tribunal. The foreign minister gives Truche only about twelve days to submit his report. "There is unfortunately no longer any doubt of the fact that particularly grave crimes are occurring on the territory of the former Yugoslavia, constituting war crimes, crimes against humanity or grave violations of certain international conventions," Dumas writes to Truche. "Such acts cannot remain unpunished, and the absence of real sanctions both offends the conscience and encourages the perpetrators of these crimes to continue the same sad path on which they are engaged. This is why France determines that it is indispensable to proceed very rapidly to the constitution of an international criminal tribunal."[22]

Still skeptical, François Mitterrand proceeds with caution, as if approaching a yellow traffic light. On January 21, the president of the French Republic is in Bonn, in the company of German chancellor Helmut Kohl. During a televised interview, Mitterrand announces, in reserved terms but for the first time, that he is in favor of the "idea" of a tribunal for Yugoslavia. "I think that the notion of an international tribunal capable of judging crimes against humanity is a good idea, however the situation evolves," he says. "In any case, that is my personal opinion and this is what I will take before the French people."[23]

On January 26, the Clinton administration takes office. As soon as he is installed in the White House, the new president tempers his campaign convictions. Using the opposition of his European allies as an excuse, President Clinton renounces his campaign proposal of "Lift and Strike," which would have lifted the arms embargo (a policy less favorable to the weaker Bosnia versus federal Yugoslavia) and then directed NATO air strikes against Serb artillery still shelling Sarajevo. Now, for want of a strategic alternative, Eagleburger's abandoned idea resurfaces.

The moment is favorable, as appeals for the creation of a tribunal are multiplying in the face of ongoing atrocities. The first designs for an ad hoc tribunal for the former Yugoslavia begin to be prepared in many countries. February 1 opens the annual session of the United Nations Commission on Human Rights, whose ambition is to be the "world's conscience." There, the Americans prepare to propose the creation of a working group charged with drawing up the statute of a future tribunal.

In the race now under way, the French government quickly catches up with Washington. French diplomats circulate their draft resolution in New York. "Little did we know that France was about to pull the rug out from under us," recalls Michael Scharf. "At the very moment we began consulting our allies on our proposal at the Human Rights Commission in Geneva, France was circulating a draft Security Council resolution in New York calling for the creation of a Yugoslavia war crimes tribunal." Scharf is recalled urgently to New York.[24]

Roland Dumas briskly ups the tempo to keep the Americans from winning yet again the political benefits of their moral position while French peacekeepers are still being shot at in Bosnia.[25] Paris—as well as London—cannot stomach Washington's sabotage of the Vance-Owen plan. Faced with a political and military impasse in Bosnia, Paris does not want to cede the monopoly on moral indignation to the United States. "The tribunal was a political weapon for threatening Karadzic and Mladic," says Roland Dumas. "It was a means to pressure them to reach a settlement. I hoped, too, that it would play a dissuasive role."[26]

The enthusiasm among the "P5" (the five permanent members of the U.N. Security Council) and the United Nations Secretariat for the French proposal for a tribunal is, to say the least, limited. Mitterrand himself is still not convinced that the initiative is well founded. Roland Dumas notes that, despite his public declarations,

> Mitterrand remained hostile to this judicial dimension that would complicate the task of the negotiators, but he let it go. The United States found itself confronting an idea that was not their own and which it feared could be turned on them, if American soldiers were ever inculpated. But, reassured on this point, they saw the benefit that could be derived from a tribunal and they invested themselves in it. As for Boutros Boutros-Ghali, he was not warm to the idea in the beginning. He thought that such a tribunal constituted interference in the interior affairs of the state. Yugoslavia had been an important state for the U.N., one of the diplomatic standard-bearers for the Non-aligned Movement.[27]

Both the French and the American military are also worried about the possible effects of the tribunal. "The defense minister was very worried by the question of testimony against the military," Dumas notes. "He feared getting burned, but he let me do it, because he didn't really have a choice."[28] The Pentagon maintains its strong reservations regarding Article 7-3 of the draft Yugoslav war crimes tribunal statute, which affirms that the crime "committed by a subordinate does not remove his superior from his criminal responsibility if he knew or had reasons to know that the subordinate was about to commit such acts or had done so and the superior failed to take the necessary and reasonable measures to prevent such acts or to punish the perpetrators himself."[29]

Not least among the war's absurdities is that the idea for an international criminal tribunal on the former Yugoslavia, so long bogged down for political reasons, suddenly lurches ahead thanks to a purely opportunistic steeplechase between France and the United States.

"Nothing to do with Tibet"

The draft resolution for the tribunal is carefully prepared by the French and combed over by the British, Russians, Americans, and Chinese. It is no longer a conquerors' court, as was Nuremberg, but one with real political roots. In creating this tribunal, the Security Council indirectly awards itself the power of a prosecutor—to decide alone whether to create special tribunals or not. Tainted by this original sin, Resolution 808 is adopted unanimously by the Security Council on February 22, 1993. Politics are omnipresent in the tribunal's birth. China is seeking to negotiate Most Favored Nation status with the Americans and does not want to alienate either the West or the Islamic states for a subject peripheral to its own interests. "The Chinese were reticent," Roland Dumas recalls. "But we explained to them that it had nothing to do with Tibet, and that it would not be terribly clever to pick sides with the butchers and the torturers at a moment when China was seeking to play a more important international role."[30] Russia is sunk in its own internal problems, but Boris Yeltsin, already thinking about his reelection, seeks U.S. support. Madeleine Albright, the newly nominated American ambassador to the United Nations, is herself an interventionist by temperament and a strong partisan for the tribunal, as is the Venezuelan ambassador, Diego Arria, who at that moment heads the Non-aligned Movement. The Islamic states, including Pakistan, then seated at the Security Council congratulate themselves on the adoption of the resolution.

No doubt, the unceasing ethnic cleansing confirmed by the intermediary report of the Commission of Experts helps to dissuade Moscow and Beijing from wielding their veto against the resolution. The report documents "murder, torture, arbitrary arrest and detention, extra-judicial executions, rape and sexual assault, confinement of civilian population in ghetto areas, forcible removal, displacement and deportation of civilian population, deliberate military attacks or threats of attacks on civilians and civilian areas, and wanton destruction of property."[31]

For the time being, Mitterrand, the skeptical man of the "yellow light," has already recouped the story for his own profit. Invited to the Academy of International Law at The Hague on March 18, 1993, to receive the Houphouët-Boigny Prize awarded by UNESCO, the president proclaims, "We French, already at the sides of the victims, believe that breaches of international law must be sanctioned with solemnity. This is why, besides our aid to U.N. peacekeeping operations wherever they are necessary, and particularly today in the former Yugoslavia, France has proposed the creation of an international tribunal charged with punishing crimes against humanity, wherever they are committed, starting first with the country I have just mentioned."[32]

Politically conceived, this court is subject to pressure from all sides even before its birth because of its potential power, with the ability to indict even a head of state. The Americans immediately recognize this power, and they begin positioning themselves to head the future tribunal. They propose that "the Security Council should create a subordinate body, comprised of the members of the Security Council, to be known as the Administrative Council." This body would exercise, among other things, "general administrative control over the staffing and operation of the chief prosecutor and the tribunal, and approve recommendations for financing the tribunal's operations."[33] By controlling the purse strings and staffing policy, the Security Council would maintain control over the tribunal. "Frankly, we did not trust the U.N. Secretariat on its own to provide the necessary budget and staff," former State Department diplomat Michael Scharf later writes. This proposal for an oversight council is directly linked to U.S. policy: maintain control, even if it means financing some of the strategic divisions of the United Nations, such as its peace-keeping operations.[34]

But the American idea is rejected. "The proposal was unacceptable," explains a member of the U.N. Secretariat. "What the United States had in mind was controlling the work of the tribunal by controlling human resources and the budget. We wanted it to be independent of political power."[35] In this underground battle for control of the tribunal, the combatants defend their own interests.

The Europeans and the U.N. Secretariat, responsible for the peacekeepers, want to set up an independent legal organ that, nevertheless, will not disrupt peace negotiations. This is why Ralph Zacklin and his U.N. team had planned, in Article 32 of the tribunal statute, that the tribunal be financed through the regular U.N. budget. "All that we wanted," explains Zacklin, the deputy director of the legal division, "was to avoid the tribunal being financed by voluntary contributions, because it would have been subject to the political imperatives of the contributing states."[36] Due to the Commission of Experts experience, the Americans worry that the tribunal will not have sufficient funds to exercise its mandate. They insist on the creation of a fund for voluntary contributions. Events will show that both the U.N. Secretariat's fears as well as the Americans' are well founded. Each state participating in the tribunal's creation has a different agenda in mind.

On paper, at least, all the states of the Security Council agree on the objectives of the future tribunal. Resolution 808 "decides that an international tribunal shall be established for the prosecution of persons responsible for serious violations of international humanitarian law committed in the territory of the former Yugoslavia since 1991."[37] The job is completed on March 25, 1993, with Resolution 827, also adopted unanimously by the fifteen members of the Security Council. This resolution obliges all states to cooperate with and assist the tribunal, to arrest suspected criminals, and to transfer them to the prison at The Hague. Madeleine Albright warns that states shirking their obligations will be subject to sanctions by the Security Council or, in the case of Serbia, to an intensification of economic sanctions.

As designated by the Security Council, the objectives of the International Criminal Tribunal for the Former Yugoslavia are threefold: "To bring before justice" war criminals, "to contribute to the end of violations of humanitarian law," and "to contribute to the restoration and maintenance of peace."[38] In other words the objectives are to sanction, deter, and reconcile. Each of these objectives addresses different periods of time: chastisement looks to the past, deterrence addresses the present, and reconciliation focuses on the future. This sociological mechanism for the regulation of conflict is perfect from a theoretical point of view. It has only one fault: It ignores reality.

To Mimic Nuremberg

Sarajevo is still under Serb artillery bombardment and sniper fire; humanitarian convoys are blocked by the belligerents; ethnic cleansing continues unabated; a new war is about to break out in Bosnia between Sarajevo and its former Croat allies; millions of refugees from the former Yugoslavia are relegated to despair and exile. None of this stops Boutros Boutros-Ghali from adopting a strangely upbeat tone in his first report on the tribunal addressed to the U.N. General Assembly and the Security Council. Indeed, the report sounds triumphant despite the continuing massacres:

> [U]nlike the Nuremberg and Tokyo Tribunals, the Tribunal is truly international. It has rightly been stated that the Nuremberg and Tokyo Tribunals . . . represented only a part of the international community: the victors. . . . By contrast, the Tribunal is not the organ of a group of States; it is an organ of the whole international community. The judges of the Tribunal come from all parts of the world, bringing with them the breadth of vision and experience needed for this complex task. . . . Even the Detention Unit where persons will be held while awaiting trial is international in nature and is not within the control and supervision of the host State.[39]

At the same time that Boutros-Ghali is enjoying the incontestable superiority of the ICTY over the Nuremberg tribunals, he neglects to mention that it is also in the name of the "whole international community" that the soldiers of the U.N. Protection Force (UNPROFOR) are allowing ethnic cleansing to grind on in total impunity. Near Sarajevo airport, UNPROFOR is even stopping the city's besieged inhabitants from fleeing the capital. Faced with the forced deportation of the civilian population, with the imprisonment of men in the sinister camps, with the destruction of places of worship, the international community responds by invoking the law—a law with no immediate power or application. It is an extraordinary sleight of hand. Rarely has the law more truly masked the feebleness of policy and morality.

The Security Council and the U.N. secretary-general knowingly manipulate the symbol of the judgment at Nuremberg without realizing that they are only emphasizing their own contradictions. The allied military tribunals at Nuremberg had, no doubt, all the defects of a victor's justice, but they at least possessed the political and military means to achieve their objectives. The Allies controlled German territory; the Nazi leaders were in captivity or flight; evidence of crimes was within arm's reach.

There are no such elements in the former Yugoslavia. Instead, the international community is behaving like a police officer who simply scolds a person committing a crime in broad daylight because he is unable to stop the criminal act. For Western governments stuck in futile negotiations with the belligerents in the Balkans, to assert the need for an international tribunal by conjuring Nuremberg is clearly an attempt to dispel suspicion of their own cowardice before the perpetual violation of fundamental democratic values in Yugoslavia.

The "new Nuremberg" is designed to soothe public opinion, to demonstrate that their governments are not in league with those who place themselves beyond democratic values. To enumerate the crimes is to express moral condemnation and to demonstrate that, while unwilling to stop the carnage, Western governments are not insensitive to the tragedy unfolding before their eyes.

For all that, invoking the Nuremberg tribunal also has its limits: For London, Paris, and Washington in 1993, the parties conducting the ethnic cleansing are still the indispensable partners in a negotiated settlement. The Bosnian Serb leaders, Radovan Karadzic and President Slobodan Milosevic, are invited periodically to Geneva in the framework of the International Conference on the Former Yugoslavia. To negotiate with those responsible for war crimes, while at the same time claiming the mantle and legacy of the Nuremberg tribunals, only serves to emphasize the contradiction of their work. The diplomats themselves raise the absurdity of the situation: "How can we invite Karadzic and Milosevic to tea at the negotiations in Geneva while pretending, at the same time, to threaten to incarcerate them?"[40]

This political reality makes the tribunal look like a well-oiled machine, spinning its wheels. This absurd, almost surreal side becomes clear in remarks by Boutros Boutros-Ghali:

> One of the main aims of the Security Council was to establish a judicial process capable of dissuading the parties to the conflict from perpetuating [sic]

further crimes. The Tribunal was conceived as one of the measures designed gradually to promote the end of armed hostilities and a return to normality. Some apprehensions were expressed lest the establishment of the Tribunal might jeopardize the peace process. In fact, the Tribunal will contribute to the peace process by creating conditions rendering a return to normality less difficult. How could one hope to restore the rule of law and the development of stable, constructive and healthy relations among ethnic groups, within or between independent states, if the culprits are allowed to go unpunished? Those who have suffered, directly or indirectly, from their crimes are unlikely to forgive or set aside their deep resentment. How could a woman, who had been raped by servicemen from a different ethnic group, or a civilian whose parents or children had been killed in cold blood quell their desire for vengeance if they knew that the authors of these crimes were left unpunished and allowed to move around freely, possibly in the same town where their appalling actions had been perpetrated? The only civilized alternative to this desire for revenge is to render justice: to conduct a fair trial by a truly independent and impartial tribunal and to punish those found guilty. If no fair trial is held, feelings of hatred and resentment seething below the surface will, sooner or later, erupt and lead to renewed violence.[41]

This erudite United Nations statement has nothing to do with the Bosnian Muslims' unrelieved suffering. Worse than a dismissal, worse than voluntary blindness, it is a deliberate public relations exercise to use morality and law as camouflage for a policy of abandonment. Why do Western governments take such pains to mask their inaction? No doubt because the "victim" has become a central, compelling image since World War II. The symbol revives an icon: that of the unarmed martyr killed by pitiless soldiers. From now on, we will identify more with the suffering of individuals than the collective experience of a nation. The illusion of proximity afforded by television reinforces this reaction. By the emotional charge that it carries, the "humanitarian" image cries out to viewers, carrying the hope for a united world. On a small planet rapidly becoming a "global village," to borrow Marshall McLuhan's celebrated phrase, universal solidarity will bind the affluent to the victims of war. Certainly, this hope is only an illusion, since the humanitarian image produces a false reality by building rapport to the Other only in the form of the victim. Nevertheless, it provokes and sustains in public opinion a moral compulsion to intervene.

That is the reason for the careful attention given by Western political leaders to the question of dissuasion and reconciliation in Yugoslavia. Their motivation is more to reassure the public than to formulate concrete responses in the domain of preventive diplomacy. The creation of an international tribunal could be a strong symbol if it is integrated into a plan of action determined to crush racial ideology. Indeed, the establishment of the ICTY makes a show of addressing itself to the people of the Balkans and reconciliation in the former Yugoslavia. In reality, its objective is less to "deter" and to "reconcile" Serbs, Croats, and Bosnians than to comfort Western public opinion through the judgment of a handful of criminals.

The moral that Western governments seek to draw from the tribunal is that of their own innocence and virtue confronting actions that negate their fundamental democratic ideals. The tribunal at The Hague has been created with a "pacifying" objective, to reestablish peace and security (Article VII of the U.N. Charter), and can only fail in this specific mission. A political body has created a legal organ to take actions it is unable or unwilling to take itself. But the law cannot substitute for political will. The events in the former Yugoslavia demonstrate this contradiction day after day, culminating in the massacres at Srebrenica.

They are decided only to be undecided, resolved to be irresolute, adamant for drift, solid for fluidity, all-powerful for impotence.
—Winston Churchill, 1938

A Tribunal Nearly Stillborn

On November 17, 1993, in the grand hall of the Palace of Peace in The Hague, seat of the International Court of Justice, the highest U.N. judicial body of the United Nations opens the first plenary session of the International Criminal Tribunal for the Former Yugoslavia. Behind the solemnity of the moment, the judges' morale is in free-fall. Despite sonorous proclamations and speeches, the U.N. Security Council and Secretariat are about to abandon the judges. With no money or resources, the international court is being neatly strangled. The new legal institution, intended to play "a dissuasive role" in the Balkan conflict, "an instrument for the reestablishment of peace," has not been given the means to perform to its duties.

Yet the situation at this moment is critical. War continues to rage in Bosnia. On September 16, the U.N. High Commissioner for Refugees reports that the war in Yugoslavia has produced 3.6 million refugees or displaced persons, of which 2.2 million are in Bosnia alone. Thorvald Stoltenberg, Cyrus Vance's successor as U.N. mediator, reports that 200,000 are dead. A new war has begun to tear apart the former Bosnian and Croat allies. Croat forces are shelling the Muslim community of Mostar in Bosnia, the intensity of which even Sarajevo has never endured. Meanwhile, the peace talks in Geneva are at an absolute impasse.

On November 16, the day before the plenary session opens, the eleven judges meet at the Hotel Kurshaus resort on the North Sea to plot their course.

"We have no offices, no statutes, no prison, no accused, no logistics, not even a prosecutor!" exclaims one judge.[1] As for salaries, it is not even worth thinking about at this point, because the tribunal's budget has not been approved by the United Nations. These are the freelancers of the international legal community, paid by the day—dignified doctors of the law fallen from on high.

The Egyptian judge Georges Abi-Saab can hardly believe the astounding negligence of the United Nations. "I would have never believed that the U.N., and in particular the states of the Security Council, could be so irresponsible," he will later say. "They produced a big bang saying in nearly celestial terms 'Let there be a tribunal,' without conducting feasibility studies, without according a budget, without thinking of anything. The result is that we were unable to hire anyone for more than three months. How do you expect us to find qualified people, with high responsibilities in their own countries, under such conditions?"[2]

The judges begin to doubt the enterprise in which they are engaged. But these accomplished legal professionals, who have left their university chairs and high positions in their national judiciaries to participate in this historic tribunal, still refuse to believe that the Security Council is manipulating them, that it has, in reality, no political will to create an effective tribunal. "A lot of things were still unclear," remembers one judge. "Would we have proof of the crimes? If yes, how? How many accused would we have? How high up the chain of command? Would we get the right ones? Nor did we know what role the UNPROFOR peacekeepers would play. We thought that they would be the police force of the tribunal. Naïvely, we thought that if the Security Council had created a tribunal, it would provide us the means to work. All the more since the ICTY had been created under Article VII of the U.N. Charter, the most muscular [provision of the Charter], which authorizes the use of force in the name of international security."[3]

But their illusions dissipate quickly. For the Security Council, it is out of the question that UNPROFOR become the tribunal's police force. Behind the diplomats' grandiloquent proclamations about their unwavering determination to fight impunity, the judges can detect no will for creating an effective and autonomous judiciary with the ability to carry out arrests and proceed to trial.[4] Deprived of material means and logistical support, the judges understand the implications clearly: The tribunal risks being stillborn. The realization comes as a shock, and they corral Carl-August Fleischhauer, chief of the U.N. Office of Legal Affairs. "With what means are we going to work?" they ask, pressing him to respond. Fleischhauer dodges their questions, thereby confirming their suspicions.[5]

The judges are, understandably, at a complete loss. It is a strange lesson in moral leadership that the Security Council is offering to the world by creating the ICTY. The tribunal resembles a theater play, with members of the Security Council acting as unusually incompetent stage managers, incapable of agreeing on the script, performance dates, production budget, or even the likely director.

The Americans see the ICTY as both an instrument that can permit them to preserve, even reinforce, their moral position in the face of the Bosnian conflict without having to deploy soldiers and one that gives them political weight they can bring to bear on events. The French want above all else to allay public rancor, while also hoping that the tribunal can have some dissuasive power over the belligerents. The British still fear that the court will threaten the search for a political solution to end the war. The Russians and Chinese are wary of the precedent created by a supranational tribunal brought into being and dominated by the West.

The ICTY is in an inextricable dilemma. It has become a shop window of the contradictions of the Western powers—particularly France and Great Britain, both heavily engaged in Bosnia. These two countries want both justice and peace, but if forced to choose between the two, they prefer peace without justice. Pragmatic, realist *raison d'état* carries them ever farther away from democratic ideals. This shameful realpolitik in effect reverses all their prior commitments to the defense of human rights. Out of this contradiction, a cynical *trompe-l'oeil* strategy emerges: to create a tribunal, yes, but without giving it the resources to operate. The ICTY will become an empty theater of justice, without defendants or prosecutor, planted in the Dutch capital as a compromise between the French and the British, crushed under the weight of the war's dire urgency and at the same time paralyzed by a complete lack of support. The member states of the Security Council do not want an effective court in wartime, for this would imply breaking off negotiations with the very leaders who are suspected war criminals. Such a court could even push UNPROFOR out of its role as "peacekeeper" (of a fictitious peace) and into direct military confrontation with the aggressors. Clearly, the ICTY has been created to curb escalation, not to accelerate it. One European diplomat puts it bluntly, "When we don't have the desire to make war, we find substitutes. Which doesn't necessarily mean that we give these substitutes the means to really exist."[6]

The Security Council is afraid of its own creation. Fearing that the new tribunal may escape its power, it bolts down everything deemed "strategic"; the choice of judges, the prosecutor, the personnel, and the financial resources are all under its political control and subject to clever bargaining. The Western governments publicly affirm the "independence" of the tribunal to build its credibility, all the while seeking quietly to keep it on a leash. The only point of divergence between the American and the French-British position is that the former understands that an active tribunal may be a more useful political tool, as long as it is not truly emancipated.

The real work of the tribunal's judges and prosecutor is to free themselves from this control. But for the moment, the member states have little to worry about. The judges have been pre-selected from a primary list drafted by the Security Council, then confirmed by the U.N. General Assembly after ten rounds of scrutiny. All candidates of Muslim origin have been dismissed. Four of the judges come from Islamic countries, but the Egyptian is a Coptic Christian; the Pakistani, Zoroastrian; the Malaysian, Buddhist; and the Nigerian, Christian. (Mohamed Sacirbey, the Bosnian ambassador to the United Nations, notes the absurdity of a court with no Muslim jurists, given that the majority of victims in the Balkans are Muslim. "Symbolically, it does not bode well for the court," he says.[7]) The Russian candidate, Valentin Kisilez, is also cut from the list for fear he will manifest his country's historic Slavic ties to the Balkans in pro-Serb decisions. In short, all the judges who could be suspected of sympathy toward one side or the other, for religious or cultural reasons, are dismissed.

It is no coincidence, then, when the U.N. Secretariat uses the ICTY's still theoretical existence as pretext to justify dismantling the Commission of Experts on War Crimes in the former Yugoslavia in December, 1993. By April 30, 1994, the investigation—still in progress—is closed. But ending the commission is not that simple. The exhumation of the bodies of patients from the hospital at Vukovar, patients who were murdered and then buried by Serb soldiers and militia, is still under way. In Bosnia and Croatia, two hundred rape victims remain to be interviewed. The investigation is behind schedule because U.N. funds appropriated for the commission arrived only in August, 1993—eleven months after adoption of the resolution establishing it.

It is not difficult to see in this situation a deliberate attempt to torpedo a disturbing truth as it surfaces. "Could it have been a purposeful political action to prevent the further discovery of the truth, which at the time was not politically propitious?" Bassiouni asks himself. "Or was it simply an unwise administrative decision? Or perhaps it is the nature of the U.N. beast—part political, part bureaucratic—that accounts for what I believe to be an unconscionable outcome, no matter what the reason."[8] Three months earlier an angry Frits Kahlsoven, the first president of the Commission of Experts, had resigned to protest the dismantling of the commission, and he had publicly denounced French and British hypocrisy in the matter. "Other major countries haven't given us any support, either, but I was very angry about these two because they are permanent members of the U.N. Security Council," he says. "If they didn't want us to participate actively, they shouldn't have voted for us."[9]

In spite of everything, the commission submits a final report at the end of April, including twenty-eight appendixes comprising three hundred pages of detailed evidence and testimony. For Bassiouni, the work is already a success in itself, because it reveals not only the scale of ethnic cleansing but also "the connection between Belgrade and the politics and tactics of ethnic cleansing."[10] The premature disbanding of the Commission of Experts is an indication of the Great Powers' hostility to the very institutions that they fear may slip from their grip. And it already presages the relationship they will have with the new ICTY.

It is for this very reason that the Western governments do not and will never integrate the tribunal into a global approach to conflict resolution. Such a tribunal would be far too dangerous. Anchored on legal principles, it risks imposing its own vision on public opinion and directing various questions to governments about their policies: Does an arms embargo violate the legal right of self-defense? Do violations of humanitarian law by the belligerents require sanctions? Is every attempt to negotiate justified? Faced with the risk of an "outburst" by the tribunal, the Western nations seek to cut off its supply of "oxygen," to limit the "nuisance factor" of the tribunal.

For the moment, the ICTY is reduced to a statute of appendixes, just good enough to put a little pressure on the warring parties. But for serious business, the Great Powers will return to their traditional instruments: diplomacy, political and economic sanctions, and the threat of military intervention. In the context of the war, the marginalization of the tribunal has an immediate effect: Its dissuasive aspect is very rapidly diminished as the belligerents realize they are dealing with a lure. "In the first weeks, we received reports from UNPROFOR about the anxiety of Serb officers over the existence of the ICTY," says the Italian judge Antonio Cassese, "but, very rapidly, their fear evaporated."[11] The tribunal is only a paper tiger.

The Judges' War

Confronted with the demoralizing reality that they are to be only a tribunal-alibi, the judges get organized. Their first act is to elect a president on November 17, 1993. The presidency is a complicated position: The office holder must be both the voice and the conscience of the ICTY in the political arena, without sacrificing judicial impartiality. The judges select Antonio Cassese.

The Italian judge has a blend of some rare qualities. This brilliant jurist and professor, nominated for his qualities as an internationalist, is also an activist.

ANTONIO CASSESE—The first tribunal president fought to increase resources for the badly underfunded and understaffed prosecution force, even accepting assistance from the FBI to pursue its mission. (Courtesy Steve Junker)

Most importantly, he is rare among the judges for his habit of confronting politicians. Born at the peak of Mussolini's power in 1937, into a family of left-ist intellectuals in a little town south of Naples, he has always seen the law as a tool for social transformation and justice. "For Cassese, the law is a weapon to improve the world," says Luigi Condorelli, an Italian lawyer who knows him well.[12] During the 1960s and 1970s, Cassese worked for national self-determination in the Third World and for the advancement of human rights. In 1979 he organized the Permanent Peoples' Tribunal at the Lelio-Basso Foundation as an extension of the Bertrand Russell Tribunal, created in 1961 to denounce U.S. involvement in the war in Vietnam. He participates in the National Commission for Human Rights founded by the Socialist Party of Italy.

Regarding the state—the "cold monster" in Hegel's words—Cassese is mistrustful. He seeks to check the abuse of state power and becomes one of the architects of the European Convention for the Prevention of Torture and In-humane or Degrading Treatment or Punishment in 1987, then president of the oversight committee created by the Council of Europe. The convention authorizes investigators to enter without warning, day or night, any police station, prison, or jail across Europe to ensure that prisoners are not mistreated.

Cassese then followed up with a tell-all book in which he describes the brutal reality of European incarceration.[13]

Cassese's qualities as a jurist and his career of public service (he had also contributed to the elaboration of additional protocols to the Geneva Conventions during the 1970s) make him invaluable as the president of a tribunal that doubts its own fundamental viability. For this international crusader of the law, the International Criminal Tribunal for the Former Yugoslavia is not an ordinary job but a cause to defend. A militant for human rights of the first order, Cassese can also see farther down the road: The ICTY is the path to the creation of true international law, the laboratory of a future international criminal court. He wants the experiment to succeed so that politicians can no longer oppose the idea, to realize at last the ancient dream of the pre-war League of Nations. He wants to clear the way.

With round glasses, short stature, and a bald spot, Cassese gives the impression of inexhaustible energy compressed to serve indefatigable determination. He immediately sets to work to bring this new tribunal to life. But despite his political finesse, Cassese commits an error in judgment by trusting the political will of the Western governments. "Everybody told me: 'Listen, your tribunal, you love it a lot, but you need to understand that it is a just a leaf on the vine,'" he recalls. "These insinuations bothered me. I told them that the political will was real. I was truly naïve. I believed it, but I was clearly wrong. The governments wanted to hide their political impotence behind the existence of the tribunal. Nobody in fact believed that it was actually going to exist."[14] Another judge goes even further: "The ICTY had been created as a catharsis, as a moral executor of the Security Council, which at its core refused to intervene politically and militarily in Yugoslavia."[15]

The U.N. Secretariat does not even bother to unblock the funds to perpetuate this delusion. "We had strictly nothing: no location, no money, no personnel, no buildings," Cassese reiterates. "The few computers were rented; the four secretaries had only three-month contracts. We had rented a meeting room and three small offices at the Palace of Peace [in The Hague] for just two weeks. I sought out the Secretary General of the Carnegie Foundation, owner of the Palace of Peace, and told him, 'I am looking for some offices for the Tribunal, because the judges will be back at the end of the month.' He told me, 'Great idea.' But when I asked to extend our rental of those offices, he gave me a categorical refusal. In diplomatic terms, he told the ICTY to hit the road."[16] The ICTY is under a black cloud. The Carnegie Foundation secretary general fears that the ICTY's poor standing will damage the "honorable" organization's reputation. The ICTY becomes a "homeless" tribunal, whose immediate survival is far from assured.

Waiting for the United Nations to allocate the resources needed, the majority of the judges are demoralized and ready to pack their bags. In a plenary session, they explain, "Let us all go home to wait for a budget from the United Nations. When the international community gets serious, we will begin our work!" [17] The new president of the ICTY opposes this plan, fearing that the tribunal will fade away before it even sees the light of day. The more dynamic judges accept his counsel.

Cassese knows that accepting the death of the tribunal will kill any hope of creating an international criminal court for a long time. Closing the "laboratory" that is the ICTY would all but end the struggle against the impunity of butchers all over the world. On the other hand, the ICTY's success would open new avenues for creating a truly international court. It is in this spirit that Cassese struggles against the manipulations of the U.N. Secretariat. "The U.N. Office of Legal Affairs threw a spoke in our wheels," one judge recalls. "It wanted to control the personnel that we recruited. It wanted to treat us as a subsidiary organ of the United Nations, which we certainly were, but not as an independent tribunal which we remained even more so." [18]

Antonio Cassese uses the only power available to him: speech. "Either I accepted the facts as they were and, thus, the asphyxiation and the slow death of the tribunal," he explains, "or I launched myself into judicial activism, even to excess. Obviously, I chose the second solution." [19] Cassese recalls that during a debate at the University of Connecticut, in the presence of American diplomats, he warned, "If, in one or two years, there are still no accused in the dock, it would be better that the judges pack their bags and go home. Our duty will be to tell the United Nations, and to the Security Council in particular, that our mission ended in failure and that we do not intend to be the alibi for the political impotence of the international community." Cassese speaks for himself only, not the tribunal, and he himself is not sure that his "colleagues would have followed." [20] The American diplomats, however, as Cassese will understand later, are attentive to his criticism.

After their year-end vacations, still faced with total bureaucratic poverty, the judges return to The Hague in January, 1994, to prepare their weapons. They begin by writing the statutes of the ICTY. It is the only work they can do in the absence of a prosecutor, but it is fundamental. By establishing rules of procedure, they demonstrate that the credibility, impartiality, and power of the tribunal to get its message across are at stake. As the first international penal code ever established, the rules must be fixed on paper because there is no precedent. As one judge emphasizes to his colleagues, "We must learn to live like astronauts—in a legal vacuum." [21]

According to legal experts, the judges accomplish a remarkable technical work. But knowing nothing about the Balkans and oblivious to how the new code will be applied beyond the tribunal, these law professors and state prosecutors can only focus on the fairness of the rules. In so doing they lose sight of a fundamental principle: the imperative that an international court address the world, not remain cut off from it. This principle is particularly essential when the court is called, like an ambulance, to intervene directly in a war that is still in progress and marked by mounting atrocities.

The unfortunate result is a body of procedure that is thick, complex, and practically impenetrable to the uninitiated, thus rendering the tribunal's message nearly impossible to communicate clearly. One judge warns his colleagues, "I will tell them like I do in school. 'Place an apple in a vacuum chamber and decrease the pressure; the apple slowly changes shape and eventually explodes. The rules of law are the same thing. They must be adapted to the environment.'"[22] "The ICTY is being crushed under a slab of narrow legalism," another judge complains.[23]

The common law judges, particularly the American judge, note problems with the new code. Under the Anglo-American system, after the pretrial hearing during which the charges are read to the defendant, the accused may remain free until trial.[24] In peacetime, this condition is perfectly reasonable. But in a war context, a decision by the international tribunal to allow accused war criminals to go free before their trial takes on another meaning, constituting an affront to the victims and a signal of impunity to the criminals. The continental judges, however, consider this narrow approach to the law absurd. Fortunately, on this point they achieve a compromise: Only ill defendants will be allowed to remain free.

But there remain many other issues to resolve. The richer debate plays out around the concept of "contumacy," which under the continental system allows trials in absentia.[25] The continental judges, traditionally more assertive than their Anglo-American common law colleagues, see this element as an essential instrument for stigmatizing criminals. They know well that the ICTY will have all the difficulty in the world in issuing indictments, particularly against high political and military officials, but they have no force capable of arresting the accused. The doctrine of contumacy allows them not only to censure the crimes but also to try and convict the criminals in their absence. This action will have immediate political effect: It will revoke the accuseds' status as respectable interlocutors in negotiations for a political settlement. But the common law judges do not see things this way. For them, a trial without a defendant is worthless and can easily turn into a legal "circus." They fear that the tribunal will sink into the complacency of reading indictments aloud to itself, going nowhere without real, effective power and penalties. In truth, both the common law judges and the continental jurists fear the discrediting of the tribunal, but each interprets the threat differently.

The American Zorro

Faced with a tribunal well down the road to perdition, the Americans suddenly understand the advantages it offers. Once mistrustful, they now transform themselves into its saviors. The Bush administration had publicly affirmed that "we don't have a dog in that fight" over Yugoslavia and did not trouble itself to learn about the conflict. But by 1993, the Clinton administration can no longer afford the luxury of indifference. War in the Balkans monopolizes the media, and the American absence in the worst European crisis since World War II threatens to damage U.S. interests in the long term.

In the tribunal, the Americans find a weapon with potential. By issuing indictments, the ICTY can help marginalize the ultranationalist political and military leaders who threaten the peace negotiations. Indeed, it is difficult to present oneself as a peace partner when you are publicly accused of having blood on your hands. The ICTY allows the United States to have "weight" in the Balkans; it postpones the need for troops while allaying public concerns by showing that the United States is on the side of "justice." Backing the tribunal is a win-win proposition.

As a result, the Americans decide to place twenty-two high-level functionaries—Pentagon military analysts, CIA intelligence specialists, and lawyers—at the tribunal's disposal for an initial period of two years. Paid for by Washington, the American personnel—at no charge to the United Nations—will form the core of the Office of the Prosecutor, the central component of the ICTY. "It is not overstating the situation to point out that the success of the Tribunal as a whole depends very much on the caliber of the investigative staff of the Office of the Prosecutor," Boutros Boutros-Ghali notes in his annual report.[26] Under the adversarial rules of procedure, the prosecutor is in effect the "engine" of the tribunal, since the judges are relegated to a common law function as arbiter between defense and prosecution. From now on, the tribunal has an engine made in America.

On June 13, 1994, the first of the twenty-two functionaries are welcomed with open arms by Graham Blewitt, the interim prosecutor. For this Australian who is the sole incarnation of the long arm of international justice, they represent assistance he had never expected. Nothing seems able to distract him, except maybe a cricket match between the Old Blacks and Great Britain. Named assistant prosecutor in February, 1994, Blewitt has, by June, been able to hire only eleven people. Originally from New South Wales, Australia, this forty-seven-year-old man comes to his post by virtue of the fact that his government had charged him with tracking down Nazis taking refuge there. In this role, he moved on to direct inquests in Yugoslavia and the former Soviet Union from 1988 to 1993, notably exhuming bodies of massacre victims.

If Graham Blewitt does not hide his relief at the massive dispatch of American personnel, U.N. headquarters in New York expresses confusion and anger. It is the classic U.N. paradox: the incapacity—indeed, the absence of will—to provide the means indispensable to a functioning tribunal combined with denunciations of American hegemony when Washington intervenes to make the tribunal work. This anger cruelly reveals the weakness and hypocrisy of the United Nations. In an almost insulting gesture, the United Nations obliges the twenty-two Americans to sign a document by which they engage themselves to respect ICTY confidentiality and not to obey a hierarchy external to that of the tribunal.

The European capitals are taken aback by this American "coup," even if it is not the first of its kind.[27] "They told us, 'This is unacceptable. Your tribunal is infiltrated by the CIA!'" recalls ICTY spokesman Christian Chartier. "But these same governments had sent us no personnel while we cried famine and did nothing even when we asked them for help," he adds.[28]

"The French, Italian, and German governments questioned me, 'Why are you accepting all these Americans?'" Cassese recalls. "I told them, 'Do the same thing!' They did nothing of the sort. But I was not duped by the generosity of the Americans. They helped the tribunal, but they wanted a hold on it. The real question is why the other countries did not do the same thing. We needed everything."[29] The answer is simple. The Europeans have no interest in creating an effective tribunal, out of fear that the ICTY will block the route to a negotiated solution. This massive injection of American personnel, nevertheless, finally gives some credibility to the Office of the Prosecutor, which was until then an empty shell. There is, however, a price to pay. The image of an independent tribunal is irreversibly tarnished, and the loyalty of these personnel, whose career and salary depend on a hierarchy exterior to that of the United Nations, is clearly put into question. Moreover, the Americans are offering the Office of the Prosecutor computers worth $3 million—the equivalent of all the voluntary contributions to the ICTY so far. Ninety percent of these voluntary contributions have been made by two Islamic countries: Malaysia ($2 million) and Pakistan ($1 million). France has not put in a dime. It is not the least of the ironies of this tribunal, created thanks to a French-sponsored U.N. resolution, that it is suddenly willed into existence by the Americans, who until then had shown not the slightest intention to act.

This turn of events determines the tribunal's life from that point on. The total lack of support by the Europeans, compensated by the Americans' activism, gives credence to the suspicion of American influence over the tribunal. France maintains a solid distrust in that regard. The appointment of American personnel to the Office of the Prosecutor never makes headlines, but it does influence political and military leaders in Europe. The ICTY's privileged relations with the United States will be paid for at a high price.

"Habemus Papem"

Having a criminal tribunal implies that there is a prosecutor, but the ICTY continues to be an exception to that rule. Of all the tribunal staff positions, that of prosecutor is the most essential because the prosecutor defines the objectives and the penal strategy and proceeds to indictments and prosecution. The Security Council has left the post vacant for fifteen months. For some European cabinet ministers, this delay in the work of the tribunal is excellent news because it permits the negotiations to continue without legal "brakes."

At the United Nations in New York, a months-long waltz of prospective candidates for the Office of the Prosecutor ensues. Cherif Bassiouni, Kahlsoven's successor at the Commission of Experts, is rejected by the British, who fear his activism. The Islamic states do not want a Brit, who is judged to be too soft. An Indian candidate is vetoed by the Russians. A Venezuelan is named by the Security Council but resigns before taking his post. Justice has broken down; the war, however, rages on. On February 5, 1993, a mortar attack on the market at Sarajevo, in the heart of the city, kills sixty-eight people and injures some two hundred others.

Boutros Boutros-Ghali asks Antonio Cassese to look for the rare pearl who can satisfy all fifteen members of the U.N. executive body. Cassese skims through the potential candidates in Latin America and Asia, but "either they weren't interested, or they were not available, or they weren't up to it," he says. Then, as he remembers with humor, the solution appears by luck through the French national counsel, Roger Errera. "He said to me, 'Listen, my dear friend, you look sad,'" Cassese recalls.

> I answered, "I am very concerned. There is no light at the end of the tunnel for my tribunal." Errera asked me, "Do you know Goldstone?" I answered, "Who's he?"

"Goldstone, the South African, the chairman of the Commission on Violence [Commission of Inquiry regarding the Prevention of Public Violence and Intimidation] committed by the police under apartheid, a really good guy."

"He's Jewish?"

"Listen, we don't ask that question."

"But no, if he is Jewish, that goes down well. Everyone suspects everyone in the former Yugoslavia. So it's better that he is neither Catholic, nor Orthodox, nor Muslim."

But he didn't want to answer me. I called Goldstone myself. I understood very quickly that he was a very intelligent man. He seemed interested. I sent him a fax with a proposal, the conditions. . . . Goldstone told me that he would soon be nominated to the [South African] Constitutional Court, but that it would be possible, maybe. . . . Boutros called [President Nelson] Mandela, who gave him his consent on one confidential condition: "Goldstone will work for you for two years. After that he will rejoin the South African supreme court." [30]

At that moment, the new South Africa is at the peak of its prestige. Madeleine Albright emphasizes that the nomination of a white South African, who, "at great personal risk, insisted that the truth be known about cruel abuses committed under apartheid in South Africa," is a powerful symbol.[31] Goldstone is in effect director of the commission of inquiry that will eventually carry his name, the commission charged with investigating violence committed by South African security forces. Born October 20, 1938, in Boksburg, South Africa, this liberal judge with a seat on the supreme court of Transvaal, this former lawyer of the Johannesburg bar, now personifies his country's peaceful transition to democratic rule. Hallowed by this image, standing out in a country that has hardly any interests in the Balkans, Richard Goldstone has the perfect profile to become the ICTY's prosecutor.

On an afternoon in July, 1994, in New York, the Security Council unanimously confirms Goldstone. "I could not calm down," Cassese remembered. "It was 9:00 P.M. and everybody had left the office. I was so excited that I could not find the tribunal letterhead. All the judges were back home in their own countries, in China, in Malaysia, in Europe. I wrote a fax to them. I started like this: 'Dear Colleagues, *habemus papem,*' we now have our pope! It was one of the most beautiful nights for me at The Hague, that we could finally get to work!" [32]

Goldstone's nomination satisfies the French, even if he does not speak French, because they are the source of his nomination. The British and the Americans are also reassured. Goldstone is neither too hot-headed for London,

RICHARD GOLDSTONE—
Secured by Antonio
Cassese, the celebrated
South African jurist
was welcomed as a
principled, neutral
prosecutor for the new
tribunal. However, his
caution and "small fry"
indictments frustrated
the judges; only after the
Srebrenica massacre did
he indict Karadzic and
Mladic. (NATO)

nor too weak for Washington. The image of a white South African who directly
opposed apartheid also suits the Russians and the Chinese.

Confrontation

Richard Goldstone takes over the prosecutor's functions in the summer of
1994. After his initial shock at joining a tribunal in total deprivation, Goldstone
quickly understands what he is up against. Born in a country that has just managed to avoid civil war, the new prosecutor has no trouble understanding the
relationships of force. To fight against political obstruction, he knows that he
has only the media and public opinion and that among the Great Powers only
the United States supports a strong tribunal.

Goldstone's imperative at this point is to show that the tribunal exists. He
is under enormous pressure from all quarters to do something. The media are

criticizing the tribunal's inaction; the judges complain of having not a single defendant in the dock; even the United Nations is pressuring the tribunal to produce results. The United Nations proposes a strange bargain: issuing indictments as fast as possible in exchange for cash. "The United Nations told me: 'If you proceed to the indictments, you will have a right to a[n independent] budget,'" Goldstone explains. "It was our reality. Each dime that they gave us was taken directly out of the [general] U.N. budget. Although the Tribunal had existed since May 1993, by the time I had arrived in August 1994, its credibility was worse than zero. I felt like I had found myself in an enormous supermarket without a single product to put on its shelves."[33]

Without delay, Goldstone issues indictments on two secondary figures: Dragan Nikolic, Serb commander of the Susica concentration camp, in November, 1994, and Dusko Tadic, Omarska camp torturer, in February, 1995. The two men are accused of torturing and murdering Muslim civilians and participating in the forced deportation of civilians. The indictments are chilling: Tadic is accused of participating in the castration of a prisoner and forcing other prisoners to torture the victim. Tadic is, fortunately, already in German custody, a stroke of luck for the new prosecutor. Goldstone finally has a defendant, and the judges are satisfied. They even consider opening a bottle of champagne, but refrain, because, according to one judge, "this is not a thing to celebrate while atrocities continue unabated."[34]

But the honeymoon between the judges and the prosecutor is brief. After the Tadic and Nikolic indictments, they expect the prosecutor to indict some "big fish." But nothing happens. The Serb and Bosnian Serb heads, the Karadzics, Mladics, as well as Arkan (Zeljko Raznatovic) and Vojislav Seselj, remain unindicted. The judges suspect Goldstone of going soft, of doing just enough to keep the doors open without having a real penal strategy, of tending to his relationships with governments and the media while the masterminds of ethnic cleansing continue their sinister business. One judge explodes, "We are not here to judge the Tadics."[35] The judges fear they are merely the honorary figureheads of international justice.

Goldstone is, indeed, pursuing a different strategy. He does not break away from politics because it is a necessary part of his design. He never puts the governments in an awkward position by reminding them of their unfulfilled commitments. On the contrary, by relying on the states most receptive to his message, he hopes to win a margin of maneuver and to loosen the financial vise strangling the work of the tribunal. But the limits of this very consensual approach are quickly reached; the majority of the states that have troops in the former Yugoslavia do not want the tribunal to target the political and military leaders who are still their negotiating partners. Periodically Karadzic returns to

Geneva for sessions of the International Conference on the Former Yugoslavia, and he is put up in the best hotels. The United Nations and European Community mediators continue to treat him as a respectable interlocutor.

Beginning in January, 1995, the judges revolt. The conflict breaks out during a private meeting when a judge directly attacks Goldstone. "Instead of running a public relations campaign," the judge chastises, "sit in your office and read the documents that we are sending you!"[36] The judges cannot understand why Goldstone refuses to indict the Serb president and his acolytes. The judges have briefed the prosecutor that the best legal strategy to indict those responsible for ethnic cleansing is the doctrine of "command responsibility." On three occasions Antonio Cassese has spoken at length on the Yamashita case of December 7, 1945, that established this principle.[37] For the judges, the urgency to act is foremost, because each day that passes means new atrocities are committed. The judges know full well that the Yamashita decision is, at best, a strained precedent, but necessity creates law to curb policies of murder and persecution. The judges are not there to render justice in peacetime but to limit atrocities in war.

But without even bothering to explain why, the prosecutor refuses to consider the Yamashita precedent. The exasperated judges feel like they are talking to a brick wall. Paul Stuebner, Goldstone's right-hand man, later justifies the prosecutor's position. "MacArthur wanted the head of General Yamashita because the Japanese commander had won battles in the Pacific," Stuebner says. "MacArthur succeeded and Yamashita was sentenced to death. Very frankly, the judgment was for me the quintessence of conqueror's justice. I did not want the Tribunal to take inspiration from this case."[38] But Stuebner's objection is only partially valid; the ICTY judges have not issued their opinion based solely on the verdict against one Japanese general cut off from his troops during World War II. They want the prosecutor to operate on the well-established *principle* of command responsibility by indicting the Bosnian Serb leaders who control the troops under their direct authority and who have committed heinous crimes.

During the fifth plenary session, January 16–30, 1995, the judges summon Goldstone to explain his inertia. The most active judges are nicknamed the Three Musketeers: Antonio Cassese, Georges Abi-Saab, and Claude Jorda, all representing continental law, and there is a strong bond among them. The first two have known each other for years. They are professors who also possess solid experience in practicing international law. In the territorial dispute case brought to the International Court of Justice by Libya and Chad, Cassese had defended Chad and Abi-Saab had served as a judge. To avoid any impression of collusion on that case, whenever the two wanted to get together on a friendly basis they would invite a mutual friend, himself a member of the Libyan team, to join them. Claude Jorda had followed a different path. Born in 1938 in Bône, in what was then French Algeria, Jorda had spent most of his career teaching at the École Nationale de la Magistrature in Paris. Named prosecutor general by the Court of Appeal in Bordeaux, then by the Court of Appeal in Paris, he joined the tribunal in 1994.

The three judges, joined by their colleagues, press Goldstone. "When are you going to indict the Bosnian Serb leaders? What are your penal objectives?" they demand. Goldstone responds by describing his "pyramid strategy," also called "strategy from the bottom up" that seeks to "start with the little fish and climb the chains of command to the summit of the hierarchy." This strategy is a classic course of action against organized crime: Start with a drug dealer on the street to get at the head mafiosi. But in a wartime context, this strategy is completely maladapted. Losing his temper, Antonio Cassese, as remembered by one of the participants in the meeting, explodes, "With a little luck, in fifteen years, after you have mounted the entire military hierarchy, you may manage to trap a general." [39]

After their failure to convince Goldstone, the judges meet again in seclusion. They decide to prepare a public communiqué in which they express "their concerns" regarding the prosecutor's penal strategy. They know that they are walking on a mine field because theoretically they have no right to comment on the work of the prosecutor, who is sovereign in matters of accusation. They know that they are making a declaration of war against Richard Goldstone, who has warned that "he, too, would take out his cartridges." [40] He, too, would retaliate and come out shooting. They also know that the public effect could be disastrous for the tribunal. Thanks to Goldstone's public relations campaign, the credibility of the tribunal is on the rise. Goldstone knows how to find the right sound bite for the press. "We are going for the jugular," he has said on many occasions, ensuring that no guilty leader would escape judgment. [41] Some of the judges warn their president that he is going too far. "I responded that I couldn't care less," Cassese says. "We were all part of this tribunal and it was necessary that Goldstone succeed in his mission, if need be by prodding the prosecutor to beef up his criminal strategy." [42] The Anglo-American judges eventually follow the Three Musketeers. They draft the tribunal's third press release, denouncing the situation.

With the press release drafted, Antonio Cassese ends the meeting momentarily to inform Richard Goldstone so that he can not claim betrayal. The meeting between the two men is stormy. "You want to attack me, fine. I am going to retaliate," Goldstone says. "I am also going to make a statement to the press. . . . We'll both shoot our cartridges and then you'll see who will remain standing with the tribunal."[43] The two men separate. But just as quickly, Goldstone comes to see Cassese on his own. "He said to me, 'OK. If you change some words, I can say that I share your position,'" Cassese recalls. Goldstone's about-face is a shrewd move; he kills the judges' revolt before it can begin. "It was great politics," Cassese remembers. "He immediately applied the principle 'if you can't beat 'em, join 'em.' We finished by haggling over the press communiqué. He had tried to get rid of a passage that took aim at the Office of the Prosecutor, then associated himself 'with the judges' concern' in the last paragraph. This was a little ridiculous, since our press communiqué had been directed against him. But in the final count, he had managed to drown the fish."[44]

The journalists are a little surprised by the tribunal's press release, which, after being redrafted, makes no sense. Entitled "The Judges of the Tribunal for the former Yugoslavia express their concern regarding the substance of their programme of judicial work for 1995," it affirms, "The judges wish to express their concern for the urgency with which adequate indictments must be made. . . . Due to the gravity and the historic dimension of this mission, the judges hold particularly to this program of indictment responding effectively to the priorities of the Security Council and the international community in its entirety. The prosecutor has been informed about the judges' concern, and indicated that he shares it."[45] When asked, the ICTY's spokesman, Christian Chartier, is justified in asserting that there is "no tension" at the heart of the tribunal and that it is "one and indivisible."[46]

The Goldstone Enigma

Why does Richard Goldstone remain so cautious? Is he a prisoner of government influence? Has he made their objectives his own? Officially, he does not indict the political and military leaders of the ethnic cleansing because his dossiers are practically empty. "The only thing that we had was the work of Bassiouni's Commission of Inquiry, which permitted us to construct the Tadic case. But there was nothing in the dossiers to indict Milosevic and the other high-ranking political and military leaders," he says.[47] But Goldstone's line of defense does not hold. The only possible explanation is politics, a terrain on which he excelled. Goldstone identifies himself as a pragmatist, never concerning himself too much with legal reflection. On the contrary, he understands the relationship of force better than anyone, capturing his audience, adjusting his strategy blow by blow. He knows that Paris, London, Moscow, Beijing, and even Washington, to which he is close, do not want to close the door on a "deal" with Milosevic. A negotiated peace must go through Belgrade. And, for a long time as well, the negotiations continue to go through Karadzic's Bosnian Serb "capital," Pale. It is for this reason that Goldstone does not push hard enough to disturb them.

The Yugoslav leaders' political impunity is backed up by de facto legal impunity. As incredible as it seems, no team of investigators at the ICTY is even trying to build a case to indict Milosevic, Mladic, and Karadzic, even while Western politicians and the media are denouncing them as Balkan pyromaniacs and the principal instigators of a bloodbath. The internal structure of the Office of the Prosecutor (which is not public information) indicates that nine teams of investigators are spread out according to the geography where crimes are committed (Foca, Prijedor, Vukovar, the Lasva valley). Only a handful of investigators have the mission of climbing the chains of command to the highest levels, and more often than not, even these few investigators are sidetracked to other, more urgent missions.

Goldstone's penal strategy consists of indicting a gang of secondary figures. The judges complain, "We are not here to fill quotas!"[48] Moreover, the preparation of the few indictments Goldstone issues has some immediate harmful effects: It directs the meager forces of the Office of the Prosecutor away from higher targets. Goldstone is falling into step with the Western governments, who feel that the tribunal must confine itself to intimidating the leadership of the warring parties, while stopping short of arresting them. Their message is "Negotiate a diplomatic solution or you, too, will be prosecuted." At that moment, they are not interested in indicting Milosevic or Karadzic, partners judged indispensable to a negotiated solution, but the less important executors of ethnic cleansing. The indictments of the latter are as much a warning shot as anything. Lord David Owen, mediator for the European Union, admits as much. "When I met Goldstone or the people close to the tribunal, I did not recommend against indicting Milosevic or the others," he says.

[Such a recommendation] would not have been wise, since I did not have a word to say about whether he must or must not issue an indictment. On the other hand, I explained to them the detail of the negotiations, showed him the difficulties [we faced]. The conclusion, that they could easily draw, was that it would not be very wise to indict the heads of state if we wanted to arrive at a negotiated peace between them and with them. I believe that Goldstone and [his successor Louise] Arbour had this pragmatic attitude, this judgment of good sense, and the tribunal only indicted Milosevic when the prosecutor understood that he was no longer an obstacle, politically. Because after Kosovo there were no more means to negotiate with Milosevic.[49]

In other words, the exercise of justice continues to be subordinate to the imperative of peace, as long as the Bosnian Serb leaders appear to be credible peace partners. The risk of this "instrumentalization" of justice is that it undermines the moral foundations of the tribunal. But even in colluding with realpolitik logic, Richard Goldstone never even indicts the heads of the paramilitaries, notably Seselj and Arkan, who commit the worst atrocities of the war against Croatia, then against Bosnia, and who were never partners in negotiation. The absence of their pursuit is difficult to comprehend unless it is that indicting them would lead inevitably toward indicting Slobodan Milosevic. An exasperated Antonio Cassese testifying before the European Parliament Subcommittee on Human Rights on October 30, 1996, wonders aloud why Arkan is not indicted, nor any of the other presumed war criminals from the list read by Lawrence Eagleburger in Geneva back in December, 1993. That list, he remembers, also included Slobodan Milosevic. To the members of parliament who press him, Antonio Cassese suggests that they ask the prosecutor himself for an explanation.

Anonymously, many judges confess that they think Goldstone has succumbed to outside political pressure. It is, indeed, the most probable hypothesis. Cherif Bassiouni, the former president of the Commission of Inquiry, thinks as much. "The United States wanted to use the weapons of the ICTY," he says.

But for that weapon to be most effective, it was necessary not to use it to excess, but to hold the indictment of Slobodan Milosevic in reserve. No doubt, Washington hoped that the Yugoslav military would call the regime into question. And in fact, in 1998, Milosevic was frightened and fired his Chief of Staff and several high-ranking military leaders. [From a legal point of view,] it would have been possible, I think, to indict Milosevic for the murder of some two hundred patients and personnel of the hospital at Vukovar, under the doctrine of command responsibility. We knew very quickly who committed these crimes. It was the Serb paramilitaries from Krajina who had murdered the people in the hospital, but it was the Yugoslav army (JNA) soldiers who had delivered them. I had myself submitted the name[s] of certain JNA officers to the ICTY. I had even transmitted a memo to the ICTY where I named the commanders who had organized the siege of Sarajevo, and I determined that, there again, it was possible to corner Milosevic. I explained at the time that the Kosevo hospital, the largest in the city, had been bombarded 289 times. Even supposing that the Bosnians had managed to fire a few mortar rounds from the hospital gardens, the hospital did not constitute a military target. And it was during visiting hours, between 12 and 2 P.M., that Serb artillery fired 70 percent of their rounds.[50]

At what point did Richard Goldstone, when confronted with this moral nightmare, implicitly or explicitly delay the indictment of the top Serbs in order to bring a quicker end to the suffering of hundreds of thousands of men, women, and children? To what degree, by personal conviction or from outside pressure, did he take the risk of violating the fundamental ethic of his role as prosecutor in the hope of facilitating the search for peace? The questions remain unanswered.

Goldstone himself remains, intentionally, an enigma. His writings contradict his actions. Was it his intention to respond to criticism or to ensure the independence of the tribunal? He possesses a rare eloquence when affirming that no true peace exists without justice, even if the pursuit of war implies an ongoing bloodbath. He says as much in an article entitled "To Judge War Criminals," in which he cites an article published anonymously in *Human Rights Quarterly* that he calls "the most eloquent and most virulent criticism ever to have been made against the ICTY." He quotes this anonymous but perfectly informed author at length: "'The demands of justice in the name of yesterday's victims must not force us to make new victims among the living of today. This is one of the lessons that defenders of human rights must take from the conflict in the former Yugoslavia. Thousands of people lost their lives for the sole reason that the moralists were in search of the perfect peace. Unfortunately, it is rare that a perfect peace can be instituted in the wake of a bloody conflict. To pursue criminals is one thing, to make peace with them is another.'"[51]

To that, Goldstone replies, "It is in the time and circumstances in which the relation between peace and justice is so profound, where these notions are so inextricably linked one to another, that a negotiated peace without responding to demands of justice would hardly be worth the paper it is printed on. In many cases, one such superficial and fallacious peace returns in reality to prepare the sly return of war, which will resurge in secret, with a face even more brutal and a savagery difficult to imagine. . . . A peace concluded by war criminals returns finally to serve their own aims, while they despise all the prescriptions and fundamental norms of international law, [and this peace] will be known to be neither real nor durable."[52]

How can we reconcile Goldstone the prosecutor and the man who writes these lines, this Dr. Jekyll and Mr. Hyde of international justice?

Chapter **Four**

These innumerable dead, these massacred, these tortured, these
trampled, these offended, are the business of us all.
—Vladimir Jankélévitch, *L'Imprescriptible*

A Court Put to the Test

Sure of their impunity, by 1995 the Bosnian Serb leaders are feeling
invulnerable. The Tadic indictment handed up on February 10, after
three years of war in Bosnia, is not likely to frighten the executors of
ethnic cleansing. On April 24, 1995, Richard Goldstone gives them even
less cause for worry. As if walking on eggshells, the prosecutor of the ICTY reveals that he "is currently investigating the criminal responsibility of the leadership of the Bosnian Serbs in Pale, particularly Radovan Karadzic, their leader,
Ratko Mladic, commander of their army, and Mico Stanisic, former political
head of their special police. The investigations regarding the three suspects
cover a wide range of alleged offenses: genocide, other serious offenses against
civilians, and destruction of cultural and historical monuments." But the prosecutor is careful to announce publicly that Karadzic and Mladic are not accused
and have the right to the presumption of innocence. The tribunal press release
reiterates this point with extreme care: "The individuals under investigation at
this stage are suspects. . . . These suspects may later become the accused."[1]

The "suspects" have good reason to feel secure, so secure, in fact, that they
prepare the largest massacre committed on European soil since World War II:
Srebrenica, which will become the tragic symbol of the West's policy of appeasement of the Bosnian Serb forces.

The tragic and preventable fall of this enclave deserves some background.
On May 24, 1995, the United Nations orders the Serb forces to surrender all
their heavy weapons around Sarajevo to the control of UNPROFOR. The Serbs

64

ignore the order. NATO aircraft bomb a Serb munitions depot, and the Serbs respond by shelling the U.N. "safe areas" for Bosnian Muslim refugees, including Tuzla, where an attack on the city center kills 61 people and injures more than 500. On May 26, NATO aircraft attack other munitions depots. In retaliation, Bosnian Serb forces take 370 peacekeepers hostage. On June 3, NATO defense ministers approve, in principle, the creation of a rapid-reaction force for Bosnia. The Serbs gradually release the peacekeepers during the month of June.

On July 4, Serb forces use heavy artillery to shell the U.N. "safe area" of Srebrenica. This attack is a clear violation of the Security Council resolution creating the safe areas, but NATO does not respond. On July 9, President Alija Izetbegovic of Bosnia warns UNPROFOR of the potential for a massacre if the enclave falls. Just two days later, Bosnian Serb soldiers overrun Srebrenica. On July 12 and 13, some twenty thousand women, children, and elderly Muslims are expelled from Srebrenica in the direction of Tuzla, and they take stories of atrocities with them. On July 16 and 17, approximately four thousand Muslim men, out of a column of fifteen thousand who have fled Srebrenica, reach Tuzla. The others have disappeared. In the presence of Serb general Ratko Mladic, about a thousand men have been executed in the woods and fields around Srebrenica. In total, six thousand to nine thousand men and teenagers are reported missing. Premeditated massacres—sometimes in the immediate vicinity of Dutch peacekeepers—have been carried out boldly in front of a passive international community.

"At the tribunal, we felt horror and anger against the Security Council for allowing this to occur, and a terrible feeling of impotence," one judge recalls.[2]

Srebrenica is a personal humiliation for all who have placed faith in the court at The Hague. They feel that their years of work have been for nothing. Lord David Owen, who has worked for a negotiated solution, lucidly recognizes the failure of his own policy. "By 1995, Karadzic and Mladic had an incommensurable contempt for the West and the international community, going so far as refusing the peace plan of the Contact Group formed by the most powerful countries on the planet," he said. "As for the tribunal, they didn't give a damn."[3]

The tragedy at Srebrenica demonstrates the ineffectiveness of the international court, which has exhausted itself condemning subordinate criminals far down the chain of command while leaving alone the principal instigators of the massacre. Out of their fear that the ICTY will become independent and complicate the bogged-down negotiations, the Western governments have forfeited the court's credibility with the warlords—to the point that some think nothing of acting out their murderous hatred.

WAR CRIMINALS INDICTED BY THE INTERNATIONAL CRIMINAL TRIBUNAL FOR THE FORMER YUGOSLAVIA
WARRANTS FOR THEIR ARREST ARE HELD BY THEIR RESPECTIVE CAPITALS

ZLATKO ALEKSOVSKI
DOB: 06/01/60
NATIONALITY: CROATIAN
DESCRIPTION: NOT AVAILABLE
ADDRESS: MOSTAR, BIH

TIHOFOL BLASKIĆ
DOB: 02/11/60
NATIONALITY: CROATIAN
DESCRIPTION: NOT AVAILABLE
ADDRESS: MOSTAR, BIH

RANKO CESIĆ
DOB: 01/01/64
NATIONALITY: BOSNIAN SERB
DESCRIPTION: MEDIUM HEIGHT AND BUILD; BROWN HAIR AND EYES
ADDRESS: BIJELJINA, POSSIBLY BRCKO, BIH

RADOVAN KARADŽIĆ
DOB: 19/06/45
NATIONALITY: BOSNIAN SERB
DESCRIPTION: 185 CM; BROWNISH-GRAY HAIR; FLAMBOYANT
ADDRESS: PALE, BIH

DARIO KORDIĆ
DOB: 14/12/60
NATIONALITY: CROATIAN
DESCRIPTION: 173 CM; DARK, CROPPED HAIR; GLASSES
ADDRESS: PRESIDENT OF CROATIAN COMMUNITY OF HERCEG-BOSNA

MILAN MARTIĆ
DOB: 18/11/54
NATIONALITY: SERBIAN
DESCRIPTION: 172-180 CM; 85-90 KG; DARK BROWN HAIR; GREEN-BROWN EYES
ADDRESS: UNKNOWN

ŽELJKO MEAKIĆ
DOB: 02/08/64
NATIONALITY: BOSNIAN SERB
DESCRIPTION: 175 CM; 65 KG; BROWN HAIR; BLUE EYES
ADDRESS: PETROV GAJ

SLOBODAN MILJKOVIĆ
DOB: 01/01/53
NATIONALITY: SERBIAN
DESCRIPTION: 180 CM; DARK BROWN HAIR; SCAR ON SIDE OF NOSE; TATOOS ON BOTH ARMS
ADDRESS: UNKNOWN

RATKO MLADIĆ
DOB: 12/03/43
NATIONALITY: BOSNIAN SERB
DESCRIPTION: SHORT, STOCKY; RED-FACED
ADDRESS: BELGRADE, SERBIA

MILAN MRKSĆ
DOB: 20/07/47
NATIONALITY: SERBIAN
DESCRIPTION: 180 CM; GRAY, WAVY HAIR
ADDRESS: CDR, RSKA ARMY

DRAGAN NIKOLIĆ
DOB: 01/01/57
NATIONALITY: BOSNIAN SERB
DESCRIPTION: 190-200 CM; BLOND HAIR
ADDRESS: UNKNOWN

DRAŽENKO PREDOJIVIĆ
DOB: 02/06/70
NATIONALITY: BOSNIAN SERB
DESCRIPTION: 175 CM; BLACK HAIR; MISSING FRONT TOOTH
ADDRESS: GRADINA, BIH

MIRSOLAV RADIĆ
DOB: 01/01/61
NATIONALITY: SERBIAN
DESCRIPTION: 180 CM; DARK, STRAIGHT HAIR; PROPORTIONAL BUILD
ADDRESS: UNKNOWN

MLADEN RADIĆ
DOB: 15/05/52
NATIONALITY: BOSNIAN SERB
DESCRIPTION: 178 CM; 100 KG; LIGHT BROWN HAIR; FAT BUILD
ADDRESS: OMARSKA, BIH

VESELIN ŠLJIVANČANIN
DOB: 01/01/53
NATIONALITY: BOSNIAN SERB
DESCRIPTION: 190 CM; DARK EYES; DARK, GRAYING, SHORT, THINNING HAIR
ADDRESS: UNKNOWN

STEVAN TODOROVIĆ
DOB: 01/01/57
NATIONALITY: UNKNOWN
DESCRIPTION: 180-185 CM; 100 KG; BROWN HAIR; BALDING
ADDRESS: BOSANSKI SAMAC, BIH

ZORAN ŽIGIĆ
DOB: 20/09/58
NATIONALITY: BOSNIAN SERB
DESCRIPTION: 175 CM; 80 KG; DARK BROWN HAIR
ADDRESS: FORMER TAXI DRIVER IN PRIJEDOR, BIH

RADOVAN KARADZIC—The self-styled Bosnian Serb president was for years the "indispensable interlocutor" during negotiations to end the war in Bosnia-Herzegovina, the war that he provoked and prolonged. Indicted for war crimes committed at Srebrenica, he remains at large with Serb general Ratko Mladic. (NATO)

Confronted with the immensity of this crime, Goldstone is obliged to change his strategy. The tribunal can no longer present itself to the world without indicting Karadzic and Mladic—the mere "suspects" of a few weeks ago—even if it means excluding them from future negotiations. On July 25, the prosecutor issues an indictment against the Serb leadership for events prior to Srebrenica, some of which go back as far as 1992.[4] The "suspects" have suddenly become the "accused" for acts committed in full sight and full knowledge of the world over three long years. Karadzic and Mladic are indicted for genocide, crimes against humanity, crimes against civilian populations and against religious edifices across the entire territory of the Republic of Bosnia-

Herzegovina, crimes relating to the sniper campaign against civilians in Sarajevo, and for taking UNPROFOR soldiers hostage. Among the other indicted leaders, they are accused of being criminally responsible for the "unlawful confinement, murder, rape, sexual assault, torture, beating, robbery and inhuman treatment of civilians; the targeting of political leaders, intellectuals and professionals; the unlawful deportation and transfer of civilians; the unlawful shelling of civilians; the unlawful appropriation and plunder of real and personal property; the destruction of homes and businesses; and the destruction of places of worship." [5]

A Foreshadowing of Dayton

Nonetheless, the Srebrenica massacre does not change the priorities of the Western governments: peace at any price, even if it is a peace without justice. Even the United States, up to now the tribunal's strongest supporter, from then on subscribes to the logic of negotiation with the Serb leadership. Following the debut of the Dayton peace talks, Washington threatens to give up on the tribunal entirely. The ICTY is suddenly no longer useful to them, save as a weapon to wave from time to time under Milosevic's nose to keep him in line. Whether it is by chance or by perfect timing, just before Dayton the ICTY indicts three Yugoslav officers responsible for the massacre of more than 260 people at the hospital in Vukovar. Are the indictments a warning in disguise for Milosevic? The Serb president appears to be playing the game of negotiated settlement perfectly.

Similarly, the rumor is circulating that the American negotiator Richard Holbrooke has struck a deal with Slobodan Milosevic, guaranteeing immunity in return for his contribution to a peace accord. The rumor is not the least bit unbelievable; if the international community can metamorphose the arsonist of the Balkans into a peacemaker, the tribunal will have difficulty pursuing him. Many people at the tribunal are convinced that such a deal has been reached. The United States, which carefully measures out the information it gives to the ICTY, has never passed on enough to indict the Serb president. "We had no, let me repeat, no information," says Paul Stuebner, the principal counselor to Richard Goldstone. "Neither the United States, nor France, nor Great Britain, nor any of the other countries aided us in building an indictment against Milosevic." [6] Milosevic remains the indispensable partner. So much the worse for justice.

The judges have often considered resigning en masse to protest their treatment, but this time the idea is real and serious. They have endured humiliation for years. Used as an alibi, constrained to impotence, then marginalized by the imminence of a negotiated settlement, they are no longer willing to be dupes in the role that they have been forced to play, marionettes of the international community. "During the summer of 1995, the idea of a deal between the Western governments and the Bosnian Serbs was spreading," Judge Georges Abi-Saab says. "All the judges, even the most conservative, agreed to resign in protest if this rumor was verified. We had spoken of it on several occasions, and no one, even the most reserved, was against it. We had even thought of sending a letter to Boutros Boutros-Ghali to warn him about it."[7]

But the judges do not resign because, evidently, they have no proof that any such deal has been reached between Holbrooke and Milosevic. Moreover, this promise of immunity for Milosevic does not need to be explicit between the American negotiator and the Serb president. Milosevic may assume that he becomes practically untouchable from the moment he participates in a negotiated solution in Bosnia. Justice is again sacrificed on the altar of peace.

Other rumors are circulating, even more worrisome for the tribunal: Mladic and Karadzic may come to Dayton as negotiators, even though the ICTY has indicted them, first in July and now, again, for the massacres at Srebrenica. Concerned by this prospect, Richard Goldstone quickly organizes a press conference and threatens to resign. Paul Stuebner is summoned by the Department of State for a sounding. Does Goldstone truly intend to resign if Karadzic and Mladic come to Dayton? Stuebner responds, "Not only the prosecutor, but many others may resign too. And they will not hold back from pointing an accusing finger at all those people who accept these presumed war criminals as participants in the negotiations."[8]

The threat by the prosecutor and the judges pays off in part: Neither Karadzic nor Mladic are present at the negotiations. But things get no better for the ICTY. Antonio Cassese pleads with the Americans not to leave the international court out of the talks. "I wanted to draft some clauses in the peace treaty referencing the work of the tribunal and that would require the establishment of a police force composed of NATO soldiers, who would be placed under the direction of the prosecutor, in order to proceed with arrests, seize documents, and participate in the investigations," Cassese says. "But the Americans told me, 'Forming a police force is out of the question. Our military are the military, not policemen at the service of an international prosecutor.'"[9] But the truer reason is elsewhere. The Americans want to avoid repeating the Somali fiasco in the Balkans; GI blood must not flow in Bosnia.

Cut loose from their only political support, the tribunal wonders if it is not condemned to disappear. Resolution 827, which marked the tribunal's birth, is ambiguous about its death; it stipulates that the mandate of the tribunal will end at "a date to be determined by the Security Council upon the restoration of peace."[10] If peace is reestablished at Dayton, will the tribunal still have any reason to exist in the eyes of the Great Powers? It could even become extremely burdensome during a peace sealed by the mastermind of ethnic cleansing.

Cassese fears a more pernicious threat. "The tribunal was like a monster. Once created, it was politically difficult to get rid of," he says. "However, one could paralyze it. A tribunal without defendants, without trials, would cost a fortune and produce nothing of value."[11]

The tribunal's president sees it coming: The Security Council indeed intends to slash the tribunal's budget. The pretext is simple: U.N. finances are in calamitous shape. The judges revolt against this umpteenth attempt at financial asphyxiation. On October 9, 1995, they make it known to Boutros Boutros-Ghali that

> [a] substantial (but not excessive) amount of travel is an essential component of the Tribunal's activities. To prohibit investigators and lawyers from travelling to the former Yugoslavia and elsewhere to conduct their investigations, interview witnesses etc., is to cut the very heart out of the Tribunal. . . . The flow of indictments will cease, leaving heinous crimes to go uninvestigated and unpunished. . . . If these witnesses cannot travel to The Hague, the entire raison d'être of the Tribunal, for which the Secretary-General has fought so determinedly, will collapse.[12]

Lastly, in an attempt that reveals their exasperation with the contempt in which their U.N. patron holds them, the judges brandish the threat of bad publicity: "Finally, the Judges note that it would be extremely difficult to justify to international public opinion (which is particularly focused on the Tribunal at this moment in time) the cessation of its activities solely for budgetary reasons, no matter how pressing."[13] For a tribunal whose entire destiny depends on public opinion, only this threat proves effective. The judges finally manage to make themselves heard.

A Peace without Justice

After three weeks of haggling, the Dayton negotiations end in success. A semblance of peace wins out over justice. Slobodan Milosevic, the Balkan pyromaniac, is indeed metamorphosed into an architect of peace. In signing the Dayton Accords with the Serb president, the international community grants him new legitimacy. In effect, he is assured of immunity from then on; how can one accuse a sitting head of state who is the necessary pivot for the reestablishment of peace?

Pauline Neville-Jones, a negotiator on the British team, confesses that a settlement was their grail. "A negotiated peace was the essential objective. It was not at all clear at Dayton that we would finish by finding an accord," she says. "The question of justice was absolutely not a priority. Our hypothesis, a little naive in retrospect, was that Karadzic and the others would capitulate. Or, at least, we expected to isolate Karadzic and Mladic, to marginalize them in order to reduce their political influence, rather than arrest them." [14]

In fact, the question of the fate reserved for war criminals tears at the American delegation. Two "realist" ideas are in conflict. If Milosevic appears assured of immunity, the State Department, and in particular the Bureau of Democracy, Human Rights, and Labor Affairs, at least wants to put the most influential war criminals behind bars at The Hague in order to weaken the network of ultranationalist power in Bosnia. The Pentagon opposes this plan, fearing that the dangerous task of hunting down and arresting suspects will put the entire mission in peril, just as the search for the Somali warlord Aidid turned that humanitarian mission into an absolute fiasco. [15] Stricken with "Somali Syndrome," the U.S. generals dig in their heels. The tension between the State Department and the Pentagon comes from their divergent goals. The State Department civilians understand that stability in the long term depends on marginalizing the war criminals, while the soldiers want to avoid making arrests that would heighten tensions.

As a participant in the negotiations, Pauline Neville-Jones sees this difference of opinion firsthand. Stressing its doctrine of "zero casualties," the Pentagon opposes the investigation by IFOR (Implementation Force for the Dayton Accords) of "past incidents, atrocities and violations of human rights." It rejects the principle of aiding civilians in the case of massive violations of human rights. The Pentagon is also hostile to the proposal that its soldiers proceed with the arrest of war criminals under warrant by the tribunal. [16]

A cool realist who knows that the Pentagon's limited vision will endanger the future peace accord, Richard Holbrooke tries to enlarge IFOR's mandate. He fears that the "ethnic cleansers" will continue to make trouble in the region. Holbrooke tries to engage President Clinton outside the final meeting of the cabinet before Dayton. "If we are going to create a real peace rather than an uneasy cease-fire, Karadzic and Mladic will have to be captured," he tells the president. "This is not simply a question of justice, but also of peace. If they are not captured, no peace agreement we create in Dayton can ultimately succeed." [17] But his message gets nowhere. On the contrary, President Clinton completely agrees with the Pentagon, as demonstrated by the decisions taken in Dayton. It is agreed that "IFOR shall have the authority, but not the obligation, to arrest war criminals." [18] Once again, justice is sacrificed. In the early days of the tribunal, the United Nations had solemnly affirmed that the tribunal could play

RICHARD HOLBROOKE—The architect of the Dayton Accords (here with Gen. Wesley Clark, commander of NATO forces). After Dayton, Holbrooke favored arresting the alleged war criminals who had been indicted. The Pentagon, however, fearing reprisals against American forces deployed in Bosnia to enforce the accords, blocked the idea. (NATO)

a key role in "break[ing] the cycle of hatred and violence" and promoting "reconciliation." But who cares about that now?

During the negotiations at Dayton, Pauline Neville-Jones finds herself alone with American general Wesley Clark, the Supreme Allied Commander, to negotiate the crucial military annexes to the peace accords.

> The French delegated to me the task of representing them, the Russians did not come, and the Germans did not speak. With Wesley Clark, the discussion was relatively brief on the question of war criminals: I myself had a very narrow margin of maneuver given to me by the British government, and I sympathized with the preoccupation of the military, whose concern was to avoid all escalating events that could not be mastered. We had considerable doubts about the feasibility of the arrests. We worried, too, about resistance that would lead to more fighting. This pessimistic vision filled us, but in retrospect, it did not turn out that way.[19]

Neville-Jones well knows the position of Malcolm Rifkind, the British defense minister: achieve regional stabilization without putting British soldiers in danger. In other words, avoid a scenario whereby the local population takes the side of the arrested war criminals, provoking reprisals.

The Pentagon wins. For form's sake, a verbal accord with the belligerents is concluded at Dayton, committing them to turn over war criminals to the tribunal. But the will of the West, and in this case the Americans, to enforce respect for this commitment is so weak that they take care not to put the agreement in writing to avoid having to follow up. "We made verbal accords because we did not want to entangle ourselves if the parties did not follow their commitments," Neville-Jones remembers. "It is for this very reason that no mechanism for arrest or sanction is mentioned in the Dayton Accords." [20]

NATO soldiers now have the mandate but not the obligation to arrest presumed war criminals. Those responsible for the massacre at Srebrenica have little to worry about. No plans are made to arrest the Bosnian Serbs (and others) responsible for ethnic cleansing. In fact, insistent rumors allege that the Americans have granted Karadzic two years of immunity if he agrees to prevent hostile acts against U.S. soldiers deployed in Bosnia.

The Dayton Accords are the point of absolute contradiction for the international community. The imperative of justice confirmed by the Security Council in creating the International Criminal Tribunal for the Former Yugoslavia would, logically, have rendered any peace with Slobodan Milosevic impossible. The only remaining roads to justice are unconditional surrender or a change of regime in Belgrade. The first road requires the political will of the Great Powers, which is clearly lacking. The second is hardly more realistic. Practically speaking, justice has been buried.

It does not take long for the consequences of this choice to be felt. The governments contributing the Rapid Reaction Force to IFOR do not want to admit that they have limited their chances of success by leaving the war criminals alone. But Richard Holbrooke, who is following the evolution of the balance of power on the ground, notes the ravages caused by this policy of impunity. "While the arrest of Karadzic would not have solved all the problems the international community faced in Bosnia, his removal from Bosnia was a necessary, although not sufficient, condition for success," he writes. "As we had told the President and his senior advisors before Dayton, Karadzic at large was certain to mean Dayton deferred or defeated. Nothing had changed six months later, except that Karadzic was rebuilding his position." [21] In one final attempt in June, 1996, this lucid realist who never embraced morality in dealing with Milosevic informs President Clinton by letter that beyond the Balkans, American policy in Europe is being hurt by the liberty Karadzic enjoys:

> The success of IFOR so far is now threatened by Karadzic's success in defying the political portions of Dayton. If he continues to thwart the Dayton powers,

the peace process will fail. The implications of Karadzic's defiance go far beyond Bosnia itself. If he succeeds, basic issues of American leadership that seemed settled in the public's eye after Dayton will re-emerge. Having reasserted American leadership in Europe, it would be a tragedy if we let it slip away again. It may seem odd that so much can hang on such a matter as the fate of two odious war criminals. But history is replete with examples of small issues leading to the unraveling of larger ones. . . . Everyday, Karadzic uses television and the controlled media to prevent local reconciliation efforts. IFOR has the ability and authority to cut these lines, but has refused to do so. These communication lines should be cut—now. This would be a devastating blow to Karadzic, and popular in the United States."[22]

Richard Holbrooke fails to convince the American president. He has tried to show Bill Clinton that arresting war criminals would bring him political benefits both in terms of public approval ratings at home and in the Balkans and throughout Europe. But it leads to nothing. In these conditions, how can the Bosnian people believe in the commitments of the international community, while the conflict's instigators—indicted by the ICTY and theoretically sought after—freely drive through roadblocks, even American ones, as late as 1996? It is not only the credibility of IFOR that is questionable; the physical security of all local opponents of the war criminals is also at stake. With warlords operating with impunity in the midst of sixty thousand heavily armed soldiers representing the leading military alliance in the world, all those who oppose the ultranationalists risk their lives if they step out of the shadows.

A Tribunal of Words

Traumatized by Srebrenica, marginalized and wrung out by the Dayton Accords, the tribunal has lost its way. During a dinner in New York bringing together Cassese, some French-speaking diplomats, and the Dutch U.N. ambassador, the morale of the tribunal president is bleak. "This is the hour of truth," he tells them. "Either [the ICTY] works now or it breaks." (In French, Cassese's remark is "Ça passe ou ça casse.") The Dutch ambassador tries to comfort him with a wry joke: "Don't worry, it will all end well, because your name is 'Passese.'"[23] Nevertheless, the future of international justice appears compromised by the failure of the ICTY.

In this atmosphere of despair and disarray, Richard Goldstone, pushed by Cassese, decides to invoke the massacres before the tribunal in July, 1995. Condemning the crimes is a pathetic attempt to bring the real stakes back to the heart of the discussion. But how to do even that much? Those responsible for the massacres are free, and a trial is, thus, impossible to organize. The only option is to use "Rule 61," a pseudocontumacy provision. "You have a weapon, use it," the tribunal president tells Goldstone.[24] Cassese seeks to stigmatize Karadzic and Mladic, for he fears that, otherwise, they will once again become interlocutors of the Western diplomats. "The idea was to counter any possibility of an amnesty for Karadzic, who still intended on returning to Paris, London, and Washington," Cassese later says.[25] A mocked court now deploys itself as well as it can, with the weapon of the weak—the Word—to assert the elementary principles of civilization following the worst crimes committed in Europe since World War II.

With no choice and no defendants, the ICTY becomes the "Tribunal of the Word." And words with little force, at that, because no punishment is possible as long as the sixty thousand soldiers of the strongest military alliance in the world refuse to arrest the Bosnian Serb chiefs, Karadzic and Mladic. It is not a trial in absentia, which the majority of judges have repudiated in the name of the right to defense.[26] It is, rather, a new idea, baptized Rule 61, whose objective is limited: to confirm the indictment by determining that a "reasonable basis" exists to establish the presumed guilt of "President" Karadzic and his military chief, Mladic, for crimes against humanity and genocide.

In reality, Rule 61 comes to little, if anything: a public reading of the indictment, the presentation of evidence, and the deposition of some witnesses. As it is not a true trial, the defense may be absent. The legal effect is nil, but the media resonance is potentially strong. Rule 61 is an exorcism by default. Since the international community does not want to arrest the guilty parties, the evil must at least be conjured by the public pronouncement of the crime.

Alarmed by the spectacle of this impotent international court, U.N. Secretary-General Kofi Annan evokes at length the writings of Italian Holocaust survivor Primo Levi to justify Rule 61.[27] To cite a writer is unusual in a U.N. report. Has the U.N. head weighed the symbol incarnated in Primo Levi, the writer who no longer believed in the force of words? Is the man who endured the indifference of the world in the death camps intended as an echo of the international community's abandonment of the victims of Srebrenica? Annan's evocation is an implicit confession of the defeat of international justice. It is no longer a matter of dissuading criminals, nor of participating in the reestablishment of peace, nor of playing some role in the reconciliation to come in some uncertain future, but merely of fighting "historical revisionism," the next generation of Holocaust deniers. It is the admission of the failure of the tribunal and, at the same time, of the international community.

In two fundamental works, *If This Is a Man* and *The Drowned and the Saved*, explains Kofi Annan, Primo Levi recalls his nightmares as a prisoner in the concentration camp at Auschwitz. In the worst of the dreams, he saw himself free, surrounded by loved ones, to whom he recounts the horrors he has suffered, only to realize that they are not listening, that they remain indifferent, incredulous:

> [M]any survivors [of the concentration camps] . . . remember that the SS militiamen enjoyed cynically admonishing the prisoners: . . . even if some proof should remain and some of you survive, people will say the events you describe are too monstrous to be believed. . . . Strangely enough, this same thought ("even if we were to tell it, we would not be believed") arose in the form of nocturnal dreams produced by the prisoners' despair. Almost all the survivors, orally or in their written memoirs, remember a dream which frequently recurred during the nights of imprisonment, varied in its detail but uniform in its substance: they had returned home and with passion and relief were describing their past sufferings, addressing themselves to a loved one, and were not believed, indeed were not even listened to. In the most typical (and cruelest) form, the interlocutor turned and left in silence. [B]oth parties, victims and oppressors, had a keen awareness of the enormity and therefore the noncredibility of what took place in the Lagers—and, we may add here, not only in the Lagers, but in the ghettos, in the rear areas of the Eastern front, in the police stations, and in the asylums for the mentally handicapped.[28]

In London in 1993, the politicians had put Elie Wiesel out front to give themselves a virtuous image. After Srebrenica, whose executioners remain free, the U.N. secretary-general summons the writings of Primo Levi to emphasize the importance of speech and memory. In doing so, he reduces the tribunal to the function of archivist—an essential function, but a derisory one when confronted with the ongoing impunity of the executioners. But this "Tribunal of the Word" will reveal itself to be stronger than could have then been imagined. And the nightmare of Primo Levi will be, at least in part, refuted.

To articulate the past historically does not mean to recognize it "the way it really was." It means to seize hold of a memory as it flashes up at a moment of danger.

—Walter Benjamin, *On the Concept of History*

Tribunal of the Word

On June 27, 1996, three judges, flanked by two United Nations flags, open the Rule 61 hearing in the case against Radovan Karadzic and Ratko Mladic. It is a show trial, yet it does hold some surprises because the hearing will shed light not only on the monstrous crimes at Srebrenica but also on something neither prosecutor nor judges expect: the responsibility of the international community.

Two empty chairs, separated by a thin partition, are reserved for the two defendants, still at large. One year earlier, nearly to the day, six thousand to nine thousand men and adolescents of Srebrenica had been murdered. The testimonies of a French investigator, Jean-René Ruez, and several peacekeepers as well as the deposition of two witnesses, an executioner and a victim, suddenly give a concrete account of this unprecedented massacre committed in a "safe area" theoretically under the protection of the United Nations.

What is most astonishing about these hearings, at which there are neither lawyers nor even defendants present, and with no real punishment at stake, is that the simple recitation of the crimes suddenly imposes its own imperative. One may well know the horrific facts of this war, but within the enclosure of the tribunal, the truth suddenly becomes indisputable and irrefutable. It is a stand against revisionism and denial. Incapable until now of rendering justice, constrained to let crimes against humanity and genocide go unpunished, the work of the ICTY subtly takes on substance: The truth can, at least, be spoken before the judges and the victims can be recognized as such before the world. Deeply moved, the Egyptian judge Fouad Riad says, "These are truly scenes from hell, written on the darkest pages of human history."[1]

The first person to testify about the deadly clockwork set in motion in Srebrenica is Jean-René Ruez, assigned to the tribunal's investigation. On July 3 Ruez tells the court in a clinical tone about the season in hell that thousands of men and women endured just one year earlier, as Europe was preoccupied with its summer vacations. His story concerns the massacre of thousands of men, the deportation of twenty-five thousand women, elders, and children, and the satisfied smiles of the Bosnian Serb general reassuring prisoners who, a few hours or days later, will be murdered en masse by stabbing, grenades, or heavy gunfire.

In an even voice, Ruez recounts the events that he has reconstructed. The hearing room is in total silence as he describes the fall of Srebrenica on July 11, 1995. Some fifteen thousand men and women fleeing desperately through the forest toward Tuzla are blown up crossing mine fields, bombarded by mortar fire, or shot like rabbits by antiaircraft cannons. By megaphone, the Bosnian Serbs encourage them to surrender. Serb soldiers even sport blue helmets stolen from UNPROFOR troops to trick the fleeing civilians into returning to their tormentors. Prisoners are forced to call out to their sons or fathers, assuring them that nothing bad will happen to them. Those who surrender are often tortured; noses, lips, and ears are cut off—"apparently, a common torture," Ruez states before the court—before being executed. Sometimes the horror reaches a paroxysm, recounts this former officer of the French judiciary police, who has reconstructed the events with the aid of witnesses:

A group that had been surrounded for a number of hours is captured. The people were put in a circle. The Bosnian Serb Army soldiers were around them. They started by taking a number of the individuals in the group and to execute them summarily. There is not just killing, there is also torture. Prior to the killing there was a woman who was slaughtered in front of everyone. There is a man who is accompanied by his young son and a soldier comes up to him, makes some comments about the fact that his father is in the process of killing off Serbian children. He takes the old man, puts the knife through his hand, sticks it to the tree, then cuts open the stomach of the little boy and then on the top of the knife he has a bit of an organ from the inside of the child's stomach and then he forces the man to eat that part of the child's innards. . . . A child is separated from its mother who is fighting with the two soldiers to try to get her son back. The son is thrown up and he is hit with bayonets before being beaten once he hits the ground. This process goes on the whole afternoon. The soldiers are taking their time. They are going around, the soldiers, picking up one or the other and executing them in front of everyone else. There as well there are in fact some survivors." [2]

Seeing what is happening to some of the prisoners, many men go insane. Others commit suicide so as not to fall alive into the hands of their enemies. In the forest, these suicides are committed in an anarchic fashion; some pull the pins from grenades, injuring or killing others. Sometimes the Bosnian Serb soldiers tease the prisoners, telling them, in front of a pile of bodies, "Choose your spot!" before executing them, Ruez recounts.

The situation of the twenty-five thousand women, children, and old people and three thousand men who have found refuge near the ineffectual Dutch peacekeepers at their base in Potocari is just as sinister. A video shows General Mladic on foot in the streets of the town, affirming, "Here we are in Srebrenica on July 11, 1995. On the eve of yet another great Serbian holiday, we present this city to the Serbian people as a gift. . . . [T]he time has come to take revenge on the Turk in this region." His soldiers embrace him. To the refugees, Mladic perversely declares, "Let women and little children go first. Do not let any of the children get lost. Do not be afraid. Nobody will harm you." A Bosnian Serb soldier asks a mother why her child is crying. "He is hungry," she responds. "Oh, well, the child will not be hungry anymore," the soldier retorts, slitting the child's throat in front of his mother and a great number of witnesses, who look away and try to flee by boarding a bus as quickly as possible. [3]

The deportation of women, interrupted sometimes by rapes and killings, the massive executions of men—the criminal clockwork follows the plan systematically. On five occasions, General Mladic visits a massacre site, toying with those who will soon perish: "Hello, neighbors. Do you know who I am? I am General Mladic," and promising they will be exchanged. [4] The men are separated from the rest and held in hangars and factories, then massacred. Here and there the methods vary. During the night of March 11 in Potocari, dozens of men are picked by two soldiers and taken behind a factory in small groups of ten. Twenty soldiers are waiting there to kill them with knives, one after another. No sign of revolt against the soldiers is recorded. The process goes on for many hours and the bodies pile up. Two prisoners are designated to put them in a pile. A truck arrives and the bodies are thrown in the back. It is covered and its direction unknown. After five trips, the two prisoners charged with speeding this work are themselves executed.

Elsewhere, men are machine-gunned:

> At Kravica, on 14 July, that entire group, there were about 500 to 1,000 individuals, were forced to enter into a hangar. The people were forced to sit down. When the last one entered into the hangar, there was not enough space for him to sit down. The soldiers ordered him to sit down and since he did not act fast enough, he was beaten. Immediately, the soldiers who were around the hangar fired into all the openings of the hangar. Grenades were thrown into the hangar. Those who tried to escape by the openings were beaten by the soldiers at the outside of the hangar. Once the smoke cleared in the hangar, the firing started again. After the firing the soldiers on the outside asked if there was anyone who still was alive, some answered. They were asked to leave the hangar and as soon as they left the hangar you heard shots on the outside of the hangar as well. Nevertheless, some people managed to survive.[5]

A video shows an unending column of refugees, men on one side, women on the other, faces emaciated by hunger, marked by fear and despair. Unbearable images. The investigator covers a map with black dots—mass graves located by planes and spy satellites.

On July 4 and 5, 1996, the court hears from Witness "A," whose identity is protected by a screen. This Muslim, a native of Srebrenica, speaks in a steady voice, without emotion, about the events that he survived one year earlier. He tells of seeing General Mladic at the execution sites, attentive to the systematic organization of the crime, a good professional in the "art" of massacre. The witness's detailed description of the Bosnian Serb general and of the men killed like animals in a slaughterhouse makes it even more unbearable that NATO has let the Bosnian Serb military leader go unpunished. "A" recounts,

> About mid-day Ratko Mladic appeared at the door. Then we all as one cried out, "Why are you choking us in here? Why are you keeping us here? Why do you not take us somewhere?" He said, "What I am to do with you when your government does not want you and I have to take care of you? I will move a group of you to Kladusa and another group to Bijeljina." "Why do you not give us water?" He says, "You will get water on the way out of the hall." Then he went away. . . . One by one the vehicles have come. Then those nearest the door got up and started walking out and so they went out and then we heard from people that they were blindfolding people. . . . So we were filing out, people were filing out. About 7:30 in the evening it was my turn to leave. . . . When I entered the lorry, two soldiers closed it and the lorry took off. . . .

When we got to a field we saw to the left, dead, a lot of dead people. Then we realized where we were going. We passed those corpses and the truck went on across some pasture land and when it turned we saw to the right the same number of dead. The truck stopped. Two Serb soldiers opened the back. They told us to come down quickly, not to look, not to look, just come out. So we came out. We were lined up. As soon as the small lorry went off, they started firing at us from behind. There were some people standing behind me and they fell on top of me. So I fell on my stomach and they fell on top of me. Then the firing stopped and then they started shooting individually. If anybody gave any signs of life he would be killed. I kept quiet. They moved away and again they would refill their automatic rifles. They were firing from automatic rifles. Then another small TAM [military] truck came near me. . . . Ratko Mladic watched as people were being forced out of the truck and lined up. . . . This went on until the evening hours. Two dredgers were digging holes behind me. A big excavator was being used. When darkness fell those removed from me were closest. Then they switched off the machines and they put on the lights, and then the other people came from the other side, killing where the lights were on. When they brought in the first truck under the lights, I crawled out from under the dead and I went to the pile of bodies where there were some small shrubs and when the lights came, I was in darkness and that is how I escaped.[6]

One judge asks Witness "A" how many Bosnian Serb soldiers were in the field carrying out the mass executions.

"There were five in one place and five in another," the witness answers. "When the truck came, two hold their rifle across their chest, then one on each side of the truck opened the back side of the truck, and then three others are standing watch with rifles ready in case anybody would try to get away. When the lorry moved away, the first three started to fire immediately and the other two would also aim and start firing. So there were five at one spot and another five at another. There was a total of 10."[7]

When the soldiers finally left, "A" stood up and called out for any other survivors. There was only one. The two men managed to reach territory controlled by Bosnian forces.

The U.N. Colonel and the Penitent

Two military men are testifying before the tribunal. One is there by profession; the other, by circumstance. The first is Captain Thomas Karremans, one of the Dutch peacekeepers charged with protecting the civilian population in the "safe area" of Srebrenica. The other is Drazen Erdemovic, twenty-five years old, an executioner in spite of himself, with the look of a pimply adolescent. A death squad member, Erdemovic is the first person to plead guilty before the ICTY. His comrades and superiors, unrepentant, are all free men; he is in prison. As for Karremans, since his return to the Netherlands following the massacre, he has been promoted to colonel. It is a promotion that rings with self-absolution by the international community, the hypocrisy of the Western governments. The only one "paying" for his guilt is the only one who has admitted it.

Judge Riad asks Colonel Karremans if he made any mention of or protest against the executions in his last meeting with Mladic and, if so, how Mladic responded. Colonel Karremans replies, "I [had] not protested in the last meeting because I did not even expect that meeting. . . . I was not aware of that. . . . [Mladic] was again a little bit monologing, and asked me how the Battalion was and how we were doing and if we were prepared to move and ready to go. There was hardly [any] opportunity to evaluate, let us put it in that way, what happened in all the weeks and days before. To be frank, I [had] not thought about the idea of asking him what happened with the refugees."[8]

One year after the murder of thousands of Muslims in the Srebrenica "safe area," Colonel Karremans does not seem to understand the full weight of his words. On July 21, 1995, when Mladic met with him, Karremans did not know everything, but he knew enough. On July 1, near the U.N. base at Potocari, he had seen twenty-five thousand terrorized women, children, and old people and a few hundred men arrive after the fall of Srebrenica. He had seen the Bosnian Serb military commander tell these terrified crowds, "Allah can't help you, but Mladic can."[9] Then, in front of U.N. troops threatened with bombardment if they resist, Karremans saw Serb soldiers tear men away from their families, then the women and children forced to board a bus before disappearing.

Karremans tells the court that he knew nothing about the massacres that took place practically in front of his eyes one year earlier. However, he has read the deposition of one Corporal Paul Groenewegen, who, with the look of a beaten dog, has told the court earlier how the Serb soldiers had executed a man right in front of his eyes, how he heard gunshots "20 to 40 times an hour . . . [m]ainly . . . from the area with the houses" where he witnessed a civilian shot in the head by Serb soldiers, how he heard the Serb soldiers shooting until twilight in the hills, with never an answering shot.[10]

Karremans had received, too, on this fateful July 13, 1995, the deposition of one Lieutenant Koster, who had taken photographs of nine bodies of men in civilian clothes, seven of whom had been shot in the back.[11]

And what did Karremans, the officer in charge of the U.N. "safe area" in Srebrenica, do? He held "his command informed minute by minute." He called in air strikes. For five days, they did not come. "When the air strikes started . . . it had no effect on the mission. . . . The air strikes and close air support were too late and too little." When General Mladic demanded to see all the Muslims between seventeen and sixty years old, "because he said there were a lot of war criminals amongst them," Karremans prepared a list of all the Bosnian men on his base. "I can remember 239. But there were about 70 which did not like that and they have not done that [did not want to be counted]." He said he did not know for sure, but he thought that the list ended up in the hands of the Serbs.[12]

When General Mladic's soldiers stripped the peacekeepers of their helmets, flak jackets, and military equipment, Karremans ordered his men to "work just in a t-shirt without helmet, without flak jacket, and without weapon."[13] Overwhelmed by the situation, by the fact that fifty-five of his men were hostages of the Serbs, abandoned by the UNPROFOR military hierarchy, Karremans is now under Mladic's orders. Testifying before the tribunal, he speaks with words that have a hallucinatory quality. "[Mladic gave us] eight days to prepare our own, let us say, departure, to rest," he said. "On Friday, the day after the evacuation, all of a sudden a convoy with food, a lot of food, a lot of diesel was accepted and came to the Potocari area. So, then we had, from that day we had food enough, diesel enough, medicines, and we had eight days to recover from what happened in the weeks before."[14] The organizer of the greatest massacre committed in decades in Europe offered "eight days of rest" to an officer of the United Nations and his soldiers, "to recover from what happened." It is a terrible euphemism for the worst atrocity committed in this war, with the deportation or death of men, women, and children that the peacekeepers were supposed to protect in the name of the international community.

At this moment in the pseudotrial, the indictment of General Mladic and Radovan Karadzic has overwhelmed its initial, anticipated scope. Rule 61 has also become a trial of the United Nations and its incomprehensible passivity, a fact that goes well beyond the responsibility of one Dutch officer. The spectacle of these days of July, 1996, is itself strange: peacekeepers with a duty to maintain a peace that does not exist, confronted by judges incapable of judging criminals accused of genocide who, instead, enjoy total liberty. To the pathetic weakness of UNPROFOR, abandoned by its hierarchy, add these judges abandoned by the international community, obliged to pantomime a trial in the absence of any defendants.

Following Karremans, enter Drazen Erdemovic. This man's fate is the perfect emblem for the absurdity of the conflict in the former Yugoslavia. Erdemovic is a Croat by birth, married to a Serb, with several Muslim cousins. He is not nationalistic. As in the book by Virgil Gheorghiu, *The Twenty-Fifth Hour,* adapted for the screen in 1967 and starring Anthony Quinn, Erdemovic had not embraced the conflict that consumed his country. When Yugoslavia began its disintegration, he was carrying out his military service in the federal army. He quit the JNA but found himself mobilized in the Bosnian army. He managed to run off to enlist in the forces of the Croatian Defense Council (HVO) of the self-proclaimed Herceg Bosna. He fled again, worried for his pregnant Serb wife, hoping to find a channel to Switzerland via the Republika Srpska, the self-styled "republic" of the Bosnian Serbs, but he ended up in the Bosnian Serb army. It was there that his unit was transformed into a death squad. With his handful of comrades, he would kill a thousand men at Srebrenica in a single day. During his testimony, his body shakes as he recounts the taking of Srebrenica:

"I heard . . . that buses with Muslims would be coming from Srebrenica."

"Did he say what you and the members of your unit were supposed to do regarding those Muslims from Srebrenica?" asks the prosecutor.

"[The officer Brano Gojkovic told us] that we have to execute those people, to shoot them."

"What happened once the bus arrived at the farm? Could you describe what happened, please?"

"When the bus arrived at the farm [around 9:30] . . . the Commander of the group, Brano Gojkovic, would tell us how to stand as an execution squad and two military policemen would bring out 10 people of Muslim nationality from Srebrenica at a time, and Brano Gojkovic and Golijan Vlastimir would bring them to the execution squad."

"Did you follow that order?"

"Yes, but at first I resisted and Brano Gojkovic told me if I was sorry for those people that I should line up with them; and I knew that this was not just a mere threat but that it could happen, because in our unit the situation had become such that the Commander of the group has the right to execute on the spot any individual if he threatens the security of the group or if in any other way he opposes the Commander of the group appointed by the Commander Milorad Pelemis."

"Do you know how many buses were brought to Pilica farm on July 16th?"

"I do not know exactly, but I think between 15 and 20 buses."

"Did the same thing that you have described just a moment ago happen to each one of those bus loads of civilian persons who came off the buses? In other words, were they executed at Pilica farm?"

"Yes."

"What time . . . did the last bus arrive at Pilica farm?"

"I really do not know exactly . . . but I know that before the last bus came a group of about 10 soldiers from Bratunac came to the farm. . . . I do not know what time it was, but maybe around 15:30 or 16 hours."

"Did they act in a way that was different to the civilians than the members of your unit acted?"

"Yes, they beat the civilians with bars. They said all kinds of things to them. They forced them to kneel and to pray in the Muslim manner, to bow their heads."

"Did it appear to you . . . that they were attempting to humiliate some of these victims before they killed them?"

"Yes. I think even that some of them from Bratunac knew some of those victims from Srebrenica."

"What was the attitude of the bus drivers who drove the victims to Pilica farm?"

"They were horrified. I think those people, those men, did not know that they were being driven to the execution ground. They probably thought they were being led for exchange and that is what this man that I talked to, the one between 50 and 60, actually told me, that it had been promised them. However, Brano Gojkovic entered the bus and gave [each driver] an automatic rifle, a kalashnikov, and ordered [them] to kill at least one of the Muslims so that they could not testify."

"Can you estimate . . . how many civilians were killed by your unit and members of the Bratunac unit on 16th July?"

"Somewhere about 1,000, 1,200, I do not know. I estimated the number according to the arrivals of the buses."

"Are you able to estimate how many people you killed?"

"I do not know exactly. I cannot estimate but, to be quite frank, I would rather not know how many people I killed."

"Did [the lieutenant colonel] see the dead bodies that were covering the field?"

"Of course, yes, he saw them."

"Did he make any comments about seeing those bodies?"

"No, no. He made no comments, but he said in . . . Pilica there were another 500 of those Muslims from Srebrenica and that we had to go to finish off that work. I said aloud that I would not, that I did not wish to kill anyone, that I was no robot for the extermination of people. Then I was supported by some individuals from my unit so we did not go, but the group from Bratunac went."

"Did you eventually . . . travel to Pilica?"

"Yes. Brano Gojkovic said that the Lieutenant Colonel had told him that he had to hold a meeting in Pilica later. . . . When we got there, where we were told to report, I heard shots and . . . hand grenades which went off in the building."

"How far were you from that particular building?"
"Some 70 to 100 meters, I think."[15]

Drazen Erdemovic said that he and two other soldiers were the targets of an attempted assassination in Republika Srpska to keep them from doing what he eventually did before the court: testifying about these crimes. He affirmed that he wished to bear witness "because of my conscience," and he pleaded guilty in his eventual trial.[16]

Condemnations and Excuses

Shaken by the evocation of the horror, on July 11, 1996, the judges draft an indictment of Karadzic and Mladic. In this document, a great surprise awaits journalists: For the first time, the tribunal has named Milosevic. The press release affirms that the Serb president controlled Plan RAM, "designed at the highest Serbian political and military level, to set up a new state through the use of violence."[17] One has the impression that, moved by emotion and disgust over the massacre at Srebrenica, the judges have finally decided to point an accusatory finger at the Serb president.

The negotiators, the mediators, and the Western diplomats are furious. Just as quickly, the judges reverse themselves, and the press communiqué is immediately withdrawn. In the final version of the Karadzic and Mladic indictment, Milosevic is not mentioned. What has happened? Have they determined that it is premature to mention the Serb president? Do they fear the consequences of this act? Have they "internalized" the constant pressure from without? No one knows for sure. In the indictment, Judge Riad settles for confirming the unsurprising condemnation of the two Bosnian Serb butchers: "The evidence tendered by the Prosecutor describes scenes of unimaginable savagery: thousands of men executed and buried in mass graves, hundreds of men buried alive, men and women mutilated and slaughtered, children killed before their mothers' eyes."[18]

In the space of a week, the International Criminal Tribunal for the Former Yugoslavia proves that it could become, according to the curious formula of one judge, a "Frankenstein" capable of freeing itself from the Great Powers that have created it. The Word, then, is not a weapon totally devoid of power. From now on, Karadzic and Mladic live under an international arrest warrant, accused of genocide and crimes against humanity. Rule 61 has permitted the expression of truth. This truth has not only exposed the mechanism of the crime to the light of day, it has also thrown a floodlight on the refusal of the international community to assume its own responsibility. One year after the events, the results are public knowledge: the deportation of twenty-five thousand women and children and the deaths of thousands of men and women in the "safe area" of Srebrenica. The work of the tribunal at The Hague has become the theater of a terrifying lesson in very recent history, but with no real consequences. Justice is not served merely by the indispensable declaration of facts and responsibilities.

The tribunal has once again demonstrated its limits on all levels. The fact that Colonel Karremans, commander of the United Nations peacekeepers at Srebrenica, had not thought to "mention" the fate of the refugees to General Mladic, although he had knowledge of the reports sent to him by his own subordinates, makes him the symbol of the international community's indifference. During those fateful weeks in July, 1995, neither France nor any other permanent member of the Security Council had wanted to intervene. In deconstructing this chain of events, where the U.N. Protection Force stood by passively, the judges have plenty of time to meditate on a reality they know intimately from having lived it: the role of alibi that the Security Council wants them both to play. But, in these conditions, what is the sense of international justice when the victims that they are supposed to protect by force of law die so horribly and senselessly? It is a terrible statement of impotence. Karadzic and Mladic, described by the tribunal spokesman as "fugitives" for whom "the world is a prison with an open sky," live freely and in defiance of the IFOR soldiers who do not deign to arrest them.[19]

For years, the United Nations has obstinately refused to recognize its own responsibility for the deportation and the massacres committed in the "safe area" at Srebrenica. Only one man, Tadeusz Mazowiecki, the special rapporteur on the former Yugoslavia, has slammed the door on the United Nations. In his letter of resignation, he affirms, "Events in recent weeks in Bosnia and Herzegovina, and above all the fact that the United Nations has allowed Srebrenica and Zepa to fall, along with the horrendous tragedy which has beset the population of those 'safe havens' guaranteed by international agreements, oblige me to state that I do not see any possibility of continuing the mandate of Special Rapporteur entrusted to me by the Commission on Human Rights. . . . Crimes have been committed with swiftness and brutality and by contrast the response of the international community has been slow and ineffectual."[20]

It will be necessary to wait four more years for recognition of the international body's numerous errors and its *mea culpa*, which appears in the report by Kofi Annan, dated November 15, 1999, prepared for the U.N. General Assembly. The United Nations is in an awkward position. While the international court pursues the war criminals of the former Yugoslavia, the United Nations reserves the right to present extrajudicial excuses for abandoning the Security

Council mandate to protect the civilian population in the "safe areas." Without wanting to put the murderers on the same footing with those who refused to protect their potential victims, the *mea culpa* by the head of the United Nations reinforces the feeling that the Great Powers have absolved themselves of any responsibility.

In his report, Kofi Annan does not evade the fundamental questions. He relates how "after three years of siege, the population [of Srebrenica] was demoralized, afraid and often hungry" and attempted to defend itself against the will of the United Nations: "Surrounding them, controlling all the high ground, handsomely equipped with the heavy weapons and logistical train of the Yugoslav army, were the Bosnian Serbs. There was no contest. Despite the odds against them, the Bosnians requested UNPROFOR to return to them the weapons they had surrendered under the demilitarization agreements of 1993. They requested those weapons at the beginning of the Serb offensive, but the request was rejected by UNPROFOR because, as one commander explained, '[I]t was our responsibility to defend the enclave, not theirs.'"[21]

In Kofi Annan's assessment, "With the benefit of hindsight, this decision seems to have been particularly ill-advised, given UNPROFOR's own unwillingness consistently to advocate force as a means of deterring attacks on the enclave." He also noted, "It is harder to explain why the [UNPROFOR] personnel did not report more fully the scenes that were unfolding around them following the enclave's fall."

The head of the United Nations also underscores the fundamental incoherence of the Security Council's policy. "[W]e tried to keep the peace and apply the rules of peacekeeping when there was no peace to keep," he writes. "Knowing that any other course of action would jeopardize the lives of the troops, we tried to create—or imagine—an environment in which the tenets of peacekeeping—agreement between the parties, deployment by consent, and impartiality—could be upheld." And, letting loose an arrow at the U.N. executive, he writes that "[t]he community of nations decided to respond to the war in Bosnia and Herzegovina with an arms embargo, with humanitarian aid and with the deployment of a peacekeeping force. . . . The arms embargo . . . left the Serbs in a position of overwhelming military dominance and effectively deprived the Republic of Bosnia and Herzegovina of its right, under the Charter of the United Nations, to self-defense."

Kofi Annan then recognizes the responsibility of the U.N. Secretariat, which refused to authorize air strikes to save the enclave at Srebrenica:

[M]y predecessor, his senior advisers (among whom I was included as Under-Secretary General for Peacekeeping Operations), his Special Representative and the Force Commander, were all deeply reluctant to use air power against

KOFI ANNAN—The U.N. secretary-general (here with the author) headed peacekeeping operations for the world body during the 1994 genocide in Rwanda and the 1995 Srebrenica massacre. "The tragedy of Srebrenica will haunt our history forever," he admitted in a 1999 report on the failure of UNPROFOR. (U.N.)

the Serbs [because] . . . [w]e believed that by using air power against the Serbs we would be perceived as having entered the war against them, something not authorized by the Security Council and potentially fatal for a peacekeeping operation. . . . [W]e risked losing control over the process . . . with grave consequences for the safety of the troops entrusted to us by Member States.

He concludes, "The cardinal lesson of Srebrenica is that a deliberate and systematic attempt to terrorize, expel or murder an entire people must be met decisively with all necessary means, and with the political will to carry the policy through to its logical conclusion. . . . Through error, misjudgment and an inability to recognize the scope of the evil confronting us, we failed to do our part to help save the people of Srebrenica from the Serb campaign of mass murder."

Kofi Annan's *mea culpa,* as courageous as it is, comes four years after the fall, three years after the Rule 61 hearing against Karadzic and Mladic, and outside all connection to the international criminal tribunal. Without detracting from the belligerents' responsibility and guilt, one has the unpleasant impression that the International Criminal Tribunal for the Former Yugoslavia has an efficacy inversely proportional to the power of the actors implicated in the conflict.

How to admit that, for fear of eventual reprisals, the sixty thousand soldiers of IFOR have not been ordered to hunt down and arrest Karadzic and Mladic? How to understand this justice where an Erdemovic is imprisoned, while neither the principal instigator of the war, Slobodan Milosevic, metamorphosed at Dayton and Paris into a peacemaker, nor the sinister militia chieftains, perpetrators of the worst crimes since the beginning of the conflict, are the least bit worried by the ICTY? Despite Vukovar, Srebrenica, and the hundreds of other atrocities committed on all sides, the diplomats insist on believing in the virtues of realpolitik and in submitting the exercise of justice to their particular interests. The Office of the Prosecutor affirms this faith without evasion in its final deposition against Radovan Karadzic and Ratko Mladic: "The world had the capability to bring these two alleged architects of genocide to justice and did nothing. It will haunt the victims and it will shame us all." [22]

Chapter **Six**

The privilege of opening the first trial in history for crimes against the peace of the world imposes a grave responsibility. The wrongs which we seek to condemn and punish have been so calculated, so malignant, and so devastating, that civilization cannot tolerate their being ignored, because it cannot survive their being repeated. That four great nations, flushed with victory and stung with injury stay the hand of vengeance and voluntarily submit their captive enemies to the judgment of the law is one of the most significant tributes that Power has ever paid to Reason.
—Justice Robert Jackson,
   U.S. opening statement at Nuremberg, 1945

The Quest for Independence

By the end of 1995, the Dayton Accords have silenced the guns in Bosnia. A relative peace is holding in the still-divided country. Some weeks earlier, on October 1, Louise Arbour succeeded Richard Goldstone. Soberly tailored and energetic, the new forty-nine-year-old prosecutor with the singing accent of Quebec does not take long to make her verdict: The tribunal is careening toward failure.

Humiliated by the massacres at Srebrenica, shunted to the side during the preparatory phase and negotiation of the Dayton Accords, the ICTY continues to be dismissed by the NATO countries that do not want to proceed with arrests. Neither Yugoslavia nor the Republika Srpska recognizes its authority and jurisdiction; Croatia gives it mere lip service. France's hostility is such that it has blocked its officers from testifying at The Hague. Great Britain, to say nothing of Russia, is still hostile to this "paper tiger," carried at arm's length by Washington.

With the exception of the United States, none of the great Western states shares information with the tribunal beyond dribs and drabs. Richard Goldstone has rained down indictments, but the cells at Scheveningen Prison, near the Dutch capital, remain desperately empty. Out of seventy-four men indicted, the tribunal has received only seven detainees: three Bosnian Muslims, three Croats, and a Serb. Camp guards and members of the death squads, they are all secondary figures with the exception of a Croat general, Tihomir Blaskic, who surrendered voluntarily under pressure from his government, itself responding to U.S. pressure. There is no immediate prospect of filling the cells.

To rescue the tribunal from this ruin, Louise Arbour intends to break radically from her predecessor's strategy. The Tribunal of the Word is not her idea of an international court. Rule 61, that pseudotrial of defendants in absentia, is in Arbour's opinion a recipe for disaster. She sees it as the court's abdication, the acceptance of being reduced to a mere voice of morality, incapable of punishing the butchers. Arbour wants to put a stop to the pathology of failure that she sees symbolized in the tribunal's almost Pavlovian recourse to Rule 61 after its use against Karadzic and Mladic. "This pseudo-trial functioned like a drug," she says. "The Tribunal people were addicts."[1] Faced with their inability to arrest the indicted, some tribunal members are calling for the formal introduction of judgment in absentia. Arbour refuses. "It would have transformed the trials into a trial by archives," she says, "serving a merely historical function. It was necessary to unblock the situation in some other way, to think about what we could do by ourselves—rather than to moan about the inadequacies of others."[2]

This strong-willed jurist has always known what she wanted. Born February 10, 1947, in Montreal, in an exclusively francophone environment, Arbour learned English only later in life in order to study law. In 1971, she was admitted to the bar of Quebec, at that time shaken by secessionist violence, and soon afterward she clerked for the Supreme Court in Ottawa. Her career took off like a rocket. From the Supreme Court, she became a professor of civil and criminal law at York University, and, by 1990, she was a judge on the Court of Appeals for Ontario. "Like the rest of my generation, I fed on the debates over the concepts of sovereignty, independence, federation, confederation, autonomy," she says. With her nomination by the Security Council to be prosecutor of the tribunal, she says she now has "the best legal job in the world . . . that of inventing a concrete international court."[3]

LOUISE ARBOUR—The Canadian prosecutor (here with Canadian defense minister Arthur Eggleton) succeeded Richard Goldstone and aimed the tribunal at the top leadership responsible for war crimes. She struggled to make the tribunal integral to the peace process, but her aggressiveness guaranteed it could not be ignored. (NATO)

   Trials, however, require arrests of the indicted. How to get the court out of this impasse, revisited already a thousand times? During the Dayton negotiations, Antonio Cassese had tried—in vain—to create a judiciary police for the tribunal. He collided with the refusal of the Americans—indeed, of all the countries constituting IFOR—to play police officer for the tribunal.

   On October 30, 1996, the tribunal president suffers another blow from the European Union. Cassese has pleaded once more for "the members of NATO to give an explicit mandate to the soldiers of IFOR, or to those who would succeed it, to arrest the indicted persons who still enjoy absolute impunity."[4] But nothing comes of it. For Louise Arbour, it is absolutely necessary to end this impotence. But how to correct this asymmetry of power between politics and the law? How does one rid the tribunal of political pressure from states, that are, in theory, "submitted to the ICTY," when some of them, as permanent members of the Security Council, have the power to dissolve the tribunal?

In an attempt to push back the politicians, Louise Arbour stands on the law. Contrary to Richard Goldstone, who searched for political support to "establish" the tribunal, Arbour quickly understands that she must be, in fact, wary of governments, especially those of the West.

Arbour's apprenticeship is as brutal as it is quick. In her first trip to Yugoslavia as prosecutor, she asserts that "nothing is more important for the survival of the Tribunal than the incarceration of criminals" and is neatly rebuffed by the military leadership as well as the diplomats of the NATO countries.[5] The "blockade" on arrests will continue to exist de facto.

A few weeks later, in December, 1996, Prime Minister John Major of Great Britain delivers a new slap in the face to the tribunal. Although he has the obligation to invite a representative of the tribunal to a conference following up the Dayton Accords, Major does not trouble himself to do so. The message is clear: For London, the tribunal is worth hardly more than peanuts. Under German pressure, the Foreign Office consents at the last minute to the tribunal sending someone to the conference as an "observer." This contemptuous invitation is couched in the following terms: "The observer will have a seat in the conference chamber, but not at the conference table."[6] Tribunal president Antonio Cassese finds worse in the meeting's agenda: The British have erased any reference to the obligation of the States to cooperate with the tribunal, including the arrests of indictees. These omissions not only demonstrate an additional sidelining of the tribunal but also violate a Security Council resolution.

Unanimously, the judges draft a furious letter to the British government. It states, "The Tribunal recalls that Resolution 922 of the Security Council begins with these words: 'The fact to put in conformity with the demands and the orders of the [tribunal] constitutes an essential aspect of the putting in place of a peace accord.' But this essential aspect does not figure in the program of the London Conference." The letter continues, "It is also regrettable that the International Tribunal has not been invited as a participant, but only as an observer, despite the fact that the international community recalls on many occasions the essential role of the [tribunal]."[7]

Faced with a public confrontation, the British government backs down, proposing that Louise Arbour, the "observer" to the follow-up talks, be allowed to express herself publicly. After listening for two days to a diverse discussion on the circumstances under which arrests might eventually take place, Arbour cuts the debate short, curtly declaring that the states are obligated to apply the tribunal's decisions because "there cannot be any discussion about it. It is the law!"[8]

This incident reveals Arbour's style; like a good attorney, she relies on her one unbending pillar, the law. Pragmatic and inventive, conscious of her mandate's historic dimension, she waits for her moment to "corner" the politicians. As a permanent reminder of her difficulties, at the bottom of her computer screen flashes the quotation declaimed by William of Orange at the beginning of the United Provinces' rebellion against the Spanish: "One need not hope in order to act, nor succeed in order to persevere." Arbour's persistent approach even colors what an editorialist will call her "Tintin spirit," the freedom to act outside conventional canons. She confesses a passion for the beloved books of Hergé ("despite the absence of women," she says), her favorite being *The Blue Lotus,* a story set in China under the Japanese occupation.[9] She who dreams of equipping the tribunal with a "strike force" to carry out arrests is exasperated by the resigned fatalism of her staff. "I wanted to change the culture at the heart of the Office of the Prosecutor," she says. "We had the habit of sniveling, complaining that the states did nothing. We had developed a psychology of dependence, about the press that did not like us enough, about the money we lacked, about the States that did not help us. It was, for me, a suicidal strategy. We cursed, giving visibility not to the tribunal, but to the impotence of the tribunal. I preferred less immediate visibility, but more success." [10]

Breaking the Blockade

To break the blockade against arrests, Louise Arbour decodes the argument made by London, Paris, and Washington: Each government is simply passing the blame to a neighbor. "The politicians said that the military did not want to proceed with the arrests, because it was too dangerous," she states. "The military said that they were obeying orders and that the political leadership did not give them instructions to do anything. When the countries were criticized for their passivity, they hid behind the Supreme Allied Commander of NATO in Europe, the 'SACEUR.' Everybody was passing the buck. In fact, the arrests for the very big fish depended on NATO headquarters in Brussels and, on the ground, on the commander of the multinational forces in Sarajevo. For the rest, the sectors had plenty of freedom of action." [11]

Louise Arbour is absolutely right. No government with soldiers in Bosnia wants to take the initiative to proceed with arrests, and each blames the others to justify that passivity. To put a good face on it, the Americans are even putting up posters of presumed war criminals and distributing matchboxes with photographs of Karadzic and Mladic labeled "Wanted" and listing a reward for information leading to their capture.

But it is all a great bluff. Milan Simic, one of the accused who voluntarily surrenders himself to the tribunal on February 14, 1998, will tell the investigators of the tribunal about his initial fear of these cowboy tactics, until, realizing that it was merely eyewash, he no longer hesitated to pass NATO checkpoints.

Paul Stuebner, formerly Richard Goldstone's principal counselor, is disgusted by the "hypocrisy" of the Western powers. In early 1996, the tribunal veteran had rejoined the Organization for Security and Cooperation in Europe (OSCE) for a few months. With his own eyes, he saw the car of Radovan Karadzic, sirens blaring, arrive near Pale at a checkpoint held by Italian soldiers: "[The soldiers] turned toward Sarajevo and pretended to see nothing. NATO pretended not to know where to find the war criminals indicted by the ICTY," he says. "It was a total lie. We were all soaking in a hypocrisy without name! Mladic himself was in the American zone and we knew it full well. But Clinton wanted to secure reelection and that meant, above all, avoiding having any boys killed in some Bosnian backwater. In derision, we in the OSCE renamed ourselves the 'Organization to Secure Clinton's Election.'"[12]

Under such conditions, it is hardly astonishing that Louise Arbour's incitement and agitation of NATO has little effect. "I told them: 'How is it that journalists meet with war criminals and you don't even know where they are?'" she says. "They responded that 'The war criminals look for the journalists, but they avoid us.' In reality, IFOR, then SFOR [Stabilization Force], avoids searching for the criminals and even avoids making the SFOR soldiers too visible."[13] The ever-present fear of reprisals, fed by the searing memory of the Dutch battalion taken hostage by the Bosnian Serbs, continues to paralyze Western governments and their armed forces.

The height of absurdity, the "Wanted" posters garner huge publicity for the Americans yet render the capture of the indicted ever more difficult. This "Wild West" tactic motivates Louise Arbour to act *a contrario*. "Since the posters warned the indicted that they were officially being sought, I said to myself, 'We are going to do the exact opposite and hold the indictments secret,'" she explains.[14] It is one of the key ideas of her mandate: From now on, NATO commandos hold the advantage of surprise, because the war criminals do not know that they are even suspects. The prosecutor's other trick is to put maximum pressure on the Western governments by threatening to reveal publicly their refusal to carry out the arrests if they continue their policy of passivity. "Officially, I told them that, from now on, the soldiers of IFOR, and then SFOR, would have the advantage of surprise for arresting the suspects," she explains. "Which was perfectly accurate. I added, as a fact and not as a threat, that if they did not carry out the arrests in the coming weeks or in the coming months, then I would make the indictments public. The intent was obvious. The media would immediately see that the indictments had been released internally and they would begin to ask some embarrassing questions of the governments that had soldiers with SFOR in Bosnia."[15]

Some members of the tribunal do not favor keeping indictments under seal, believing that doing so violates the rights of the defendants. Antonio

Cassese is among those members, and he raises the question in a plenary session. "I was very disturbed with this procedure," he says later. "In Italy, there is an obligation to render the indictments publicly. Arbour answered that not every country recognizes the same rule as Italy and that, faced with the lack of cooperation—indeed, the intransigent refusal to cooperate—from the local Serb and Croat authorities, it was the only means for SFOR to capture the accused, since they were not on their guard. She expected strong results from that policy." [16] Arbour pleads to the judges to give her a chance. "I had been against the trials in absentia, and I beseeched Cassese and [Claude] Jorda to give me six months before going back to the beginning," she says. "I wanted a real trial. I wanted the ICTY to be legitimate to the Anglo-American world, which did not accept trials in absentia." [17] She wins the debate.

But the NATO governments are afraid to act. They try to get Louise Arbour to return to a less determined strategy. "The governments criticized me," she says.

> They did not want secret indictments, because they realized that this was pushing them to act. I said to them, "You use your means, I use mine. I obey instructions that are given to me. The ICTY is an organ of the Security Council created under Article VII of the U.N. Charter. You are all subject, as I am, to the resolutions of the Security Council." As soon as I put the discussion on legal terrain, they did not insist, but they began to conjure some apocalyptic scenarios. "You understand, the Serbs, it is important not to run them over, . . ." they told me. Certain politicians warned me of the imminence of a third world war. For me, all this talk was due to a policy of appeasement.[18]

The Russians are particularly hostile to sealed indictments. In December, 1998, Russia's foreign minister, Igor Ivanov, reiterates "their serious displeasure" with the use of secret indictments that are not authorized for the tribunal and that impede the states from "voluntary cooperation" with the tribunal while depriving the indicted persons of their right to surrender themselves. Ivanov tactlessly rebuffs Louise Arbour's reminder that the Republika Srpska and the Federal Republic of Yugoslavia "had plenty of opportunity to show their willingness" to arrest the twenty-five people on their territories who are already publicly indicted.[19]

The Western governments still balk, they say, at "provoking the Serbs." Despite her will to go ahead, Louise Arbour worries about the soundness of her strategy of secret indictments. "I had dark moments of anxiety," she recalls. "I knew that it was necessary to make arrests. Just one, and the rest would follow. I got pressure from the non-governmental organizations, especially the Americans and Human Rights Watch, who were saying, 'What is she doing? She's been there for weeks and there hasn't been a single tangible result.' I knew very well what I was doing, but I could not reveal it and I was not sure that it was going to work; now and then I was close to discouragement."[20]

To try to improve cooperation with the states, the tribunal president makes the rounds but is treated like a leper. The president of Italy, Oscar Luigi Scalfaro, receives Antonio Cassese. "[Scalfaro] said to me: 'Your tribunal will not be credible as long as Karadzic and Mladic are not judged,'" Cassese says.

> I responded to him: "Give me a hand, Mr. President." He organized a meeting for me with the minister of defense, but the political will to act was absent. In France, President Chirac canceled our meeting at the last minute. I met instead with one of his aides and the minister of justice, Jacques Toubon. They made me a ton of promises, notably to send five investigators. They never came. In Great Britain, I saw the minister of foreign affairs, Malcolm Rifkind. "I'll give you fifteen minutes," he said. He met me in his office with his chief of cabinet and his legal counsel. Then, he started coming out with banalities. After seven minutes, I couldn't take any more of it. I told him, "Mr. Minister, I know that your time is precious, good-bye," and I left. As irritated as I was disappointed.[21]

In Russia, Cassese hears the tribunal accused of partiality. The interview with Prime Minister Yevgeni Primakov turns into confrontation:

> "You are prejudiced, you are anti-Serb, you are a Western tribunal, you don't have a Russian judge, you are not fair, . . ." Primakov said. I defended myself. I explained that we took on all the belligerents, that he only had to look at the indictments. . . . In the Duma, an old prosecutor general accused the tribunal of being paid by the CIA, of corruption, of being in the pay of the Americans. Myself, I thought it would be better to commit this man to a psychiatric hospital. They told me later that I was an extremist. So, I better understood the pressures that the communists and the nationalists put on Primakov.[22]

Given the lack of cooperation from the politicians and the reticence of NATO in Bosnia, the first arrest does not take place in Bosnia but in eastern Slovenia. It is Croat territory occupied by the Serbs, with a U.N. presence represented, at the moment, by Jacques Klein. This American diplomat, born in Alsace, has the physique and temperament of a bulldozer. He cites Kafka, Camus, and Dostoyevsky in his analysis of the Balkans and implements the U.S. State Department's approach as advocated by Richard Holbrooke: Proceed with arrests as a signal to the ultranationalists that the era of impunity is over.

In June, 1997, tribunal investigators and U.N. soldiers manage to seize Slavko Dokmanovic. The former president of the municipality of Vukovar, he is accused of crimes against humanity for ordering, with others also under indictment, the deaths of more than two hundred Croats seeking refuge at the hospital in Vukovar.[23] For Arbour, the arrest in Slovenia is a psychological boost: It will clear the road for others to follow. An added bonus is that her orders have finally been carried out by U.N. soldiers. It will now be difficult for NATO soldiers to keep their arms crossed.

This tactic pays off at the July 9, 1997, NATO summit in Madrid. After a discussion between Tony Blair, Bill Clinton, and NATO Secretary General Javier Solana, British Special Air Services commandos get the green light. The next day, they go into action and attempt to arrest Simo Drljaca in Prijedor, but he defends himself and is shot and killed. This failure raises doubts that NATO will be able to carry out the arrests effectively. However, the British attempt proves that the population of the Serb Republic will not oppose them. All the fears of reprisals have been unfounded.

On December 18, just after the NATO summit at Brussels, Dutch commandos go into action near Vitez. Wounded, suspect Vlatko Kupreskic is transferred to The Hague. On January 22, 1998, the Americans arrest the man nicknamed the "Serb Adolf," Goran Jelisic, accused of many crimes, including genocide against Muslims and Croats. He had directed the camp at Luka near Brcko and boasted of killing at least ninety-six detainees. Although he claims to be wearing a twenty-kilo belt of dynamite, Jelisic is arrested without violence.

The arrests accelerate. Arbour's strategy continues to pay off. She secretly indicts the militia leaders, which the ICTY will later reveal. Several more shadows remain on Louise Arbour's list, however. She never gets the NATO countries to mount an arrest operation for Karadzic and Mladic. As for the Serb president, Slobodan Milosevic, the guarantor of the Dayton Accords, she does not really seek to build a case against him. The evidence is too weak, she says, to support his indictment before the judges. In reality, prior to the Kosovo crisis, she never makes a serious effort to indict the strong man of Belgrade. Is Milosevic the limit the tribunal's independence?

Confrontation with France

In the wake of the Dayton Accords, the deployment of U.S. forces in Bosnia changes the balance, giving a central role to the Americans. Washington and London put their acrimonious relations behind them. The "special relationship" between the two countries returns, and the arrival of Tony Blair in the spring of 1997 breathes new life into it. The new British prime minister is at

Number 10 Downing Street barely twenty-four hours before he decides to support the tribunal, notably to demonstrate publicly his will to conduct a foreign policy respectful of human rights. Under the impetus of Arbour, the Western governments begin to realize how they can take domestic political advantage of the arrests. Only one country resists, finding itself more and more isolated: France.

Paris, the wellspring of the tribunal's creation, has for a long time obstructed any cooperation with it. It has been a strange evolution in any event. French soldiers control the Foca sector, the epicenter of Serb extremism and the location where a good number of war criminals are dug in, but they refuse to make arrests. Only French officers refuse to testify in person at The Hague. The French, contrary to the British and the Americans, provide no intelligence to help advance tribunal investigations. Each time that the tribunal wants to get information from a former peacekeeper, the procedure is incomprehensibly burdensome: The tribunal must submit questions in writing, a judge or prosecutor must affirm the legality of the request, and then the court receives the responses weeks later. With the British or the Americans, the prosecutor merely has to pick up the telephone. "This procedure was truly so slow and complicated that it became surreal," Louise Arbour notes.[24]

From the beginning, the dominance of the common law system, followed by the Americans' activism in the tribunal, has France convinced that Washington is "dictating" justice in the former Yugoslavia. The fact that French—with English, one of the two official languages of the tribunal—is considered by the Office of the Prosecutor to be a kind of exotic dialect spoken by a handful of people, only bolsters this feeling. To France, the tribunal is an instrument at the service of Washington. Though the Americans have imposed order on Bosnia, the French are paying the heaviest tribute of the war.

Louise Arbour tries in vain to win over the bitter and frustrated French:

> It was impossible to have a dialogue with the French military. They argued that the arrests depended on a unified command. That was false. In fact, they could have caught the small fish anytime they wanted. No doubt, for the big fish like Karadzic, a decision from a unified command would have been necessary. But they didn't like it at all when the British began to make arrests in their sector. It was rapid, quickly done, and it showed their own absence of will. I told them, "Look what was done at Prijedor." So they tried to hide behind the errors of the British, saying, laughing, "The Brits were fooled by twins!" (which did, in fact, happen) or, "It's too complicated." In fact, the political will to act was totally absent. No doubt, the French believed that the ICTY was the property of the Americans. They did not understand that, after centuries of conflict,

for the first time, we had a relatively inexpensive instrument permitting us to put into question—both in terms of their career and their freedom—those political and military leaders who were responsible. And that this could have an effect, that we could get rid of these scoundrels.[25]

But nothing was done:

At the bottom of it all, the French were bitter. They had lost men in Bosnia-Herzegovina when the bullets were flying, while the Americans were nice and warm in their homes. The Americans could afford the luxury of a moralist discourse, while the French feared that the ICTY could turn on them and investigate decisions made by General [Bernard] Janvier or others, while Washington was unthreatened, having no troops in the war. I am convinced that the United States would have slammed on the brakes, too, if American soldiers had been implicated like the French and if their testimony could embarrass their own authorities.[26]

It is in this sensitive climate that on December 9, 1997, French defense minister Alain Richard declares that he will "never go to The Hague" since the tribunal is carrying out a "spectacle of justice" and that it is out of the question that French officers will testify in "this circus" (the ICTY).[27] Embarrassed by the public impact of this declaration, French authorities play down Richard's outburst, implying that his statements are a personal blunder. In reality, the minister is only stating publicly and in less diplomatic terms the French government's attitude toward the tribunal. An article by Henri Rochereau, "*le contrôleur des armées*" and one of the top officials in the French defense ministry, published in *Revue armées d'aujourd'hui* on February 1, 1996, is indicative of that spirit. He militates against the dangers of an international court, using the same terms that Alain Richard will eventually take as his own a few months later, setting off a hue and cry:

The most recent experience demonstrates that the international jurisdictions are more often used as media tribunes than as organs charged to speak the law, not to speak of legal customs that are not universally accepted. Is it worth taking the risk of having such or such Third World country reproach the former colonial powers with old facts pulled from history, reactivated by an artifice of procedure? Must we give certain international organizations a new tribunal through which they can make unacceptable and unfounded complaints, while granting them a high-profile platform like a trial to attract attention to their accusations? Short of the power to interrogate and judge those responsible for the atrocities committed, the temptation will be great for the International Criminal Court [the ICC, to be created] to justify its existence by multiplying the interrogations of witnesses. From the role of witnesses, we could slip into that of collaborator. The polemic that is developing on the role of France in Rwanda outside of Operation Turquoise, on that of the Dutch forces of UN-PROFOR in the enclave of Srebrenica, leaves us to believe that such a hypothesis may not be a simple case study. Ineffective without punishing particularly grave crimes, the ICC would result in the paradox of redoubling accusations regarding the Western states, blamed for allowing the dramas of the world to develop. . . . The creation of an international criminal court is a noble objective. But, in this state, the advanced project appears compatible with neither the interests of the most active states in the area of humanitarian law, nor with the legal protection of their withdrawal, nor with simple political realism.[28]

Alain Richard merely follows the path of this analysis to its logical conclusion.

After the French defense minister's thundering statement, Louise Arbour feels "that she must profit from such good fortune." Rochereau has freed her from the confidentiality she had imposed on herself: "I did not want to expose myself publicly on the issue of French reticence in cooperating with the tribunal. But, if provoked, I wanted them to know that they effectively risked me being myself."[29] In an interview published in *Le Monde* on December 14, 1997, she retaliates:

I find these ideas unbelievable. . . . [T]he Minister spoke of a spectacle of justice. His remarks insult more than 200 witnesses who presented themselves before this international authority. . . . To suggest that they made a spectacle out of themselves is insulting and shocking. As for the refusal to authorize the French military to testify at The Hague, I have two worries. Given the speed at which we have access to their written testimony, it is worrisome to think that this is France's chosen procedure. We have to negotiate question by question with the lawyers at the Ministry of Defense. This leads us to believe that the true intention is to control the Tribunal's access to the truth: it is a firm signal that suggests a will not to cooperate with the Tribunal and corresponds with the extremely disappointing position of the military authorities concerning their opposition to the arrest of presumed war criminals . . . [I]t is in the French sector that many war criminals are found, but they feel absolute security there. . . . The only arrest undertaken in Bosnia has been in the British sector. The vast majority of the indicted, including the most important suspects, are in the French sector. There are considerable opportunities for action in the French sector, yet we confront complete inertia. Thus, our conclusion that this inertia constitutes a concerted policy. This is unacceptable. . . . We would have expected that NATO demand that the first priority of its mandate be the arrests of war criminals. We have faced, on the contrary, a resistance, sometimes passive, sometimes active, of the military.[30]

The charge is blunt. Everything is now out in the open: the noncollaboration, despite the obligatory resolutions of the Security Council; the will "to control the Tribunal's access to the truth"; and the fact that the French sector in Bosnia, Foca, is a peaceful haven for war criminals. The French foreign minister, Hubert Védrine, swoons; "France cannot accept these scandalous and false accusations," he says.[31] Prime Minister Lionel Jospin goes one better on December 16 before the National Assembly. Calling Arbour's accusations "unacceptable," he says, "In our eyes, no war criminal must escape judgment, no crime must remain unpunished."[32]

Jospin does not explain the passivity of the French military, however. He hides behind the fact that France does not enforce a unique policy but rather a common and long-standing one—that the military obeys only an "integrated command." This argument is unfounded, as Louise Arbour notes, since the military has a considerable degree of autonomy in each sector. In addition, Jospin has not responded to France's alleged lack of cooperation with the tribunal, both regarding trials already under way and those to follow.

Fortunately, neither the denials of Lionel Jospin nor those of the Quai d'Orsay prove credible. L'Express, a French news weekly, issues a list of alleged war criminals residing in the hamlet of Foca:

> Janko Janjic, 40 years old, offers to recount his exploits to anyone who will pay him 5,000 deutsche marks. Like his stooges, Gojko Jankovic, 43, Radomir Kovac, 36, or again one of the most cruel, Dragan Zelenovic, 32, who beat his victims with an axe-handle, Janjic is accused of having arrested, isolated, brutalized, and repeatedly raped the Muslim women of Foca, and to having given them over to the Serb militias. Between July and August, 1992, at least 70 of these women, some of whom were adolescents of 13 or 14 years old, were locked up in the Partisan Sports Hall. Dragan Gagovic, 37, named local chief of police by Karadzic's party, of which he himself was a member, controlled this concentration camp designed for the gang rape of women.[33]

But Louise Arbour's strong rejoinder to Alain Richard's protestations bears fruit. France's foreign minister, Hubert Védrine, visits The Hague, impressing upon observers that Paris intends to clear up a simple "misunderstanding." And from March, 1998, on, French officers are authorized to testify before the tribunal, though most are generally *in camera*. On January 9, 1999, French commandos attempt to intercept Dragan Gagovic as he flees in his vehicle with six children aboard. Apparently, when he sees the commandos, Gagovic charges the SFOR soldiers, who quickly shoot him to death. Fortunately, none of the children is injured. In August, 1999, the French arrest Radomir Kovac.

While the French government is normalizing its relations with the tribunal, however, tensions are emerging between the French and American military commands in Sarajevo because of diverging visions of Bosnia's immediate future. Driven by the tribunal to act, the Americans are now convinced that the arrests of war criminals are marginalizing opposition to the Dayton Accords. This view collides with that of the French military commanders, who do not want to be the running dogs of American hegemony in the Balkans and who again balk, in the summer of 1999, at carrying out arrests. "The Anglo-Saxons wanted to sweep away the old leaders at the risk of destabilizing the entire region; the pursuit of war criminals risked provoking reprisals; the exhumations tore open old wounds," explains a top French commander.[34]

This rivalry between the militaries turns bitter. (The judicial division of the Quai d'Orsay confirms, not in so many words, that the French military are dragging their feet and are faced with a mandate that has evolved.) With a certain bad faith, on June 24, 1999, American Ambassador at Large for War Crimes Issues David Scheffer accuses French troops of not wanting to arrest Radovan Karadzic: "Karadzic is generally known to be in the French sector," which he labels a "sanctuary." "In general, the means [to arrest him] exist," he says.[35] The French government replies by inviting the United States to take responsibility for tracking down war criminals in Bosnia-Herzegovina: "We expect our American allies to show as much determination as we do concerning Radovan Karadzic or any other war criminal."[36] At the SFOR headquarters in Sarajevo, protected by American soldiers, the relations between the allied military are so bad that the superior French officers are sure that their American counterparts are "feeding" the Bosnian press, whose articles claim that the French passivity toward arrests is due to "the fear of the military and the French government that Radovan Karadzic will speak of the close collaboration that he, as well as General Mladic, has maintained with General Bernard Janvier, the French UNPROFOR commander in Bosnia, under the direct command of [French president] Jacques Chirac."[37] This game of tit-for-tat accusations between the French and Americans suits both sides; by tossing the responsibility back and forth, they avoid taking action individually that in any event should have been taken in concert. Karadzic's arrest would have by necessity implied support and cooperation between the French and the Americans.

Despite all her efforts, Louise Arbour can only deplore her failure. "All the politicians, whether it was Madeleine Albright, Hubert Védrine, or others, told me: 'It's too complicated, too dangerous,'" she says.[38] This policy of impunity for Bosnian Serb chiefs accused of genocide continues for years, although it is shameful in a moral sense, politically dangerous, and contrary to the spirit of the founding resolutions of the tribunal.

Resolutions 808 and 827 of the Security Council had confirmed that the international court was an instrument for the reestablishment and maintenance of peace in Yugoslavia. This dimension is never really incorporated into the process of the reconstruction of Bosnia-Herzegovina, and the result is that ethnic divisions persist. Warnings of such a result, however, have been numerous. In an ironic reversal of roles, the United Nations criticizes the passivity of NATO as endangering the reconstruction of a united Bosnia. "If [NATO] had been tougher, things would be different," declares Kris Janowski, spokesman for the U.N. High Commission for Human Rights. "We're seeing a multiethnic Bosnia being flushed down the toilet."[39]

The Marginalization of the Tribunal

The marginalization of the tribunal in the reconstruction of a multiethnic Bosnia has heavy consequences. By arresting the nationalist chieftains indicted by the ICTY, the international court could have created a climate of security favoring the return of minorities to their region of origin, shaping propitious conditions for effective economic aid from the international community. In practice, however, a negative dynamic takes shape. Jacques Klein, the head of the United Nations mission in Bosnia, complains that Karadzic, still free, has even influenced the most recent elections:

> How can we be taken seriously while Karadzic lives in liberty, still accused of genocide? In Germany and Japan, the high authorities of the regime were put out of the game after World War II. Here, they continue their fight. And the international community is letting it happen. It is a pathetic expression of its weakness. The instigators of the war have retained their power, contrary to the support of 80 percent of the population. As a result, the ethnic vote continues, because the structures of power remain the same. The Western states have lost view of what Toynbee said: Each civilization must master its own agenda if it is not to be the victim of the agendas of others. The Americans want a rapid solution in order to clear out, the Europeans are divided as usual, while the local anti-nationalists tell us, "I am willing to get involved and risk my physical security, if I am convinced that you will not leave me in a lurch. Because if you leave, the nationalists will have my skin."[40]

A chaotic international administration is set up under the theoretical patronage of the High Representative of the International Community for Bosnia, of which Jacques Klein is deputy director. "When I took office, I held a meeting where I said that we must act in concert," Klein says. "It was the first time that somebody had taken the initiative to harmonize the different policies of the World Bank, the Organization for Security and Cooperation in Europe, bilateral American aid, the United Nations Development Program. . . . I realized, with a start, that I depended on Geneva, on Vienna, on New York, on Brussels, on Washington."[41]

In reality, the Office of the High Representative for Bosnia has only limited powers. It cannot even open a blocked road without calling on soldiers of the multinational forces. This weakness is the will of the Americans, who, through NATO, want to control the base of any situation, without taking the risk of arresting the Bosnian Serb leaders. The two sole successes of the Office of the High Representative are the introduction of the convertible deutsche mark and freedom of movement. On this last point, there is a tart exchange between Bosnian Serb leader Momcilo Krajisnik and Klein. "In an interminable discussion, he told me that his people would never accept the Latin alphabet for the car license plates," Klein recounts later. "I asked him, 'Why are you talking about Latin letters? The new license plates carry only the six letters that belong both to the Cyrillic and Latin alphabets: T, J, A, E, M, K. Look. There are three numerals, a letter, and three more numerals.' He looked at me, stunned. I thought he was going to have a heart attack. Then he yelled at me, 'You think that with your tricks, you are going to succeed in deceiving us?' The license plates were introduced without a problem, because people understood the advantage of free movement."[42]

Regarding the evolution of the situation, Richard Holbrooke writes,

> Of all the things necessary to achieve our goals in Bosnia, the most important was still the arrest of Radovan Karadzic. But Karadzic surfaced after a few months of near seclusion and began issuing orders and giving interviews, signaling his followers that they could still safely pursue their separatist goals. With his military forces neutralized, Karadzic used the "special police," a vestige of the communist police state, to threaten any Bosnian Serb who showed support for Dayton. Even though these units were also covered in the Dayton agreement, IFOR pointedly ignored these "police" as they crossed the Serb portion of Bosnia intimidating anyone who cooperated with Muslims or spoke favorably of Dayton. . . . While the arrest of Karadzic would not have solved all the problems the international community faced in Bosnia, his removal from Bosnia was a necessary, although not sufficient, condition for success. . . . Karadzic at large was certain to mean Dayton deferred or defeated.[43]

But Holbrooke is preaching in the desert. Several years after their indictment for genocide, the warlords who had torched and bled Bosnia remain free men—so free, in fact, that one of them surrenders to The Hague of his own free will, confident of the justness of his cause.

Secret Contacts with Radovan Karadzic

In May, 1996, Radovan Karadzic is preparing to hold a ministerial cabinet meeting when he is told that an American visitor is in the reception area and wishes to meet him. It is Paul Stuebner. Frustrated by the inaction of the OSCE, Stuebner has resigned and is preparing to rejoin the tribunal again. On his own initiative, Stuebner has made the trip to Pale, officially as a "private citizen." In fact, Goldstone's former right-hand man nurtures the hope that he can convince Radovan Karadzic to surrender himself voluntarily to The Hague to face those who accuse him of high crimes. After a preliminary, extended verbal exchange, Stuebner says, the discussion turns to the life of the subject:

> As the Number Two at OSCE, I had met Karadzic on several occasions to discuss the questions of the dispatch of humanitarian aid. This time, I appeared in Pale in my capacity as a private citizen. I asked to see Karadzic. He accepted immediately, canceling the ministerial cabinet. We talked for two hours. His first words were: "If NATO comes to search for me, there will be blood on the floor." I retorted that, if the political will to arrest had existed, no country in the world could resist the strongest military alliance in the world. And that, if NATO had decided, he would have been either arrested and humiliated, or killed if the operation turned out badly, and in that occurrence the blood that would flow on the floor would be his own.
>
> He dropped the subject. We then explored the possibility that he could appear before the tribunal, in granting him some minor concessions. Thus, we had envisaged the hypothesis where he would not stay in a little cell in a prison near The Hague, but that he could remain at the NATO military base. We had similarly envisaged that he could be judged on a NATO base and not in the tribunal, but there was no obligation in this sense.
>
> My objective was very simple: I wanted Karadzic to testify before the tribunal and I wanted above all to do it so that he did not get killed. The last thing that I wanted was to create a martyr in the eyes of the Serbs for the next five hundred years. It was necessary thus to assure him of a fair trial, the definition of justice that applies also to those who are responsible for the worst crimes. Karadzic, his counselors told me, was very worried. He feared that, if ever he decided to surrender to The Hague, a member of his personal guard, a "turncoat" in the service of Milosevic, would simply kill him.

We also discussed the possibility that he be taken by NATO forces with his consent, leaving behind a recorded message that would be broadcast. In this message, Karadzic would have said, in substance: "I have not been kidnapped by NATO. I have surrendered of my own will to The Hague to defend the honor of the Serb people." In fact, he dreamed of becoming the hero of the Serb people.

But the idea was abandoned. Karadzic said that the tribunal was "partial," that he would never have a right to a fair trial, that too few non-Serbs had been indicted. I told him that in my sense the Serb forces were responsible for 80 percent of the atrocities of this war, and even 90 percent before Operation Storm launched by the Croats. And that the accusations of the tribunal reflected these differences in the responsibility for criminal acts. In fact, he knew perfectly well why he was being pursued. At the moment we parted, he asked me, "When will we meet again?" I told him, "When I escort you to The Hague." Afterwards when I rejoined the tribunal, I pursued this dialogue with one of his advisers.[44]

But Karadzic's dreams of justice do not go much further. A few weeks later, in early 1996, Antonio Cassese is touring the former Yugoslavia. The tribunal president is preparing for the Florence Conference that will report on the tribunal's application of the Dayton Accords. To his great surprise, an American army intermediary offers Cassese a discreet contact with Radovan Karadzic. "I was in Sarajevo, in my hotel room, when I received a telephone call from a colonel in the American army," Cassese says.

She proposed my meeting a defense lawyer in Pale. She told me that she would handle the security of transport. The suggestion was curious, to say the least. I said that it was out of the question that, as tribunal president, I meet persons indicted by the tribunal over which I presided. But I added that I was ready to talk to his lawyer at a NATO base. This was done. The next day, one of Karadzic's official lawyers asked me if I would agree that his client come to The Hague, remain in a hotel while awaiting his trial, and be allowed to hold press conferences. I said that it was out of the question, and that put an end to the discussion.[45]

At the Florence Conference, June 13–14, Antonio Cassese does not mince words. In front of the media and other observers, he excoriates the international community for its inaction in tracking down war criminals pursued by the tribunal. He demands that before the elections planned for September 14, "certain leaders like Radovan Karadzic, Dario Kordic, Milan Martic, and Ratko Mladic must be arrested." And he exhorts all the states and all the international

organizations to act in the name of "moral principles." The Western delega-
tions are furious to see their hypocrisy exposed in broad daylight by a little Italian judge, even if he is president of the ICTY. Cassese's proposal is met with icy
silence. Only the Bosnian delegation applauds. Impassive, Cassese proposes
the imposition of "selective economic sanctions as well as a sports boycott" to
punish the former belligerents who refuse to cooperate with the tribunal. The
Olympic Games are soon to open in Atlanta.

In the chamber is Karadzic's counselor, who serves as his communication
link to the tribunal. This man later confides to Stuebner, "Cassese was so eloquent in his demonstration that, at one moment, I myself wanted to arrest
Karadzic and send him to The Hague!"[46] But the counselor adds that, after
Cassese's proposal, exploring the conditions under which Karadzic might surrender himself voluntarily to the tribunal is out of the question. It is the end of
the exploratory discussions with Karadzic that began in May, 1996, and that no
doubt were doomed to failure in any event. Cassese is not the cause of this failure. He has only put the spotlight on NATO's inertia.

Hostility of Serbia and Croatia

During the war, the tribunal is ineffective. After Dayton, it collides with the
refusal of the Republika Srpska and the Yugoslav authorities to cooperate.
The authorities do not recognize the tribunal's jurisdiction and even forbid it
to open an office in Belgrade. With Croatia, relations are hardly better. That
country refuses to recognize the tribunal's jurisdiction over the matter of atrocities that took place during the re-conquest of Croat territory occupied by the
Serbs in 1995. Only when the Americans threaten to pull a loan of ten billion
dollars promised by the World Bank does President Franjo Tudjman of Croatia reverse his decision forbidding ten Croats indicted by the tribunal to surrender "voluntarily" to The Hague. He does not cut his ties to some of them,
however. Tudjman even lends his personal translator to Dario Kordic when
Kordic says his good-byes at the Split airport on October 6, 1997. Kordic is no
choirboy. The tribunal has accused him of crimes against humanity for help-
ing to orchestrate a massive campaign of persecution against Muslims in the
Lasva valley in central Bosnia. Tudjman's support is a clear signal that the Croat
president is not abandoning him. For Richard Holbrooke, it is obvious that the
two men have "reached some sort of private understanding regarding the future." (Eight weeks earlier, Robert Gelbard, American ambassador and special
envoy to the Balkans, had threatened Tudjman that he " 'must send [Kordic] to
The Hague if you want things to change between us.' " The Croat president
protested that he had no idea of the place where Kordic was hiding, a performance that was unconvincing to his American interlocutors.)[47]

The tribunal at The Hague never manages to get its message across in the former Yugoslavia. The evidence for this failure appears all over the city of Foca with small posters displaying a photograph of Karadzic and the caption "Hands Off." The tribunal has always appeared to be a Western instrument in the eyes of the former Yugoslav governments. The fact that the arrests are carried out primarily by British troops has only confirmed this perception. The U.N. secretary-general's successive annual reports on the tribunal attest to this ongoing hostility:

> The Republika Srpksa has failed to execute any of the scores of arrest warrants which have been addressed to it, or to explain its inability or failure to do so, as required by the Tribunal's rules. More troubling is the fact that two indictees—Radovan Karadzic and Ratko Mladic—each twice indicted by the Tribunal, inter alia, for genocide—not only have not been arrested but have remained (or still remain, in the case of Mladic) in official positions, contrary to the express terms of the Dayton Accord. The only cooperation of Republika Srpksa with the Tribunal evinced to date has been allowing Tribunal investigators access to sites, notably mass grave sites. At the same time, however, there are numerous media reports that such sites have been emptied of corpses or otherwise tampered with, which would constitute destruction of evidence. . . . The Republic of Croatia occupies a middle rung in this ladder of cooperation. It recently enacted a law on cooperation with the Tribunal, which, however, has the undesirable feature of reserving a certain amount of discretionary power in executive organs. It has arrested one accused in its territory, Zlatko Aleksovski. A Bosnian Croat indictee, Tihomir Blaskic, has surrendered to the Tribunal of his own accord through the mediation of the Republic of Croatia. The Republic of Croatia has, however, failed to exercise its acknowledged authority and influence over other Bosnian Croats with a view to effecting their apprehension. Furthermore, so far it has failed fully to investigate and prosecute serious violations of international humanitarian law allegedly committed by Croatian forces in August 1995 during and after "Operation Storm."[48]

The 1997 report is even more pessimistic: "Contrary to the terms of the Dayton Peace Agreement, a number of persons indicted by the Tribunal appear still to hold official positions. In particular, Zeljko Meakic (who has been indicted for genocide), Mladen Radic, Nedeljko Timarac and Miloslav Kvocka are all reported still to be working as police officers in the Prijedor area of Republika Srpska. In November 1996, local police in Prijedor confirmed that two indictees, Pedrag and Nenad Banovic, were working as police reservists, while two others, Radomir Kovac and Dragan Selenovic, were working at a police station in Foca."[49]

In August, 1996, Radovan Stankovic, accused of participating in the gang rape at Foca and still a police officer in this locality, is almost arrested by the police of the Bosnia-Herzegovina Federation. Afterward, he visits a post of the International Police Group to lodge a complaint of harassment against the federation police. The height of absurdity! A spokesman for the police group declares that it is not their duty either to arrest Stankovic or to inform IFOR of his presence at its offices.

On January 2, 1997, the president of the Serb Republic addresses a letter to the U.N. secretary-general and to the members of the Security Council: "'The present position of Republika Srpska is that we are unwilling to hand over Dr. Karadzic and General Mladic for trial in The Hague, as we believe that any such trial now falls outside the scope of the Tribunal's constitutional framework.'"[50] Kofi Annan notes,

> The Federal Republic of Yugoslavia, for its part, is both failing to ensure Republika Srpska's compliance with the Dayton Peace Agreement, as it undertook and is obliged to do, and has failed to pass implementing legislation to enable it to cooperate with the Tribunal. It has further indicated that it has no intention of enacting such legislation in the future. It has visibly failed to arrest the three senior army officers on its territory—Mrksic, Radic and Sljivancanin—who were all indicted in November 1995 by the Tribunal for their alleged roles in the destruction of Vukovar and the murder of 261 unarmed men after its fall. . . . [U]ntil very recently IFOR/SFOR has refrained from apprehending, or indeed encountering, indictees, stating that it did not intend to send out "posses" to arrest indictees but would only arrest them if they came across them. This approach has recently changed dramatically with the arrest by SFOR, on 10 July 1997, of Slavko Dokmanovic, indicted on charges of complicity in genocide for crimes committed in the Prijedor area.[51]

In December, 1998, the new tribunal president, the American Gabrielle Kirk McDonald, after having written five replies to the U.N. General Assembly, addresses herself in Madrid to fifty heads of state and governments participating in the follow-up to Dayton. In a passionate speech, she asserts,

> [T]he problem of non-co-operation looms larger than ever. In particular, the authorities of the Republika Srpska and the Government of the Federal Republic of Yugoslavia persist in refusing to arrest and transfer indictees on their territory to the Tribunal. . . . [T]he Government of the [Federal Republic of Yugoslavia] is blatantly violating international law. It is violating its obligations under numerous Security Council resolutions and the Dayton Agreement. Its

conduct and statements are an affront to the Security Council that established the Tribunal, and to this Council that is charged with overseeing the implementation of the Dayton Agreement. I urge you: end this obstruction now. Failure to do so will imperil all of the Tribunal's work to date. One state must not be allowed to dictate the agenda of the international community. One state must not be allowed to impede the work of the Tribunal, the first practical measure in the last half-century to create a world in which human rights, equality and justice, are more than words on paper.[52]

But not once, neither at the Madrid Conference nor in the Security Council, does the international community take the slightest measure against Yugoslavia for its refusal to cooperate with the tribunal. Such is the weight of international justice.

It happened, therefore it can happen again: this is the core of what
we have to say. It can happen, and it can happen everywhere.
—Primo Levi, *The Drowned and the Saved*

The International Court on the Spot

On May 25, 1999, President Slobodan Milosevic is publicly indicted
by the ICTY for atrocities committed by Serb forces in Kosovo.
Never has an indictment received such instantaneous media cov-
erage worldwide. For the first time, a sitting head of state is accused of war crimes and crimes against humanity. The indictment of President
Milosevic by a competent tribunal without retroactive effect is a major event.
Its range and symbolism go far beyond the Balkans. His indictment, coming at
the end of a chaotic process, escaping at the last minute from the supporters of
realpolitik, marks the entry of justice into international relations. One side effect of his indictment will be questions about the tribunal's margin of maneuver, now that its principal backers and political supporters have themselves become parties in the conflict.

Ten years earlier, before a million of his agitated fellow citizens assembled
on Blackbirds' Field in Kosovo, the mythical cradle of his fatherland where, six
hundred years earlier, King Lazar had been defeated by the Ottoman Turks,
Slobodan Milosevic had made himself the hero of Serb nationalism. "Six cen-
turies later, now, we are again facing battles. They are not armed battles, although such things cannot be excluded yet," Milosevic thundered.[1] His speech
would soon be followed by acts. As president of Serbia, Milosevic quickly
abolishes the political autonomy of Kosovo Province. The repression of the
ethnic Albanian population begins: purges of functionaries from the state ap-
paratus, expulsions of ethnic Albanians from public enterprises, the revocation

of officers and subordinates, arbitrary arrests and detentions, the use of torture. The repression sparks a resistance movement, the Kosovo Liberation Army (KLA, known locally as the UÇK), which itself sets off a stronger repression. On February 28, 1998, the special troops of the Yugoslav president, backed by tanks and helicopters, launch murderous raids against the villages of Drenica, a bastion of the first Albanian armed groups. They leave almost no survivors in any family that has a member suspected of belonging to the UÇK.

On March 10, 1998, the tribunal extends its jurisdiction over Kosovo for the first time. Louise Arbour affirms that she "is in the process of collecting information and evidence" in order to determine if the deaths of eighty-eight ethnic Albanians from Drenica can be considered a crime prosecutable by the ICTY.[2] Louise Arbour procrastinates for several days before taking this decision. At first, she determines—privately—that Kosovo cannot be considered an armed conflict as defined by international law, since the command of the UÇK is not clearly identifiable. But accounts of the summary executions of civilians by Serb forces push her to revise this judgment. She also feels pressure from the West to extend jurisdiction to Kosovo. The nongovernmental organizations, notably Human Rights Watch, are counting on the dissuasive dimension of the tribunal to stop crimes before they start.

It is in the name of geopolitical considerations, however, that the American government is encouraging the prosecutor to intervene. The United States determines that the threat of Milosevic's indictment is an effective weapon for breaking the cycle of violence in the Balkans. The Americans are not satisfied with merely pleading their case; they dip into their pockets to show their determination, to the point that they seem to be "buying" justice. On March 12, Madeleine Albright announces that the United States will give the tribunal a million dollars to pay the ICTY investigators in Kosovo. The day before, James Rubin, the State Department spokesman, affirms that ethnic cleansing is under way in Kosovo and that the Yugoslav president carries the ultimate responsibility for crimes committed in the province. Morton Abramowitz, a former American diplomat who is about to become political counselor to the UÇK, believes in the dissuasive impact of the tribunal. "Any sign that the international community is ready to punish Milosevic personally is going to get his attention better than anything short of a military strike," Abramowitz says.[3]

For both political and technical reasons, Louise Arbour does not want to invest her forces in Kosovo now. She has no desire to begin the race to indict that put Goldstone under such pressure, particularly from Washington. (A third of his indictments were annulled for inconsistency.) For this stubborn lawyer, dismantling the organization that she put in place in Bosnia with such great difficulty is out of the question. She knows only too well the cynicism of

American policy from having experienced it so many times in the past. Behind its pronouncements on international morality, the United States uses the tribunal for its own purposes to put political pressure on Belgrade. As soon as it gets satisfaction, however, the legal weapon is set aside.

Louise Arbour carries a bitter memory from only a few weeks earlier. In mid-February, 1998, Ambassador Robert Gelbard, the American special envoy for the former Yugoslavia, had humiliated her by declaring that the United States was in the process of assessing the indictments to determine which suspects merit a risky arrest operation in Bosnia. "The United States believes that a significant number of indictments will not stand up in court," he had said. "We will not risk the lives of any soldiers or anybody else to try to apprehend indicted war criminals if we believe the cases are weak."[4] It was a declaration with a certain irony: It was the United States that had encouraged Goldstone to proceed with indictments as quickly as possible, only to denounce their insufficiency. Hearing Gelbard's declaration, Louise Arbour had lost her temper. She reminded the Americans that they did not necessarily know all the evidence at the tribunal's disposal. "The Prosecutor regards [Gelbard's remarks] as without any foundation and purely speculative since no State, including the United States of America, has access to the evidence upon which the indictments have been confirmed," she had said in a statement. "[A]rrest warrants issued by Judges of the Tribunal, upon the confirmation of indictments, constitute the legally binding and sufficient authority for the arrest of indicted accused and their surrender to the Tribunal."[5] But nobody has any illusions about who holds the power in this relationship.

Meanwhile, the situation in Kosovo continues to deteriorate. In the summer of 1998, Serb troops launch a large offensive supported by artillery, heavy armor, tanks, and helicopters; 200,000 terrified ethnic Albanian men, women, and children flee their homes. Louise Arbour confirms on July 7 that "the Prosecutor believes that the nature and scale of the fighting indicate that an 'armed conflict,' within the meaning of international law, exists in Kosovo. As a consequence, [I intend] to bring charges for crimes against humanity or war crimes, if evidence of such crimes is established."[6] But her rhetorical intervention does not satisfy the bastions of human rights defenders. They want the tribunal to make it immediately known that it has opened an investigation, in hopes of curbing the coming repression. "She was unaware of the dissuasive dimension of her mandate!" exclaims the former American diplomat John Fox, director of the Open Society Institute.[7] In August, representatives of Amnesty International and Human Rights Watch broadside the tribunal prosecutor during a stormy meeting in Washington. "Human rights advocates are taking insane risks in Kosovo to assemble and transmit to the Tribunal evidence of crimes committed, while you remain sagely sitting on the evidence gathered!" Arbour recalls them charging. Arbour replies that she "did not intend to play district attorney" while the Yugoslavs forbid her investigators access to Kosovo.[8] In September, the former American diplomat James Hooper writes in the *Toronto Star,* "With her low public profile toward the war in Kosovo, Justice Arbour is strangely timid about applying the great moral power of her office effectively to deter further ethnic cleansing. . . . There is no compelling reason for Justice Arbour to forgo her responsibility to conduct an aggressive and well-publicized investigation that could also deter ethnic cleansing, in real time, when hundreds of people are being killed, mass graves are being discovered, and hundreds of thousands of people are being driven from their homes."[9]

Even at the ICTY, within the Office of the Prosecutor, the investigators and lawyers are dissatisfied with Louise Arbour's inaction. "We wondered if her passivity resulted from the lack of resources, her traditional prudence, or political pressure that she must submit to," one of them recalls.[10] The tribunal is no longer the small, embryonic structure that it was in 1994 or 1995. Now it has a budget of tens of millions of dollars, dozens of investigators, and real experience. All the more reason to act, think some in the Office of the Prosecutor who propose entering Kosovo via Montenegro, the only republic that still grants federal visas. But Louise Arbour opposes this idea, judging that the risks, both in terms of the physical security of tribunal members as well as political security for the ICTY, are too high. If the Yugoslav authorities should learn that a team of the ICTY is operating incognito on the territory of Yugoslavia, the impartiality claimed by the prosecutor would collapse.[11]

"Bitter and disappointed by the attitude of Louise Arbour and Graham Blewitt," four young lawyers approaching the end of their tenure at the tribunal decide to send themselves, at their own risk and peril, to Kosovo to gather information necessary for the Milosevic indictment. They have nothing to lose and want to demonstrate that the obstacles are not as insurmountable as Louise Arbour claims. "Kosovo was on the minds of each of us at the tribunal," explains Nicolo Figa-Talamanca, who directed the operation. "It was necessary to act, because we wanted to change the spirit within the tribunal, by saying, 'Here is what we have collected acting on our own. You can get much more.'"[12]

The four lawyers warn Graham Blewitt, with whom they are in direct contact, but they do not know if he has alerted Louise Arbour to their enterprise. They also tell European Commissioner for Humanitarian Action Emma Bonino, herself in contact with NATO Supreme Commander Wesley Clark, in case their operation goes badly. No one dissuades the group from leaving. On the contrary, they allow the four to act. The Europeans and Americans have several irons in the fire. The political will of the West to indict Milosevic is still lacking, since they continue to negotiate with him. But they no longer have any objection to putting together a case against the Yugoslav president.

On October 15, 1998, Nicolo Figa-Talamanca's team is in Skopje, the capital of Macedonia, then drives on to Belgrade and Kosovo. Equipped with a vehicle, computers, and coding materials, supported by an exterior logistician, and acting under the cover of a humanitarian organization with a transparent name, "No Peace without Justice," the former lawyers of the ICTY worry about becoming victims of an attack faked as a roadside accident. They are looking for "sensitive" information. "Our objective was to reconstruct the order of battle, the chains of command, to see how the different units of the MUP [special police forces of the Yugoslav government] and the VJ [Yugoslav army] interacted and how the paramilitaries were themselves implicated in the ethnic cleansing in Kosovo," Nicolo Figa-Talamanca says. "In determining who did what, it was possible to determine at what echelons the events were decided," he adds.[13] The team of pseudo-humanitarians returns to Kosovo in December to complete their research. Some of their interlocutors think that they are a secret official team of the tribunal. The report is finished in February, just before the Rambouillet Conference. It is quickly transmitted to Denis Milner, head of the Kosovo team at the tribunal. The authors are convinced that the information contained in the report is sufficient to indict Milosevic.

Meanwhile, in early October, Louise Arbour meets Aryeh Neier of Human Rights Watch. The discussion revolves around the strategy of indicting Slobodan Milosevic. Neier pleads for a rapid indictment of Milosevic for crimes against humanity. The evidence, he says in substance, is already available or relatively easy to obtain. "The forced displacement of the Albanian population of Kosovo already in itself constitutes a crime against humanity," he says. "It is easy to document. One sees the Serb forces operating with the same model of behavior, which implies a concerted strategy, decided at the top: the troops surround the villages, they let the population flee, then the pillage and destruction of surviving houses occurs."[14] It is this information that is being documented by Nicolo Figa-Talamanca and his team.

But Louise Arbour opts for a radically different strategy. She determines that the indictment against the Yugoslav president must be made on the most serious grounds. "She wanted to concentrate on the massacres, but I doubted the soundness of her approach, because it was much more difficult to prove that the local commanders had acted on orders from their superior officers all the way up to Milosevic," Neier says.[15] No doubt Louise Arbour wants an exemplary indictment against Milosevic, in the name of the inevitable precedent that it would constitute. And what is more exemplary than a head of state prosecuted for perpetual massacres, a serial killer with an army at his disposal? But in raising the bar, by wanting to accuse the Yugoslav president of the absolute worst crimes, Louise Arbour delays an immediate indictment: "I did not want a minimal charge aimed at the 'head.' I wanted Milosevic personally to be accused and not simply by virtue of the criminal responsibility of his subordinates," she explains.[16]

Is she responding implicitly to the fact that the West does not want to indict Milosevic? Or is she acting as a conscientious lawyer, determining that she does not have what she needs to indict the Yugoslav president? On several occasions, she will later reiterate her anxiety at being the first prosecutor in history to indict a sitting head of state—without sufficient proof. One thing is sure: Her prudent strategy suits the politicians, who all of a sudden have changed their line. The West, with the Americans in the lead, now wants to reach an accord with Milosevic. They threaten him with the tribunal, like a handy scarecrow, but avoid turning decisive intelligence over to the ICTY. "We had one foot on the accelerator and the other on the brake," confides a diplomat.[17]

On October 13, Slobodan Milosevic and Richard Holbrooke sign a new accord, which very temporarily reestablishes a cease-fire in Kosovo. According to the *Times* of London, the American negotiator has even exchanged a stronger international presence in Kosovo for the promise of judicial immunity for Slobodan Milosevic. A re-play of Dayton? The truth? Misinformation? No one knows. An immunity accorded by Richard Holbrooke would, in any case, have no legal value. But Louise Arbour fears that the Americans, as at Dayton, will let the tribunal down. In the end, the accord remains mute on Yugoslavia's obligations with regard to the tribunal, a prodigious annoyance for the tribunal president, the American Gabrielle Kirk McDonald, and Louise Arbour, who once more sees *raison d'état* taking precedence over justice. McDonald reacts with a public statement that the tribunal's jurisdiction is not subject to negotiation.[18] To drive the point home, on October 15 Louise Arbour writes to the Yugoslav president, hardly forty-eight hours after the "deal" is signed with Holbrooke, and makes the letter public. She informs Milosevic that she herself will lead the next mission of investigation in Kosovo and will visit the sites where crimes under the tribunal's jurisdiction have been committed. She urges him to furnish visas to her, her second-in-command, and to eight tribunal investigators, which Milosevic refuses in early November.[19] With extraordinary aplomb, Milosevic's minister of justice, Zoran Knezevic, explains that the ICTY has nothing to do with Kosovo, since nothing was provided for it in the Milosevic-Holbrooke accord.[20]

For years, Yugoslavia has violated the resolutions of the Security Council. The members of the tribunal have the obligation, imparted to them by the United Nations (Resolutions 1160 and 1203), to investigate in Kosovo. For the umpteenth time, Louise Arbour and Gabrielle McDonald write to the Security Council to denounce Belgrade's systematic policy of obstruction.[21] Ordered to act by the prosecutor and the president of the ICTY, the Security Council remains deaf. The Western diplomats, in particular the Americans, do not want to endanger the accord reached with Milosevic. For them, the international court is not an end in itself but only a means, an instrument, without realizing that their myopic approach only prolongs the problem. For years, they have believed that, each time they signed an accord with Karadzic or Milosevic, they are making real political advances. Each time, they have been wrong. The series of crises and crimes in the former Yugoslavia has not stopped demonstrating this lack of progress. Perhaps if they had really applied the tribunal's decisions, the crisis and the crimes in Kosovo would never have taken place. On October 13, 1998, the Western states once more accept that Milosevic may play pyromaniac/fireman with impunity. And he does not wait long to strike a new match.

Racak: Justice in Real Time

"A village burned every day; but no more, so as not to upset NATO." It is in these terms that NATO secretary general Javier Solana will later define Milosevic's tactics in the autumn of 1998, when, reassured by the accord of October 13, the Serb president continues to pursue his policy. On January 15, 1999, a new level in the escalation of tension is breached, set off by the massacre at Racak. For many days, pressure has been rising dangerously. For the first time, the international court is called to act on the spot in a context of extreme crisis, which at any moment could degenerate into a major confrontation. The sole fact that the prosecutor of the ICTY is in the Balkans, has opened an inquiry, and is visiting the massacre sites changes an equation that, up to now, has been purely political. Louise Arbour's inquisitory role contributes to this new balance of power. Rule 61 has been left far behind. Now, at the very moment that crimes are being committed, a prosecutor is at the sites of the killing. This confrontation between Belgrade and the West becomes a powerful symbol. The prosecutor, once an impotent "truth-teller," can now force the entire international community to bear witness while indicting high criminals of the state. In the same way that the mortar attack on the Sarajevo market in August, 1995, was the catalyst for air strikes in Bosnia and that the massacre at the end of September, 1998, in Gornje Obrinje, Kosovo, was the opening of a new phase in the conflict with the deployment of Organization for Security and Cooperation in Europe (OSCE) verifiers, the massacre at Racak will change the fundamental parameters of the conflict. Racak, the top news story for the world's media, has strategic importance. For its barbarity, for the collective emotion it revives, for the political imperative to act that it imposes, the massacre creates a new dynamic. Racak becomes one of those events capable of reversing the course of things. It obligates politicians to take sides. It modifies the relationship of military and political forces, whether by air strike or by negotiation. The ICTY has never carried such weight in a crisis. Certainly, everyone is attempting to use the tribunal or to orient its conclusions in one direction or another, but even this manipulation is recognition of its effective existence. The ICTY is no longer an alibi. It has itself become a stake in the game.

To understand the unfolding chain of events, a chronology is necessary. On the dawn of the killing, January 14, 1999, President Clinton and his aides devote a meeting at the White House to Kosovo. Entangled in the Lewinsky affair and threatened with impeachment, the American president does not participate. American intelligence reports that Milosevic is preparing to execute a vast plan of ethnic cleansing. Madeleine Albright pleads for a threat of force against Belgrade in order to secure real negotiations on the status of wide autonomy for Kosovo. But she does not get satisfaction. The American secretary of state leaves the meeting, furious. "We're like gerbils running on a wheel," she exclaims. The goal of the White House is still to keep the lid on the Kosovo cauldron, not to intervene.[22]

On January 15, Slobodan Milosevic's vice prime minister, Nikola Sainovic, orders Serb forces to strike hard at the village of Racak as a reprisal against a UÇK attack on Serb police officers. At seven o'clock in the morning, Serb forces attack the village located near the city of Stimje, about forty kilometers from Pristina. The village is taken and some local combatants of the UÇK are killed as well as about forty civilian victims, among them a twelve-year-old child, one or two women, and a few elderly residents. According to author Jean-Arnault Dérens, it appears that a sizable UÇK force stationed not far from the village makes no attempt to intervene, leaving Racak defenseless against the Serb offensive, "which would help explain the UÇK's confusion about the exact unfolding of the massacre."[23]

On Saturday, the day after the massacre, former American general William Walker, head of the OSCE observer mission, visits Racak. Emotions there, as well as in the outside world, are unrestrained. At the entrance to the village, across from the mosque, is the house of Azeme Banos, sixty-two years old. General Walker goes into the inner courtyard. Blue socks and brown pants and what remains of Azeme Banos lie in front of his door. His fifty-five-year-old brother, Bedri, searches for Azeme's head. The villagers will find it later. In the village is another body of a man, clearly mutilated. A thirteen-year-old boy finds the bodies of his three murdered brothers. Some survivors then show

General Walker around the village. The slope is steep. Suddenly, the first bodies appear. Most of them have one clean little hole in the skull. Then, in the ravine, are the bodies of twenty or so men, all entwined, "many shot at extremely close range, most shot in the front, back and top of the head," General Walker confirms. Some women discover the bodies of their neighbors. One of them cries to the men of the OSCE, "You are here today, but it was yesterday that we needed you. While the Serbs were killing us." A kneeling woman prays. Another intones, "What a horrible life," over and over again. The cell phones of the men of the OSCE and the journalists keep ringing. Shuki Buja, a local commander of the UÇK, declares, "I am waiting for orders, but I will propose that we no longer respect the cease-fire." "It is about as horrendous an event as I have seen, and I have been in some nasty situations," General Walker declares.[24]

Emine Bekiri recounts the deaths of her twelve-year-old son, Halim, and her husband. "Careful, Mama, they are going to kill you," her son had said. Those words were his last. "A bullet struck him in the neck," Bekiri says. "He had blood on his mouth. I was only two meters away. The Serbs were shooting everywhere. I could not approach him while he was dying. They also shot my husband. He was standing beside my son, so close to me."[25] Through eyewitness accounts, the chronicle of the massacre becomes more precise: At the bottom of the village, the Serb policemen, their faces masked, entered into the houses and separated the men from the women and children. Hanemsha, an eighteen-year-old girl, tried to save her brother and was killed. The men were divided into many groups. Twenty of them were brought outside the village. "They said that we were going to the police post. But shooting was everywhere," explains Rame, a forty-year-old man.[26] A bullet grazed his forehead, but he managed to escape. The rest of the group was brought into a ravine where Serb police were waiting to slaughter them, methodically. It is the bodies of these twenty men that General Walker saw, all entwined, their deaths precise, abrupt, planned, and coldly executed. Other bodies are scattered about. The indictment of Slobodan Milosevic issued by the ICTY describes what happened, specifically: "After shelling by VJ units, the Serb police entered the village later in the morning and began conducting house-to-house searches. Villagers, who attempted to flee from the Serb police, were shot throughout the village. A group of approximately 25 men attempted to hide in a building, but were discovered by Serb police. They were beaten and then were removed to a nearby hill, where the policemen shot and killed them. Altogether, the forces of the FRY [Federal Republic of Yugoslavia] and Serbia killed approximately 45 Kosovo Albanians in and around Racak."[27]

At the summit of the village, the Bekiri family tries to flee. "I woke the children. We were in our pajamas," explains Halim's mother. "We took some

WILLIAM WALKER—The former U.S. general (at left with NATO chief Javier Solana) reported the massacre at Racak, sparking the crisis over Kosovo. Finally mustering the will to intervene decisively in the Balkans, NATO found the tribunal to be a convenient political hammer for striking at the Yugoslav leadership. (NATO)

clothes to dress ourselves while we fled. The Serbs were waiting for us up the road. They were less than 150 meters, maybe 100 meters, from us." A neighbor adds, "They were masked. We were sure that they were going to kill us." [28] The shooting continues without interruption from 7:00 in the morning until 3:00 P.M. The survivors of the Bekiri family stay hidden. At 5:00 P.M., the Serb forces withdraw.

The massacre at Racak occurs just in time to open that night's television news. The martyred village has become a strategic stake. At six o'clock on Saturday evening, on the return to Pristina, a visibly defeated William Walker improvises a press conference. "I accuse the police forces and military forces of the [Serb] government of responsibility for this massacre," he states. "A few days ago, the Kosovo Liberation Army had freed eight Serb soldiers. We wait for a measure of reciprocity on the part of Belgrade. And what do we have? The murder of some forty innocent civilians. Is this, thus, the response of the government?" He adds, "I want to know who gave the orders and who executed them. Justice must be done. . . . I am not a lawyer, but, to my sense, a crime against humanity has been committed. I ask the International Tribunal for the

Former Yugoslavia to send their experts in the next twenty-four hours, with or without a visa, and I advise the Serb government to let them enter Yugoslav territory." [29] It is the first time that the ICTY has been officially called to intervene on the spot, at the site of a mass murder—to transform itself, in effect, into a district attorney. The head of the Kosovo Verification Mission then reads a paragraph from the OSCE report describing the crimes committed at Racak: "Arbitrary detention, extra-judicial killings and the mutilation of unarmed civilians by the security forces of the FRY." [30]

The political, military, diplomatic, and legal events are telescoped under the eye of the media. Slobodan Milosevic finds himself indirectly accused of responsibility for a crime against humanity and, thus, answerable to the ICTY. But the international presence in Kosovo is in danger. Milosevic orders General William Walker, labeled "a liar" by Serb television, to leave the territory within forty-eight hours. The entire OSCE mission will be compromised if its leader is chased out by the host government. The American secretary of defense, William Cohen, affirms that the United States is ready to launch air strikes against the Serb forces, if the members of NATO so decide.

On the ground, however, the fighting quickly resumes. The new Serb offensive now has only one objective: to seize the bodies stored at the mosque in Racak in order to block the international court from mounting its inquest. Like an assassin who seeks to repossess his victim's corpse in order to erase the evidence, the morbid battle speaks volumes about the febrile nature of the Belgrade regime. Milosevic, evidently, understands the ICTY's newly acquired importance. Kosovo, decidedly, is not Bosnia; impunity is coming to an end. And the Yugoslav president realizes that one indictment by the ICTY will make him a leper, a pariah among heads of state.

On Sunday, January 17, at 8:45 A.M., the assault is prepared. In the locality of Stimje, close to Racak, an old woman is crying. A police officer of the special Serb forces taunts her: "Cry, cry, you haven't seen anything yet." Nine o'clock in the morning at Racak: The orange vehicles of the OSCE are in the village. The international verifiers have slept there to keep the Serb forces from committing new atrocities. The dissuasive capacity of the OSCE does not last long. The forty-five bodies of the victims are still in the mosque. Their families are gathering. The survivors of the Bekiri family are in their house, at the top of the steep village. The children are in a state of shock; the women are crying. Emine, the mother of Halim, mourns her dead son. Suddenly, a man cries out, "The Serbs are coming back!" A teenager begins to shake all over. [31]

Eleven o'clock in the morning: Gunfire snaps. The verifiers get into their vehicles and leave at top speed. The shots of automatic weapons grow closer. Noon: In the tarred road, at Stimje, two kilometers from Racak, a verifier admits, "I obeyed my orders, but I feel bad about leaving behind the villagers of Racak."[32] Some hundreds of meters farther away, one sees the vehicles of the special Serb police forces. Some dozens of men are marching on foot toward Racak. One hears the noise of automatic weapons. Inmates at the local psychiatric hospital stroll in the garden behind the high gates as if all this commotion does not concern them; they are waving or calling to those who are close by. This island of so-called "insanity" has become the only place where Serbs, Albanians, and Roma still live together. On Monday, supported by antiaircraft cannon and T-55 tanks, Serb soldiers manage to seize the bodies in order to store them at the morgue in Pristina under their control. They forbid access by the OSCE observers but permit the entry of Belarusian doctors, who conclude that Serb forces are not responsible for the massacre. According to the thesis of the Serb authorities, these victims are, in fact, terrorists of the Kosovo Liberation Army, whose uniforms have been replaced by civilian clothing to fake Serb culpability. A Finnish team of lawyers arrives in Belgrade as advisers, but on some obscure bureaucratic pretext the Yugoslav authorities delay their departure to Pristina. It is only on Thursday that the Finnish team arrives. Helena Ranta, head of the Finnish team, has in vain asked that the Serb and Belarusian doctors stop their autopsies. On the contrary, they have accelerated their pace, clearing four bodies on Tuesday and seven on Wednesday.

Meanwhile, back at The Hague, the spokesman for the tribunal, Christian Chartier, exclaims on Sunday night that Arbour was demanding "immediate and unimpeded access" to Racak. The prosecutor's efforts to lead a team to investigate earlier charges of atrocities in Kosovo have been rebuffed by Serbian authorities, who do not recognize the jurisdiction of the tribunal and refused to issue visas. "For this we don't care," said Chartier, adding, "We are no longer prepared to discuss jurisdiction."[33]

It must prove that it is not only a tribunal for history but also that it can weigh directly on present events. On Monday, January 18, Louise Arbour, accompanied by six members of her office staff and four investigators, arrives in Skopje, Macedonia, the first stage before returning to the massacre site. She recalls,

> I had a 5 to 10 percent hope of returning to Yugoslavia. I spent all of Sunday on the telephone, calling all the NATO ambassadors, asking them to make a public declaration saying that if I presented myself at the Yugoslav frontier, they would help me enter. They said that they had only the force of extraction in Macedonia, and, as I wanted, on the contrary, to enter Kosovo, they were not prepared for this kind of operation. In fact, they did not want to encroach

upon the national sovereignty of a state. I knew that, but I wanted to put pressure on them so that they would put it on Belgrade.[34]

The Western governments do not back up the prosecutor. The ICTY is only one variable of a larger equation that they are trying to master.

Installed in her room at the Alexandra Palace hotel in Skopje, Louise Arbour tries again to persuade Belgrade to authorize her to enter Yugoslav territory: "I then spent two hours on the telephone with Zoran Knezevic, the Serb minister of justice. I and my legal counselor were sitting on the bed in my room, with an interpreter at each end. Zoran Knezevic rambled for ten minutes without interruption, then, he suddenly said: 'Are you still there?' It was an interminable sermon." She tries to persuade her interlocutor of the necessity to let her enter Yugoslavia. She supports her argument with some articles published in France on the hypothesis that the macabre massacre has been perpetrated by the UÇK to provoke an international incident:

> I had seen that only articles in the French press doubted what had happened in Racak. I was not naïve; it signified something about the attitude of the French government. But I told myself: I could use it on the Yugoslavs. So I said to Zoran Knezevic: "Look, the French press expresses doubts about the responsibility of the massacre. I have no *a priori* knowledge about what happened at Racak. Let me go there and send my experts and they will determine the truth." I told him that, if he refused, it would signify, in the eyes of the world, the responsibility of the Serb forces in the massacre. But he didn't want to hear it. I proposed that he let me enter, but I accepted as a compromise that I would say that Yugoslavia did not recognize the jurisdiction of the ICTY so that Belgrade would not lose face. I even proposed this through a Russian intermediary to show that I was serious. But nothing doing. He proposed one or two ideas, but they were laughable: that I go to investigate in Racak alone or that he, Knezevic, would accompany me. He was mocking me! What would I do down there all alone without my experts, squatting in the grass taking samples? It was very demoralizing. I thought for a moment that I would get there. Then I saw evidence of the failure. I was at the point of sending my letter of resignation to the Security Council.[35]

However, she plays her cards until the end, even if she feels that the West has abandoned her. She wants to make Milosevic pay as much as possible for his victory. For a very long time, Belgrade has mocked the ICTY. But, being a good strategist, Milosevic knows that the tribunal could become a dangerous weapon against him. He understands that all the media interest is concentrating on the presence of Louise Arbour in Skopje, so he decides to create a diversion to shift the media's attention. How? By giving a twenty-four-hour reprieve on the expulsion of General Walker from Kosovo. Louise Arbour understands that Milosevic is seeking to marginalize her in focusing the confrontation around the presence of Walker in Kosovo. The prosecutor warns the American diplomats, "I told the Americans, do not play Milosevic's game. His goal is to diffuse the tension around Racak. He wants to shift to a less difficult political conflict for himself. When Walker leaves, his successor will pursue his mission in exactly the same manner. We are interchangeable, but the mission remains."[36]

Diversion or not, the United States does not want to submit to the demands of Belgrade. The American secretary of state, Madeleine Albright, warns that the international observers will leave the Serb province if the order is maintained. She emphasizes that the international community must show itself to be "persuasive" vis-à-vis the Yugoslav president: "We will maintain the credible threat of force, which has proven again and again to be the only language President Milosevic understands."[37] "It was an escalation," Arbour says later. "It was a pissing match. It was a show that, at bottom, Milosevic had won: Walker remained in Kosovo, and I stayed in Skopje. It was exactly what the Yugoslav president was looking for. But the Americans wanted Walker to remain, and so they let me fall."[38]

On Tuesday, Louise Arbour returns to the border accompanied by a squad of journalists. It is, literally, a photo opportunity whose audience is international public opinion and the Western governments. Arbour presents her passport to the border guard and, as expected, is refused authorization to enter Yugoslav territory. Her failure is anticipated; Louise Arbour expects no about-face by the Yugoslav authorities. She knows full well that they will not authorize her to put one foot on their territory. But she wants to demonstrate in front of the world Belgrade's policy of obstruction. In this game of power, the domination of the media is an important element, because it shapes the perception of reality. For years, the ICTY has uselessly denounced to the Security Council the obstacles that Belgrade has put up against the international court. But suddenly, under the glare of cameras, this obstruction gains an unexpected tangibility. At the same time, it revives the image of a tribunal no longer disconnected from the reality that it has pretended to judge, year after year, in the comfort and boredom of a peaceful, middle-class suburb of The Hague. "What is crazy," Arbour notes, "is that this failure has become one of the great successes of the tribunal, but I did not understand that until much later. It showed the world the difficulty the tribunal experienced in doing its work."[39]

After being waylaid in Kosovo, Louise Arbour moves quickly when she finds herself solicited by the OSCE. She has become the "district attorney" that, a few months earlier, she had refused to be. The political interests of the West and those of the tribunal have momentarily converged until the NATO countries glimpse, once more, a negotiated solution in the discussions to be held at Rambouillet.

The War and New Pressures on the ICTY

At the end of January, 1999, eleven huge boxes arrive at the tribunal offices. Each is covered with a poster of Slobodan Milosevic and a caption proclaiming, "We must arrest this man." They contain more than 100,000 signatures of Nobel Prize winners and ordinary citizens from around the world supporting the indictment of the Yugoslav president. From then on—and this is new—in the spirit of public opinion, the tribunal is about to become a true actor, one that can apply itself directly.

In the Balkans, the escalation of violence continues. A bloody chain of events is under way, warns CIA director George Tenet, testifying before the U.S. Senate on February 2: "We assess that if the fighting escalates in the spring as we expect, it will be bloodier than last year's. Belgrade will seek to crush the KLA once and for all, while the insurgents will have the capability to inflict heavier casualties on Serb forces. Both sides will likely step up attacks on civilians. . . . Heavier fighting will also result in another humanitarian crisis, possibly greater in scale than last year's." [40]

On February 6, the Rambouillet negotiations open. *Raison d'état* again triumphs over the international court, according to the well-worn playbook. On February 15, Gabrielle McDonald writes to the French and British foreign ministers, Hubert Védrine and Robin Cook, respectively, warning them against "sacrificing the principles on which the Tribunal is founded for short-term political interest. . . . In recent days I have received worrying reports . . . that the text currently under consideration by the parties does not contain provisions that would require them to recognize the competence of the International Tribunal or to take specific measures to co-operate with the Tribunal. . . . It is axiomatic that there can be no peace without justice." [41] It is then Louise Arbour's turn to warn Védrine and Cook that "to compromise on those fundamental principles would not only be damaging to the ICTY in the short term, but would also erode the long term prospects of international peace and justice." [42] Nevertheless, the negotiations are at a standstill. The delegation of Kosovo Albanians balks at accepting the accord and finally does so only under Western pressure. The Serb president refuses any substantial autonomy for Kosovo and opposes NATO's proposal to deploy an international force of thirty thousand men to guarantee autonomy for the province. The Western demands are unacceptable for Milosevic, but he again underestimates the determination of the Americans to act. The West has reached the point of no return. On March 13, Christopher Hill, the American ambassador to Macedonia, interrupts a meeting at the White House devoted to the crisis to announce that in his opinion Milosevic will not back down, even at the very last moment. The chances that Milosevic will accept the accord, he says, are "zero point zero percent!"[43] Facing a failure of diplomacy, the Americans manage to convince their allies to proceed with air strikes.

On March 24, sirens ring out in Belgrade. Operation "Allied Force" has begun. The secretary-general of NATO, Javier Solana, has just ordered strikes against Yugoslavia. The NATO bombing campaign is, no doubt, illegal, because the U.N. Charter forbids recourse to armed force against a sovereign state in the absence of a Security Council resolution. But as the Swiss jurist Nicolas Levrat puts it, "[T]he regime in Belgrade has rendered itself beforehand capable of 'deliberate behavior, substantially and massively illegal,' in violating the Convention against Genocide, as well as the international pact relating to civil and political rights and the prohibition against the recourse to armed force in the U.N. Charter, that being against Bosnia-Herzegovina, Croatia and Slovenia."[44] That issue is up to the International Court of Justice, rather than the tribunal, to decide on this point because the tribunal passes judgment only on violations of the Geneva Conventions, war crimes, crimes against humanity, and genocide.

The regime in Belgrade declares a state of war and on March 25 breaks off diplomatic relations with Washington, London, Bonn, and Paris. Ignoring the destruction of his country, the Yugoslav president empties Kosovo of its ethnic Albanian population. On March 28, the exodus of Kosovars crests. Hundreds of thousands of Albanians flee in terror or are deported on trains or on foot to the Macedonian and Albanian frontiers. Murders, massacres, and rapes become daily events of this war.

Tribunal investigators only later reconstruct the chronology of these crimes. The likely scenario is as follows: On March 29, 1999, Serb forces attack the village of Bela Crkva in the municipality of Orahovac. A large number of inhabitants flee and find refuge under a railroad bridge. A patrol of Serb police opens fire and kills a dozen people, including ten women and children. The police separate the men from the women and young children. The police order the men to undress and then strip them of all objects of value. The women and the children are ordered to leave. The village doctor tries to negotiate with the chief of police, but he is shot, as are his nephew and other men. About sixty-five Kosovar Albanians are killed this way.

The next day, Serb police spot villagers in the forest near the villages of Velika Krusa and Mala Krusa. The police order the women and children to leave for Albania. Then they search for the men and boys, confiscate their identity papers, assemble them inside a house, and shoot them all. After several minutes of firing, the police pile hay on top of the bodies and set it on fire in order to burn the bodies. Some 105 Albanian men and boys die in this attack.[45] The same methods are used across the province.

In Pristina, on April 1, 1999, Serb police give the Kosovar Albanian residents only a few minutes to leave. Several people are killed during these forced expulsions. A great number of those who have been constrained to leave go to the train station while others find refuge in neighboring quarters. Hundreds of Albanians, guided at each crossroads by Serb police, board trains or packed buses, after waiting for a long time without food or water.

Serb police order the Kosovar Albanians leaving the trains to walk the length of the rails until they reach Macedonia, because the land around the tracks is mined. Simultaneously, FRY and Serb forces invade the villages in the municipality of Pristina, where they shoot and kill a large number of Kosovar Albanians, steal their money, pillage their goods, and burn their homes.

On April 3, the first NATO bombings on the center of Belgrade begin, striking the Serb and Yugoslav ministries of the interior. On April 6, NATO accidentally bombs a residential area in Aleksinac, about two hundred kilometers south of Belgrade. Such "mistakes," resulting in the deaths of dozens of civilians, multiply, provoking a spike in negative public opinion—indeed, more and more cutting criticism—in the West about NATO's strategy, based on the doctrine of zero casualties for bomber pilots. On April 12, a NATO airplane fires on a bridge near Grdelica, south of Belgrade, striking a passenger train. On April 23, allied aircraft mistakenly strike a convoy of civilian vehicles in the Djakovica region in southwestern Kosovo. On April 21, NATO bombs the headquarters of the Serb Socialist Party of President Milosevic, then his residence. Two days later, the studio of Serb RTS television and radio is bombed. The next day, the allies use graphite bombs to neutralize Yugoslav electrical installations. The Chinese embassy is bombed in Belgrade, killing three people. President Bill Clinton apologizes to Beijing for this "mistake." In the icy jargon of the military, the civilian victims are "collateral damage."

A battle over the public perception of these events is added to the real war between NATO and Yugoslavia. In this propaganda war, demonizing the adversary becomes indispensable, so the tribunal's role as the voice of the "truth" becomes central. The Western governments, which have never really wanted to indict Milosevic, change their minds again. On the contrary, after having signed so many accords with Milosevic, accords that he simply violated one after another, it has now become imperative for them to criminalize the strong man of Belgrade.

On the other side, the regime in Belgrade seeks condemnation of the "criminal policy" of NATO's bombing campaign. Belgrade and many international organizations ask Louise Arbour to open charges against "Clinton and Associates" for "genocide, crimes against humanity, grave violations of the Geneva Conventions," and for "their illegal and criminal aggression" against Yugoslavia.[46]

In this game where each belligerent seeks to use the tribunal, Louise Arbour exploits the opportunities presented to her, without being duped by the parties' individual rationales. She knows that from now on she has a green light from the Western governments to indict Milosevic. But their unprecedented enthusiasm to collaborate with the tribunal only feeds her suspicions. Is she being manipulated? Is she the legal arm of the Atlantic alliance? As the Canadian daily *Globe and Mail* editorializes, "Is war crimes prosecutor Louise Arbour becoming a pawn of NATO?"[47] Arbour energetically refutes these accusations. "There are circumstances in which justice and political interests coincide," she says.[48] From her mouth, it is an implicit criticism of the West, which demonstrated no such devotion to the tribunal when Bosnia was burning and bloody. One judge finds an appropriate formula to describe the limits of the tribunal's autonomy: "The ICTY has escaped its creator, but not its environment. I am convinced of the independence of the judges with regard to the Security Council. The more complex question remains on the relationship between the prosecutor and the states. The governments want to measure out the oxygen that they feed to the tribunal, to tell it when to speed up and slow down, even if it is not simply a marionette in their hands."[49] It is a more matter-of-fact way of saying what Louise Arbour already said in April, 1999. "The question is not whether we are free to [indict Milosevic], but whether we will now be better equipped by those who may hold relevant information to move forward with this investigation," she had said. "The Tribunal's investigators are now assembling a body of direct witness testimonies. Refugee accounts are critical, but they are not enough on their own. The victims didn't see the command structures or the people giving the orders at the highest level. We therefore need the sophisticated kind of assistance that only states can provide."[50] The tribunal's dependence on the most technologically advanced countries is a serious limit to its autonomy. The most "political" indictments depend, in part, on the goodwill of certain states and their cooperation with the tribunal.

The tribunal cannot refuse such precious help, nor can it be the servile agent of those who decide, according to their own schedule, when to pass on crucial information. "We have neither satellites, nor spy planes, nor means of electronic interception," Graham Blewitt once admitted. "We are dependent on the states to obtain this information."[51] It is in this fluid space, pulled between two contradictory imperatives, that the tribunal finds its margin of maneuver. But very quickly, it will be put to a difficult test.

Up to now, no government with sophisticated listening technology—that is, the United States, Great Britain, France, or Germany—has judged it useful to give the tribunal evidence that could incriminate Milosevic. In the eyes of the West, the Yugoslav president has remained a man with whom it is imperative to do business. But after the fruitless conference in Rambouillet, Milosevic is no longer the solution. According to State Department press secretary James Rubin, "He is not simply part of the problem; Milosevic is the problem."[52] From then on, the Western governments even push the tribunal to indict Milosevic as quickly as possible. "Criminalizing" the Milosevic regime, they think, will permit them to calm a public that is increasingly questioning the wisdom of NATO's bombing campaign. Louise Arbour begins to be strongly pressured to act without delay.

On April 7, Arbour goes to NATO headquarters in Brussels to declare that she sees a possibility of indicting Milosevic. Speaking to journalists, she explains that the Western governments will have to bring "the best possible access to information that is usable in court." After her discussions with NATO leaders, she expresses satisfaction: "We have had a very useful dialogue with a lot of our information providers, so that there is a much better understanding of our needs." Two days later, on Friday, April 9, the prosecutor meets the American undersecretary of state, Harold Koh, who visits the tribunal to "discuss ways to improve the timely delivery of information about events in Kosovo to the Office of the Prosecutor." "The American government supports this unprecedented collaboration to document these cases to help ensure that all potential sources of information will be tapped and that those who commit these crimes will be held responsible," Koh says.[53] The same day, the British name a coordinator charged with delivering information to the tribunal. "The converging interests" are such that they carry "unprecedented levels of cooperation," Graham Blewitt exults.[54] On April 19, the German defense minister transmits to The Hague some aerial photography documenting the destruction of villages in Kosovo. The next day, Foreign Minister Robin Cook of Great Britain declares that an immense file containing information on more than fifty incidents during the previous month in Kosovo will be furnished to the tribunal: "We have authorized the handover of British intelligence material to the War Crimes Tribunal. . . . [It is] one of the largest releases of intelligence material ever authorized by the British." The French government also promises its complete cooperation.[55]

In early May, Louise Arbour makes the rounds in Washington, London, and Paris. The Americans are preparing to transmit thousands of pages of documents to the tribunal. Robin Cook insists on making a grand show of publicly handing over the files to the prosecutor, who is obliged to accept the condition. "Myself, I wanted to make a discreet trip," Arbour says. "But it couldn't be helped. It was the price to pay for their cooperation. They told me, 'It is important to demonstrate that we are working together.'"[56] During her visit to Paris, Arbour receives documents that the tribunal can use on the condition that it does not reveal the technology used to collect them. Often, in fact, the governments remit information that has already been on the Internet or CNN for three days. For practical reasons, cooperation between the intelligence services and the tribunal is difficult. "For a minister, what is important is the information: which country is in the process of preparing what or who does what. For a prosecutor, what is important is the source, to which politicians are indifferent," Arbour explains. "The military said, 'We already gave you an enormous amount of material. Don't ask for any more.' They never gave us a human source. On our side, we need to know who ordered the troops that committed these atrocities. The army? The ministry of the interior? Was it a combined operation? Who was responsible? Who was on the periphery of the action? Who gave the orders? And at what level?"[57]

The Tribunal Addresses the NATO Bombing

The Western governments have confidence in the work of the tribunal. They feel that an indictment is approaching, but they are stunned to hear the second half of Arbour's message. Although she knows that she is playing the West's political game by indicting Milosevic thanks to their sudden cooperation, she does not intend to become NATO's puppet. She warns that she holds them responsible for potential crimes committed by the countries of the Atlantic Alliance. "They were staggered. I reminded them that I had jurisdiction over them," she says.

> I told them, "Ask your legal counselors." They did not believe me. I had warned them, "Pay attention to your targeting objectives. For if you violate the Geneva Convention, then you will be prosecutable before the Tribunal." They did not like that at all, but it was the truth. They said to me, "Whaaat?" I told them, "Did you sign the Geneva Conventions?" They said, "Yes, and we apply

them." So I added, "Very good, so everything is clear." They told me, "How dare you put on the same footing a just war and a war of repression?" I replied that I was speaking to them about the universality of the rule of law.[58]

Invited to a forum on the creation of an international criminal court, Louise Arbour makes public her position. "On 24 March 1999, 19 European and North American countries have said with their deeds what some of them were reluctant to say with words. They have voluntarily submitted themselves to the jurisdiction of a pre-existing International Tribunal, whose mandate applies to the theatre of their chosen military operations, whose reach is unqualified by nationality, whose investigations are triggered at the sole discretion of the Prosecutor and who has primacy over national courts," she tells the forum.[59] In deciding that she would not hesitate to open an inquiry into the NATO bombing, Louise Arbour wants to liberate herself from the American protection that has been so necessary to her.

It is one of the first signs of the tribunal's will toward emancipation. NATO does not at all appreciate her declaration. NATO spokesman Jamie Shea reprimands the prosecutor by recalling the old saying, "Don't bite the hand that feeds you." Reminding the tribunal that it is a tributary of political, financial, and military support of the West, he notes, "The people of NATO are the ones who apprehend the war criminals indicted by the Tribunal." He hammers the point home, saying, "We all want to see war criminals judged and I am certain that, when Prosecutor Arbour returns to Kosovo and sees the facts, she will indict the Yugoslav nationals, and no other nationality." He follows with a reminder to Louise Arbour that she can return to Kosovo only under the aegis of the Atlantic Alliance. "NATO is a friend of the Tribunal and will allow Prosecutor Arbour to go to Kosovo to investigate," Shea concludes.[60]

Afterward, Louise Arbour will, in fact, determine that NATO has not committed war crimes, despite the civilian victims of the bombing. She joins Human Rights Watch in judging that there has been no deliberate targeting of civilians and that the bombings were not indiscriminate, although the use of fragmentation bombing in populated areas was inappropriate. But as prosecutor, she does not dodge the question and asks her legal counselors to determine if any violations of the Geneva Conventions were made during NATO's target selection process. She will leave this highly emotional and politically charged investigation to her successor, Carla Del Ponte.

Carla Del Ponte, who becomes prosecutor on September 15, 1999, will send contradictory signals. At first, she affirms, "If I was not ready to do that [indict NATO if evidence of violations of international law is available], I would not be in the right job and I would have to resign!" and adds that this investigation "is not my priority, because I have investigations concerning the crimes of genocide and crimes against humanity." Then, faced with the general outcry in the Western capitals over her remark, she will say flatly, "No investigation of the Tribunal is open against NATO."[61]

Carla Del Ponte's mixed message is explained in part by the fact that the new prosecutor has neither the disposition, nor probably the taste, for multilateral diplomacy. A Swiss influenced by Germanic law, she belongs to that rare breed of judges that includes Giovanni Falcone, Baltasar Garzón, and Jean-Louis Bruguières. The anti-mafia judge Falcone is, in fact, her idol, and she had escaped an assassination attempt with him in Sicily in 1988. (Judge Falcone died in another mafia attack on May 23, 1992.) This fifty-two-year-old Swiss native of Tecino who prefers action to austere reflection about the law, attributes her nomination to the tribunal, in the fall of 1999, to her Swiss nationality. After the intervention of NATO in Kosovo, the Russians do not want a national of the Atlantic Alliance as prosecutor. Del Ponte has the support of the Americans, who are aware of her "supercop" reputation. FBI director Louis Freeh has credited her with all the progress made in Switzerland against money laundering and organized crime, calling her "my dear friend and colleague."[62]

Does this American "sponsorship" influence Del Ponte's judgment of the NATO air strikes? Speaking before the U.N. Security Council on June 2, 2000, she bluntly puts a stop to any idea of an investigation into the air campaign of the Atlantic Alliance: "I am now able to announce my conclusion, following a full consideration of my team's assessment of all complaints and allegations, that there is no basis for opening an investigation into any of those allegations or into other incidents related to the NATO bombing. Although some mistakes were made by NATO, I am very satisfied that there was no deliberate targeting of civilians or of unlawful military targets by NATO during the bombing campaign."[63] The judges have no word in the matter and even less to instruct. They have just been shunted to the sidelines. We may never know if, in their eyes, the NATO air war, or at least certain bombings during it, would have constituted war crimes or grave violations of the Geneva Conventions.

The prosecutor's refusal to investigate such an important question provokes persistent criticism, even at the heart of the tribunal. Put on the defensive and obliged to justify herself, Carla Del Ponte takes the unprecedented step in June, 2000, of making public a report of the internal commission of jurists charged with examining this issue for the Office of the Prosecutor, in order to explain how the conclusions were reached.[64]

CARLA DEL PONTE—Famous in Switzerland and Italy for her struggle against the Mafia, the Swiss prosecutor (here with NATO chief George Robertson) took over from Louise Arbour and carried her indictment of Slobodan Milosevic to trial. (NATO)

The tribunal's assessment clashes not only with that of the Yugoslav authorities and a Russian commission but also with that of Amnesty International. The lawyers of that London-based organization had determined that, in four cases at least, war crimes were committed by the Atlantic Alliance. Besides the bombing of such civilian targets as the Serb radio and television studios, NATO pilots had also violated the law of war in attacking three bridges—Grdelica on April 12, Luzane on May 1, and Vavarin on May 30—after determining that civilians were present. Other victims were killed due to insufficient precautions taken to avoid collateral damage. By requiring their pilots to fly at a high altitude beyond the range of antiaircraft artillery, NATO failed to take the precautions necessary to avoid hitting civilians by mistake. Former tribunal judge Georges Abi-Saab notes that "NATO intervention was 'to protect the Kosovar populations against Serb atrocities.' NATO should have limited itself to military objectives and avoided all indiscriminate strikes likely to hit civilians. It is, thus, not acceptable that an army, intervening without having been attacked, in the name of ensuring respect for international law, act in a manner that minimizes risks for itself while maximizing them for civilians. And that is what the American policy to avoid any casualties among NATO soldiers implies."[65]

A Prosecutor under the Influence?

The criticisms do not stop there. Another report, just thirteen pages long, confidential and for strictly internal use, is prepared by the International Committee of the Red Cross (ICRC). Its conclusions are overwhelmingly against the commission named by the tribunal prosecutor, to the point of putting into profound doubt its reliability and impartiality. The Red Cross report concludes with these words: "Neither the ICTY, nor international law in general nor international humanitarian law has come out greater from the report of the commission established by the prosecutor of the ICTY. . . . The clear partiality taken in the establishment of facts, the legal approximations and errors, render the document little credible or indefensible before a lawyer who knows international law well." Even more damning: "This document also helps one understand better the frankly negative positions of the FRY and of Russia vis-à-vis the ICTY. Such a difference in approach, depending on whether the alleged war crimes are ascribed to the FRY or to NATO, is indeed shocking."[66]

The ICRC is the guardian of the Geneva Conventions, the keystone of international humanitarian law, and has actively participated in the development of these conventions as well as their additional protocols, notably Protocol I, adopted in 1949, on the protection of civilians in times of hostility. This protocol, which has been ratified by neither France nor the United States, notably forbids attacks that cannot distinguish between military objectives and civilian persons or goods, as well as any attacks on military objectives whose impact on civilian persons or goods "would be excessive in relation to the concrete and direct military advantage anticipated," known as the Rule of Proportionality.[67] These rules require that specific precautions be taken in launching attacks, notably the requirement to verify that the target is effectively a military objective and the obligation to warn civilians if they risk being harmed. The ICRC has analyzed the work and conclusions of Carla Del Ponte's internal commission on the NATO bombings, but without ever making its assessment public.

First salvo: In a subchapter titled "A Commission and Prosecutor under the Influence?" the Red Cross jurist is astonished by the extraordinary indulgence toward NATO, so extraordinary that it puts in question the impartiality of the prosecutor's commission: "We are struck (and ill at ease) in reading the report to note to what degree the commission relies on the public declarations of NATO or of its Member countries to establish the facts that form the foundation of its analysis." In other words, the commission starts with the principle that the declarations of representatives of NATO and its member states reflect reality, without making any effort (so far as one can tell from the report, in any case) to verify these declarations by other sources or by an investigation in the field. It is all the more strange that the commission recognizes that it has received from NATO only general answers to its questions and no information on particular incidents. "We may reasonably ask the question if this *a priori* favoritism to one of the parties of the conflict is compatible with the Prosecutor's avowed impartiality."[68]

Reviewing some NATO air strikes, the Red Cross jurist again notes the partial, indeed partisan, approach of the tribunal commission regarding respect of the rule of law. Invoking the attack on the bridge near Grdelica (which caused the derailment of a passenger train), the commission admits that it "has divided views concerning the attack. . . . Despite this, the committee is in agreement that, based on the criteria for initiating an investigation . . . this incident should not be investigated."[69]

"But," notes the Red Cross report,

> the rules on the conduct of hostilities specify that an attack must be interrupted notably when it appears that one can expect that it causes incidental loss of human life among the civilian population, injuries to civilian persons, damage to property of a civilian character, or a combination of these losses and damages, that would be excessive in relation to the concrete and direct military advantage achieved. It is doubtful that this rule has been respected in this specific case, and the commission admits elsewhere having doubts on the subject. One can, in consequence, only regret that the prosecutor has refused to pursue its investigation further.[70]

So invoking the criminal responsibility of pilots and their commanders, the ICRC determines that "the least that one can say, is that the commission has not made special effort to establish the individual responsibilities of the different protagonists of the bombings." It deplores "the opinion of the commission that the crews implicated in the bombings should not be subject to any responsibility for scouring orders for an attack on the wrong target. Similarly, that it is inappropriate to try to impute criminal responsibility to responsible superiors, because they received false information coming from another organization." The commission's approach clearly flabbergasts the Red Cross, which asks why the commission has given not "a single word of explanation" for reaching such a conclusion. At the base, the Red Cross jurist criticizes the biased approach of the ICTY lawyers: "When one thinks of the meticulous work the prosecutor must have put into establishing the individual responsibility of

persons like Milosevic, Karadzic, or Mladic, one wonders about the dispro-
portion of efforts invested in the other direction." [71]

Finally, regarding NATO's attack on the studios of Radio-Television Serb
(RTS) in Belgrade, the Red Cross is merciless toward the commission's analysis. The ICRC lawyer is astonished by the superficiality and partiality of the
tribunal lawyers in not seeking to verify NATO assertions that the primary
objective of the attack on the RTS building was to destroy the Serb army's system of command and control: "The least that one can say is that, given the importance of the public controversy on this affair (without speaking of its in-
trinsic importance), a more thorough investigation to establish the facts and,
thus, the nature of the military objective or otherwise of the studios would
have been useful in order to establish whether a criminal procedure was justified." The ICRC is also amazed that the commission lawyers have not more
clearly stated that in no case may a television studio be considered a military
objective, even when it transmits propaganda: "It is profoundly regrettable
that the report was not more clear on this point." With a touch of irony, it
adds, "It is true that more clarity would, no doubt, have forced the prosecutor
to open an investigation." [72]

NATO may equally have violated another requirement of Protocol 1 of the
Geneva Conventions, that of giving "effective advance warning . . . unless circumstances do not permit" to civilians situated in proximity to a military objective taken as a target. The Red Cross jurist protests one "theory" of the
commission "which nears perversity." In the reasoning of the commission,
"Foreign media representatives were apparently forewarned of the attack. As
Western journalists were reportedly warned by their employers to stay away
from the television station before the attack, it seems that some Yugoslav officials may have expected that the building was about to be struck. . . . [That]
may . . . imply that Yugoslav authorities could be held partially responsible for
civilian casualties in the attack and that the warning given by NATO could, in
fact, have been sufficient under the circumstances." The Red Cross expert dis-
mantles this analysis: "In other words, the fact that NATO had warned foreign
journalists (but not Yugoslav ones) of the attack and that these foreign journalists were, therefore, not in the studios the night of the attack substitutes for
warning the Yugoslav authorities. As they did not react to this subtle warning
to evacuate the studios, the Yugoslav authorities are, therefore, at least partially
responsible for the fact that the attack caused civilian casualties. Nice logic!" [73]

Finally, the Red Cross lawyer finds "edifying" the conclusions of the prosecutor's internal commission absolving the Atlantic Alliance:

> NATO has admitted that mistakes did occur during the bombing campaign
> and that errors of judgment were made. The selection of certain targets may be

subject to legal debate. On the basis of our information, however, the committee is of the opinion that neither an in-depth investigation of the bombing campaign as a whole nor investigations related to specific incidents are justified. In all cases, either the law is not sufficiently clear or investigations are unlikely to result in the acquisition of sufficient evidence to substantiate charges against high-level accused or against those of lower rank accused of particularly serious offenses.[74]

The Red Cross lawyer concludes, in turn, "So, it suffices to admit certain errors, to be part of a powerful military alliance, to not answer questions posed by the Tribunal, and to manipulate the law in order to escape international justice."[75]

The rules of war can, undoubtedly, not be completely abstracted from the international balance of power. What is, in effect, the margin of independence of a tribunal carried financially, politically, and logistically by the United States and, to a lesser extent, by other Western countries, when these countries themselves become belligerents participating in the conflict?

Never had the Western powers imagined, in establishing the tribunal, that they could become parties to a conflict in the former Yugoslavia, much less that they might risk finding themselves in the dock of the accused at The Hague.

After balking for so long at actively supporting the investigative work of the ICTY, the Western powers suddenly want to make use of this formerly scorned instrument to demonize Slobodan Milosevic, by at last providing the evidence needed for his conviction. What they did not realize is that they could also end up in the dock for other reasons. Threatened, they manage to escape from the tribunal, which they had presented as the precursor to a more just international order. There is a certain hypocrisy in the Western states posing as champions of human rights, while refusing themselves to submit to rules that they recommend for other, less powerful countries. The American attitude is a clear double standard. The fierce opposition in many American circles to the idea that U.S. soldiers could one day be brought before an international tribunal triumphs, on June 14, 2000, in the American Service-Members' Protection Act of 2000. Its object is to block the transfer of any American soldier to the future International Criminal Court for trial.

The great Western states have put pressure on the Achilles heel of the tribunal: the prosecutor. Dependent on the financial means granted principally by NATO member states, dependent on intelligence from the NATO countries to build the case for indictments and to arrest suspects in Bosnia, still dependent on their political support, could the prosecutor ignore their demands? Would any other prosecutor have reacted differently from Carla Del Ponte?

How far did the pressure go? Would the great Western states have abandoned all support for the tribunal, as they had threatened under their breath for so long? Or would this threat, carried out in the open, have backfired and revealed their hypocrisy? No one knows. Western pressure on the tribunal did resurrect the old ghost of "victor's justice." Yet, in applying that pressure, NATO's leading nations gave indirect and unintentional homage to the judges' independence; it was because these Western states believed in the ICTY's impartiality that they wanted to escape its judgment.

As it is, no one can prejudge the position taken by the tribunal regarding the NATO bombing campaign. In managing to dodge any examination by the judges, however, the members of the Atlantic Alliance have given the unpleasant impression that they could escape from the scrutiny of a court that they had themselves shaped.

The Indictment of Milosevic: The West's Reversal

On May 6, 1999, the G8 countries agree on the "deployment to Kosovo of an effective international civilian and security presence" under the aegis of the United Nations.[76] For the umpteenth time, speculation and rumor grow regarding a possible "understanding" reached between the West and Milosevic, according to which he would accept the deployment of an international force in Kosovo in exchange for the abandonment of an investigation under way against him. Having pushed for a rapid indictment of Milosevic, the West is now suddenly less in a hurry. In the transparent theater of *raison d'état,* the behavior of the main players has become ritualized. This time, however, Arbour resists. Profiting from intelligence transmitted to her in recent weeks by the NATO countries, she refuses to become the politicians' instrument: "[O]ur jurisdiction covers any person of any nationality who violates the laws or customs of war [or] the Geneva Conventions or commits a crime against humanity on the territory of the former Yugoslavia. So that would include, hypothetically, the NATO leadership."[77] The Western governments have loosened the reins during the bombing campaign and can no longer check a process they themselves began. A margin of maneuver lies within this perimeter, and Louise Arbour intends to make the most of it.

In Belgrade, a foreign affairs ministry spokesman says that the G8 declaration "represents an element of the peace process and we are open to that despite some of our reservations."[78] The president of Serbia, Milan Milutinovic, confirms this position in a telephone conversation with Lamberto Dini, the Italian minister of foreign affairs.[79] On May 19, there is intense diplomatic activity across Europe to reach a negotiated solution. Back in Belgrade, Milosevic and the Kremlin's emissary, Victor Chernomyrdin, propose a resolution through the United Nations, with the participation of Belgrade, to solidify the G8 principles. They also call for a preliminary suspension of the NATO bombing campaign. On June 3, Milosevic accepts the peace plan presented by Russia and NATO. But an irreversible event occurred several days earlier: The president of Yugoslavia has been indicted by the ICTY.

By mid-May Louise Arbour and her closest advisers, bound to secrecy, know that the case for Milosevic's indictment is almost airtight. For weeks, the four or five lawyers working on the case against the Yugoslav president have been meeting with the prosecutor every morning to discuss the progress of the investigation and to lay out the flow charts to show which connections are still missing in the chains of command leading to Milosevic. From the beginning, Milosevic has taken precautions. During the war in Croatia, and later in Bosnia-Herzegovina, he hid behind the fact that he was president of Serbia, which was not officially implicated in the war. It was the federal Yugoslav army (the JNA, later the VJ) that was engaged in the fighting, not the Serb police. When the conflict begins in March, 1998, in Kosovo, Milosevic hopes once again to get by with this trick, but this time in reverse. In the meantime, he has become president of Yugoslavia, and now it is mainly the Serb police and paramilitaries who are responsible for the atrocities in Kosovo, not the Yugoslav army. To overcome this ruse, the tribunal lawyers determine that the Yugoslav president is the man who has de facto control of the forces of Serb repression in Kosovo.

On Friday, May 21, Graham Blewitt calls tribunal spokesmen Christian Chartier and Paul Risley into his office. Louise Arbour is already there. "Prepare yourself, Milosevic is going to be indicted," they tell the spokesmen.[80] The meeting focuses essentially on one practical problem: The U.N. mission led by Sergio Vieira de Mello is still in Yugoslavia. Louise Arbour is concerned about the security of the U.N. mission personnel in the event of an indictment, and for good reason: When she learned indirectly that the United Nations was going to return to Yugoslavia, she managed to slip in one of her men. Belgrade accepts that a member of the tribunal is traveling under another identity so as not to lose face. Officially, however, they continue to reject the tribunal's jurisdiction. Louise Arbour fears that, if the news of Milosevic's indictment spreads, the life of her investigator will not be worth much. "God knows what could happen to him," she says.[81] She prepares to ask Judge David Hunt, who is required to countersign the indictment, to embargo it until noon, Thursday, May 27. According to the itinerary, the U.N. mission is scheduled to leave Yugoslavia at 8:00 A.M. that day. Until then, a total blackout on information has to be respected for obvious security reasons. The spokesmen consult their agendas. Good news: May 23 is Pentecost Sunday, a three-day weekend, which limits the potential for leaks.

A few days earlier, Louise Arbour and the lawyers had been divided on two essential points. First, must they indict Milosevic for crimes of genocide? "The debate, purely legal, was agitated," recalls Louise Arbour. "Did we have sufficient evidence to make it? To my sense, the charge of genocide was premature, so I renounced it. The majority shared that point of view. The other crucial question was with whom should Milosevic be indicted. Should he be alone? With four others? Six? Twelve? It was a strategic question, because once an indictment is decided, adding names is always complicated. The debate was intense. The final agreement was to have a mix of leaders from the army and the police forces."[82]

On Saturday, May 22, Louise Arbour and the team working on the Milosevic case draft the indictment. "It was a crazy and terribly tense time," she says. "Anything that could go wrong, did go wrong. Saturday night, the computer crashed while we were working on the final draft of the indictment, and we had to find some technicians."[83] Louise Arbour finally signs the indictment. On Sunday, Judge Hunt receives three thousand pages, complete with maps and flow charts designed to help him read the indictment without getting lost. In the introduction, Louise Arbour writes, "This indictment is the first in the history of the tribunal to concern a head of state while a military conflict is ongoing, in the course of which serious violations of international humanitarian law were committed. To force the appearance of the accused raises questions about the practice of arrests not previously known by this institution."[84] To rule out any attempts at a deal between the West and Milosevic, and to prevent him from enjoying a gilded retirement in South Africa or elsewhere, Louise Arbour asks each state to seize property owned by Milosevic and his four co-defendants. This unprecedented indictment is a formidable legal advance; from now on, national sovereignty will no longer be absolute when crimes against humanity are committed.

"It was hell from Saturday night on," she says. "From that moment on, I was on the alert. What was going to happen? Would there be a leak? When? With what consequences? How would the politicians react?"[85] In the final phase, twenty-five people in the Office of the Prosecutor, including the translators, know about the indictment.

Louise Arbour has developed a strategy to avoid immediate pressure from the Western governments. She has brought into confidence one of her friends, Dutch foreign minister Joss Van Aarsteen, asking him to play mailman. Once he receives a code indicating that Judge Hunt has signed the indictment, he is to contact the Western capitals about the Milosevic indictment, according to a precise schedule. At the tribunal, neither Louise Arbour nor Graham Blewitt can be contacted from the outside. "Many of the politicians believed that I would not be so presumptuous," Arbour recounts.

> That I would talk to them before indicting Milosevic, that I would consult them. But I gave myself one piece of advice: "Never ask for anything they can refuse." So, I said nothing. In any event, afterwards, it would have been too late to go back. I had signed the indictment; the judge, [he had signed] as well. There was nothing more to do. I did it to avoid embarrassing the politicians, to avoid saying things that they would regret later, to avoid their embarrassing themselves by asking me to nullify the indictment. I feared the politicians' interminable, apocalyptic speeches, as if their crystal ball was clearer than mine, the unending repetition of the necessity not to back the Serbs into a corner. I believed, on the contrary, that it was necessary to hit hard. The indictment against Karadzic and Mladic had, in part, left the political game.[86]

On Monday, Kofi Annan is in Stockholm for a conference. Louise Arbour makes the trip to see him. A few minutes were enough to give him the picture. "I told him that the indictment would be made public on Thursday," she says. "I added that in case . . . the U.N. team in Yugoslavia had not left by that time, the judge was required to keep the indictment secret."[87]

On Tuesday, Kremlin envoy Victor Chernomyrdin is in Belgrade. There is still a diplomatic impasse, but discussions continue. Kofi Annan's advisers, plunged in secret negotiations, are lukewarm about the decision to indict the Yugoslav president, but there is nothing they can do about it. "We could no longer hold it back," a close aide to Kofi Annan recalls. "We were left to ask ourselves if this indictment was going to ruin the chances of a peace accord. After all, it is easy to condemn crimes: we keep our hands clean, while leaving populations to be sacrificed. Sometimes it is more important to reject truth-telling to save the lives of civilians."[88] In other words, they are still searching for a deal. The prosecutor, however, is pursuing her work contrary to any political schedule. No one now can slow down the process that is under way.

On Tuesday, May 25, Judge Hunt signs the indictment. In the Office of the Prosecutor, Louise Arbour and her aides share a bottle of champagne. The man who has led his country into four wars, in Slovenia, in Croatia, in Bosnia, and in Kosovo, has finally been indicted. But he does not know it yet.

Joss Van Aarsteen receives the password: "The golf balls have been struck." He plays his part, alerting Washington, Paris, London, Brussels, and the rest. With each, he tries to head off any offense being taken at the circuitous notification by explaining the tribunal's concern for the security of diplomatic personnel in Yugoslavia.

For Louise Arbour, interminable days have begun. "I asked myself how the heads of state and public opinion would react," she says. "I did not want to be accused of prolonging the war. The worst was the silence. It was the waiting. It is a true miracle that there had been no leaks earlier. I worked with a lot of people, and if just one had had a reason to talk . . ."[89]

On Wednesday, May 26, the three tribunal spokesmen, Christian Chartier, Jim Landale, and Paul Risley, eat together at the restaurant Rousseau, near the tribunal offices. They agree that they will stick to a policy of "no comment" in case rumors begin to run rampant. A leak has occurred the day before. An acquaintance of CNN reporter Christiane Amanpour thinks he is giving "more force to the story" by giving it to her, but the situation moves quickly beyond his control. On the same day the spokesmen meet, Amanpour boards the Concorde for Europe. Landing at Heathrow, she thinks that the BBC is about to broadcast the same story. Unwilling to be "scooped," she immediately broadcasts the indictment of Milosevic, feeding a little more information hour by hour, but in fragments. The frenzy begins with the entire world media calling the tribunal. Reuters obtains an official confirmation from an anonymous source on Wednesday night. The governments begin to speak to the press.

Exhausted by the work and tension of these last few days, Louise Arbour understands the historic importance of the unprecedented press conference she gives on Thursday, May 27. For six uninterrupted hours, she gives interviews continuously, alternating between French and English, to live broadcasts, radio, television, newspapers—twenty minutes with each. In a packed press room, Louise Arbour officially announces the indictment of Slobodan Milosevic: "On May 22, I presented an indictment for confirmation against Slobodan Milosevic and four other persons, accusing them of crimes against humanity, which includes deportation, persecution and murder. The Yugoslav President is accused, from January 1, 1999 on, of having 'planned, instigated, ordered, committed, or otherwise aided and abetted a campaign of terror and violence directed at Albanian civilians living in Kosovo.'"[90]

The indictment continues in detail:

Beginning in January 1999 [to the present date], Slobodan Milosevic, [Serbian President] Milan Milutinovic, [FRY Prime Minister] Nikola Sainovic, [General] Dragoljub Ojdanic, and [Serbian Interior Minister] Vlajko Stojiljkovic planned, instigated, ordered, committed or otherwise aided and abetted in a campaign of terror and violence directed at Kosovo Albanian civilians. . . . During their offensives, forces of the FRY and Serbia acting in concert engaged in a well-planned and coordinated campaign of destruction of property owned by Kosovo Albanian civilians. Towns and villages were shelled, homes, farms and businesses burned, and personal property destroyed. As a result of these orchestrated actions, towns, villages and entire regions were made uninhabitable for Kosovo Albanians. Additionally, forces of the FRY and Serbia harassed, humiliated and degraded Kosovo Albanian civilians through physical and verbal abuse. The Kosovo Albanians were also persistently subjected to insults, racial slurs, degrading acts based on ethnicity and religion, beatings and other forms of physical mistreatment. . . . On March 24, 1999, NATO began launching air strikes against targets in the FRY. The FRY issued decrees of an imminent threat of war on March 23, 1999, and a state of war on March 24, 1999. After the air strikes commenced, forces of the FRY and Serbia intensified their systematic campaign and forcibly expelled hundreds of thousands of Kosovo Albanians. In addition to the forced expulsions of Kosovo Albanians, forces of the FRY and Serbia also engaged in a number of killings of Kosovo Albanians since March 24, 1999. . . . By May 20, 1999, over 740,000 Kosovo Albanians, approximately one-third of the entire Kosovo Albanian population, had been expelled from Kosovo. Thousands more were believed to be internally displaced. An unknown number of Kosovar Albanians were killed in the operations by forces of the FRY and Serbia.[91]

To the journalists who ask her if this indictment comes at a good time, Louise Arbour responds, "From the point of view of the accused, actually, it's never a very good time. . . . I say it came perfectly appropriately because it was governed by the requirements of our mandate." She insists that justice must accompany any peace. "No credible lasting peace can be built upon impunity and injustice," she says. "The evidence upon which this indictment was confirmed raises serious questions about [the accused parties'] suitability to be the guarantors of any deal, let alone a peace agreement. They have not been rendered less suitable by the indictment. The indictment has simply exposed their unsuitability." In fact, the indictment of their adversary reduces the margin of maneuver for the NATO governments. Unable to go back on the moral principles in whose name they have fought the war, they can no longer cobble together yet another accord with the Yugoslav president, who is from now on labeled a presumed war criminal. "This may seem naive, but I would not be in this business if I did not think that their case can be tried," she continues. "We certainly proceed on the assumption that this indictment is the first chapter. The next one has to be the apprehension of the accused."[92]

Without doubt, no indictment in history has benefited from such an immediate and considerable impact. Television networks broadcast Louise Arbour's press conference live. The text of the indictment is immediately posted on dozens of Internet sites. The indictment makes headlines in the world press, with one notable exception: Serbia. The reactions of the Western dailies are generally good, even if they question the political effects of the indictment. *Libération* headline, May 28: "Milosevic the Pariah." *The Financial Times:* "Russia Pursues Peace Deal Despite War Crimes Charges." *Le Figaro* notes that "[d]espite the indictment of the Yugoslav President, Washington does not challenge Milosevic." The *Wall Street Journal* suggests "[t]he indictment of Milosevic complicates the field for NATO in war." As for *Le Monde,* it states that "the decision of the prosecutor caught the Western leaders unawares, who, while encouraging the investigations of the Tribunal, did not expect that it would succeed so rapidly." [93]

The reactions of the Western governments are positive on the surface. In reality, many Western diplomats are furious but unable to show it. They can hardly take public offense at this indictment after ferociously denouncing the Milosevic regime for weeks. For many days, secret diplomacy had been under way to usurp the tribunal, and an accord was close at hand.

The French interior minister, Jean-Pierre Chevènement, is rare among Western Europeans to condemn openly "this initiative that does not serve peace. . . . If we want to reach an agreement, we avoid criminalizing our adversary." [94] Cautiously, the German foreign affairs minister, Joschka Fischer, declares, "We will know in a few days probably whether it will make our work more difficult or make it easier." [95] In the same vein, Moscow coolly receives the announcement of the indictment of Slobodan Milosevic, judging the decision of the ICTY to be "politicized," regretting that it complicates the search for a solution. [96] But the governments that long ago publicly gave their open support to the tribunal can now only with great difficulty retract themselves, apart from some isolated voices. Thus, the French government "forgets" its old grudges against the tribunal at The Hague. Jacques Chirac is the first head of state to react. In a televised address on Thursday, May 27, he greets the indictment of Milosevic as "a major event . . . a great progress of universal conscience . . . showing that, from now on, no person leading a criminal policy can claim impunity." [97] Similar satisfaction is expressed by Prime Minister Lionel Jospin: "France, who supported the creation of the International Criminal Tribunal, has vowed to collaborate with it and to respect its decisions." [98] President Bill Clinton, on vacation in Florida, is pleased, expressing the hope that it "will make clear to the Serbian people who is responsible for this conflict and who is prolonging it." [99] But another tune indeed is played by the Yugoslav ambassador to the United Nations in Geneva, Branko Brankovic, who declares, "This court for us does not exist. This so-called indictment is, I think, the last attempt by the NATO countries to avoid what is obviously inevitable: a total collapse of the policy of aggression against the Federal Republic of Yugoslavia." [100]

Pursued for crimes committed in Kosovo—ironically, the least "dirty" war Milosevic has led—the next step is to indict him for crimes committed earlier, in Bosnia-Herzegovina. At least, that is what is implied in Article 21 of the initial indictment: "Although Slobodan Milosevic was the President of Serbia during the wars of Slovenia, Croatia and Bosnia and Herzegovina, he was nonetheless the dominant Serbian political figure exercising *de facto* control of the federal government as well as the republican government and was the person with whom the international community negotiated a variety of peace plans and agreements related to these wars." [101] On October 8, 2001, Milosevic will be indicted for war crimes and crimes against humanity committed in Croatia and one month later, on November 22, for genocide, war crimes, and crimes against humanity in Bosnia-Herzegovina.

Ever since U.S. secretary of state Lawrence Eagleburger, in his speech of December, 1992, in Geneva, affirmed that Milosevic was a presumed war criminal, the indictment of the Yugoslav president has been expected. Richard Goldstone and then Louise Arbour have always insisted they were going where the evidence led them. It has taken seven years to get there—seven years during which the West has not deigned to provide the information in their possession to indict the man who has bathed the Balkans in fire and blood, the man responsible for four wars, insane destruction, civilian exodus, massacres unknown on European soil since World War II.

After reducing Vukovar to cinders in November, 1991, after putting Bosnia-Herzegovina to fire and sword, after bombarding and laying siege to Sarajevo for more than three years, after deporting 740,000 Albanians from their province, President Milosevic has finally been indicted. Until October, 1998, the West still considered him an acceptable partner. Created as a poor substitute for a real intervention, the tribunal for a long time did not possess the means to achieve its ambitions. Then, when it had finally obtained those means, the Office of the Prosecutor never put to use the forces necessary to mount an indictment of the Yugoslav president. It is the legacy of Dayton: Peace with impunity as a bonus for Slobodan Milosevic. Thanks to all that, Milosevic enjoyed a practical immunity that contributed to his belief that he was invulnerable. For eight years, the Western democracies continued to deal with him, to negotiate innumerable accords, to make him the guarantor of stability in the Balkans—all while he was its gravedigger. It took the war in Kosovo and the indictment by the ICTY to destroy his image as the indispensable fireman for a conflagration that he himself had set. It has taken the international court to put an end to the West's temptation to make deals with the man who has led his own people and others into war. Slobodan Milosevic has benefited too long from the guilty indulgence of the West, under the pretext that he was the unique credible partner. In deferring this indictment for so long, for lack of evidence and political will, the tribunal gave the unpleasant impression that it was obeying orders, right up to the moment when the NATO bombing campaign failed to deliver the expected results. All justice, no doubt, is born in ambiguity. All the same, the indictment of the Yugoslav president could have been, should have been, accomplished earlier.

Chapter Eight

In God, we trust. All others will be cross-examined.
—Inscription on an ICTY lawyer's T-shirt

The Interminable Trial
of Slobodan Milosevic

July 3, 2001, Hearing Room 1, ten o'clock in the morning. Case number IT-99-37-I. Behind this bureaucratic and from now on routine number for this new trial lies the ideal image for international justice: "The Prosecutor *v.* Slobodan Milosevic," the unhoped-for duel, the first trial of a head of state indicted by an international criminal court.

Highly symbolic, this case is the most important legal event since the Nuremberg trials and it is a key moment as well in the history of human rights and international relations. But a bitter aftertaste quells any excessive enthusiasm. This trial comes late, very late—two years after the ICTY's indictment of the Serb president, an indictment that came only in the middle of the 1999 NATO air campaign in Yugoslavia. Left unanswered is an insistent question: If Milosevic had not launched his bloody repression in Kosovo, would he have ever been indicted for the years of atrocities committed in Bosnia and Croatia?

On this Tuesday morning in summer, nearly six years to the day after the massacres in Srebrenica for which he is charged with genocide, Slobodan Milosevic appears before his judges. He must respond to sixty-six counts, including charges of war crimes and crimes against humanity committed in Kosovo, Croatia, and Bosnia. He risks spending the rest of his life in prison.

It is an interminable trial that begins with hundreds of witnesses called to the stand. It is both a showcase for and the greatest threat to international justice. This trial is the hour of truth for the tribunal: Will it be a trial like Nuremberg, the watershed for all to follow? Three judges—the Briton, Richard May, who is president of the chamber, and his assistants, Patrick Robinson from Jamaica and O-Gon Kwon from South Korea—will try Slobodan Milosevic. But public opinion will also pass judgment on the evidence and the functioning of this international court. Is it capable of freeing itself from the control of the Great Powers that, due to their initial passivity and internal divisions and then because of their military involvement, have at every moment and in very different ways weighed heavily on the conflict? Will the tribunal manage to dispel the impression of partiality created by the Office of the Prosecutor's decision not to open an investigation into the NATO bombings?

Inside the Office of the Prosecutor, the preparatory work for the trial is enormous. Despite repeated avowals by Richard Goldstone and Louise Arbour that they would pursue the mandate to the very end, each had understood in reality that this objective was unattainable, as Milosevic continued to be a key to balance in the Balkans.

This understanding was so pervasive that the individuals charged with pursuing an indictment against Milosevic for the crimes of Bosnia and Croatia had done practically nothing. Why waste energy for a useless task? Carla Del Ponte remembers her surprise when she discovered a nearly empty dossier. "This was a shock for me," she explains. "Louise Arbour had directed an indictment against Milosevic acting on crimes committed in Bosnia and Croatia, but practically nothing had been done. Why? I see only one possible explanation: Nobody seriously believed that Milosevic would one day be tried at The Hague."[1] It would take Del Ponte two more years following the initial indictment against Milosevic on Kosovo to issue supplementary indictments, on October 8 (amended October 23) and November 22, 2001, for crimes committed in Croatia and Bosnia, respectively.

For Croatia, Slobodan Milosevic is accused of participating in "a criminal enterprise" between August, 1991, and June, 1992, seeking "forcible removal of the majority of the Croat and other non-Serb population from the approximately one-third of the territory of the Republic of Croatia that he planned to become part of a new Serb-dominated state through the commission of crimes." He is accused of the expulsion "of at least 170,000 Croats and other non-Serbs civilians," of the murder "of hundreds of civilians," and of the detention of thousands of others "in inhumane conditions."[2]

The indictment relative to Bosnia accuses Milosevic of having "planned, instigated, ordered, committed or otherwise aided and abetted the planning, preparation and execution of the destruction, in whole or in part, of the Bosnian Muslim and Bosnian Croat national, ethnical, racial or religious groups, as such, in territories within Bosnia and Herzegovina." The indictment also says that "[t]his campaign of destruction had resulted in the death of at least 9,000 persons," including victims from massacres in Srebrenica and the detention camps of Omarska and Keraterm. He is also implicated in the expulsion of at least 268,050 non-Serbs.[3]

As soon as Milosevic arrives at The Hague, "delivered" by a NATO transport aircraft on June 28, 2001, following a brief stop at Tuzla, the tribunal's eight years of relative tranquility is transformed instantly into a high-stakes trial run. The three judges have the unique charge of trying the criminal policy of a head of state, which poses serious difficulties. First, the Office of the Prosecutor must establish the evidence that Slobodan Milosevic was at the top of the chain of command while atrocities were being committed. But the documentary evidence remains beyond the reach of the tribunal. Yugoslavia balks at cooperating. Parts of the army and the secret services remain loyal to their old president and threaten those who would be tempted to leave the circle of loyalty and cooperate with the tribunal.

Plenty of other challenges are added to this one. Can the Milosevic trial stigmatize crimes against humanity beyond the tribunal's walls without turning into a "legal circus," in the words of former French defense minister Alain Richard?

Finally, the ICTY cannot work outside the political environment that it inhabits, for the court is itself the object of the debate on international justice. The administration of U.S. president George W. Bush, fiercely hostile to the International Criminal Court (ICC), has succeeded the Clinton administration, which was itself already very reserved about the new court. Washington fears that, in the case of an intervention, its soldiers could be pursued by an international prosecutor and judges politically biased against them. American opposition to the ICC hardens further after the terrorist attacks on New York and Washington on September 11, 2001.

How, then, to establish the credibility of international justice when American policy itself has a double standard? The problem is that while Washington supports the ICTY, it is trying by all means to torpedo, or at least to free itself from, the pending ICC. This policy is symbolized geographically in The Hague: On one side of the town is the ICTY, kept afloat by the United States; on the other side are the ICC provisional offices, whose most formidable enemy is the same American superpower.[4]

As seen from Washington or Texas, this unequal policy toward international justice may make sense, but how can the rest of the world not read into it the arrogance of the sole superpower seeking to shelter itself from any eventual pursuit? This is the same superpower that holds the court at arm's length for the former Yugoslavia yet has forced Belgrade to transfer Milosevic to The

Hague. How will the Milosevic trial and international justice not suffer from the opportunism of American policy?

President Kostunica: European Principles in Parentheses

In fact, Milosevic's "delivery" to The Hague would never have occurred without American will. At the end of September, 2000, events in Serbia accelerate during national elections. On September 24, the opposition declares Vojislav Kostunica winner of the presidential elections. The Milosevic regime refuses to recognize its defeat. On October 2 a general strike is called, and on October 5 thousands of demonstrators storm the parliament. They are supported covertly by elements of the army and the secret services. On October 6 the electoral commission recognizes Kostunica's victory, and Slobodan Milosevic withdraws. The special correspondent for *Libération* writes, "The story of this day is that of a crowd, of a few men and of a regime that has turned on itself rather than being overthrown."[5] The cutting loose of Milosevic by his own friends will weigh on the events that follow. The same day, October 6, ICTY prosecutor Carla Del Ponte sends "a message to the elected president," Vojislav Kostunica, in which she affirms "that The Hague court is ready for Milosevic 'at any time . . . if there is to be a true and lasting peace in the Balkans and if the people of Yugoslavia are to be fully accepted back into the international community.'"[6] She obtains a dry public response from Kostunica: The ICTY, he says, is a "tool of political pressure of the U.S. Administration." "Every time I am asked the question over the Milosevic issue, I resolutely say no," he tells Serb state television."[7]

The discarded president has lost none of his bite. One and a half months after being chased from power by demonstrators in the streets of Belgrade, here is Slobodan Milosevic in perfect health. Wearing a red tie with a sober suit, on November 26 he is acclaimed by twenty-three hundred supporters, who triumphantly elect him head of the Serb Socialist Party. Who would have believed this image possible? Indicted for war crimes and crimes against humanity by the international court, the man now takes on the mantle of the perfect democratic opposition. Reversing roles with disconcerting aplomb, he tries to pass himself off as an inoffensive victim persecuted by the "new Gestapo," which is, according to him, the ICTY: "Large sums of money are being distributed and significant privileges given to those who would agree to anything against this country: the loss of independence, the secession of Montenegro, Kosovo and Vojvodina, humiliation and extinction of the Serbian people, the extradition of national heroes to the new Gestapo in The Hague," he claims.[8]

Slobodan Milosevic, still powerful and free, mocks the international court and at the same time accuses the West of wanting the destruction of Yugoslavia. Like the distorted mirror at an amusement park, his strange destiny reflects the ambiguities not only of the new regime in Belgrade but especially of the Western governments relative to international justice. The latter's primary objective is to integrate the new power in Belgrade as firmly as possible into the international community, even if it means temporarily closing their eyes to Yugoslavia's obligation to cooperate with the ICTY.

While the Croat president Stjepan (Stipe) Mesic has abjured nationalism without garnering any real Western support, Kostunica, on the other hand, benefits immediately from all the favors of Europe. Still, he is hardly moved by the ethnic cleansing perpetuated during the war in Bosnia. In fact, not long before, he labeled the ICTY "not even international . . . it's an American tool for exerting pressure."[9] Since then, he has tempered his remarks but continues to assert that cooperation with the tribunal "is not a priority."[10]

That the new Yugoslav president balks at collaborating with The Hague is one thing. Undoubtedly, he does not want to provoke the army, which during the crazy days of October did not block him from ascending to power (and perhaps even gave him assurance, according to some, in exchange for his commitment not to hand over certain persons indicted by the tribunal). On the other hand, the attitudes of the European governments and the special U.N. rapporteur for violations of human rights in the former Yugoslavia are infinitely more worrisome, as seen from The Hague. Certainly, political calculations enter into the will to do everything possible to solidify Kostunica's power: "Let us wait for Kostunica to be democratically elected next December 23. After that, he will have freedom to act," is the official explanation. There is no question of putting the slightest pressure on the man who made possible "the Europeanization of the Balkans," in the words of French foreign minister Hubert Védrine. So after October 5, the European Union lifts its sanctions on Yugoslavia: "We are not there to impose conditions," French president Jacques Chirac explains. To be sure that his message is clear, he uses a popular expression to indicate that the policy does *not* imply a quid pro quo: "The spirit of the [European] community is not at all 'scratch my back and I'll scratch yours.'"[11]

In an editorial, the Paris daily *Le Monde* warns the European Union against sacrificing its principles in this way: "It would be frankly immoral to treat the international criminal court as a pariah, a hindrance to good relations with Belgrade, because Mr. Kostunica has decided that he will not hand over Mr. Milosevic. To lift sanctions unconditionally raises a Pascalian wager, expressing faith in the democratic dynamic at work in Serbia. But this bet must be made in good conscience and clarity, which is to say in holding close the principles that brought Europe to the Balkans. Not to have done this is either a mistake or naïveté."[12]

Endorsed by the European Union, Vojislav Kostunica leaves the European summit in Biarritz, France, on October 14 without promising to deliver Milosevic, nor even to free the thousands of Kosovar Albanians held in Serb prisons, but with a check in hand for 200 million euros. This extraordinary prejudice by the Fifteen against the international court is, of course, nothing new. Diplomats and high functionaries have never liked the tribunal, seeing it as a hindrance to negotiation. The West's ambivalence toward the tribunal culminated days earlier, at the beginning of October, with the public intervention of Jiri Dienstbier, the U.N. human rights rapporteur for Yugoslavia. This old Czech dissident is the first high-level foreign functionary to go to Belgrade during the period of transition. Now, he forcefully demands the lifting of the indictment of Milosevic in order to facilitate the democratic transition: "We have to ask ourselves whether from a moral point of view the fate of a single dictator is more important than the fate of millions of people in the Balkans."[13] The idea—illegal in itself (one cannot annul or suspend an indictment)—is rejected. U.N. Secretary-General Kofi Annan reprimands Dienstbier, but the idea of amnesty from justice imposes itself de facto.

Before the Security Council on November 21, 2000, Carla Del Ponte can only deplore the "flexible" approach of the international community that is apparently so little pressed to see Milosevic judged for his crimes: "The world has embraced President Kostunica despite the fact that he has repeatedly said that co-operation with the ICTY 'is not a priority' for him. If he chose that phrase himself, I admire him—it is a clever line, one capable of different interpretations—a true politician's phrase," she says. She warns the international community against the temptation to conclude a "deal" with Belgrade that not only would constitute a grave reversal of justice but would also be dangerous for regional stability:

> Milosevic must be brought to trial before the International Tribunal. There simply is no alternative. After all the effort the international community has invested in the Balkans to restore peace to the region, after the weeks of NATO bombing to prevent massive human rights abuses against the citizens of Kosovo, and given the enormous residual power and continuing influence of the hard-liners in Belgrade, it would be inconceivable to allow Milosevic to walk away from the consequences of his actions. It is not enough to say that the loss of office is punishment enough, nor is it satisfactory to call him to account for election offences or some such national proceeding. We have already seen

that there can be no "deals" with figures like Milosevic. It is to the great credit of the international community that the temptation to offer him an easy escape route was resisted. The consequences for international criminal justice would have been devastating, if that had happened. I urge the Security Council not to allow the same result to be achieved in slow motion by lingering inactivity. It is of crucial importance that double standards be avoided in dealing with the FRY, Croatia and Bosnia and Herzegovina.[14]

It is a declaration as strong as it is useless. Claude Jorda, the president of the ICTY, warns the U.N. General Assembly,

History has taught us that so long as the duty of rendering justice is not truly discharged, the spectre of war can re-emerge, sometimes even several generations later. We are all now accountable to these generations for the success of our undertaking. Our success is especially important since that of the future International Criminal Court is to a great extent dependent upon it. We must not let slip through our fingers this unique and historic opportunity to demonstrate that the court which you have established can contribute to restoring a just and lasting peace in the regions battered by conflict.[15]

At The Hague, members of the tribunal no longer hide their concern, judging that "the ICTY has its best days behind it." [16]

Once again, the wars' victims feel abandoned by the world. How can such a wounded population ever accept that the primary instigator of the wars in the former Yugoslavia is a free man? Or that the Bosnian Serb leader Radovan Karadzic has still not been arrested in the tiny Bosnian territory controlled since 1996 by NATO, the strongest military alliance in the world? How could this de facto impunity not provoke a bitter reaction from the victims, feeling once again cheated in their thirst for the justice that had been promised by the international community? How could all this not transmute itself through pressure and frustration in Bosnia and Croatia into dangerous nationalist tensions?

Prior to the Zagreb summit of November 24, 2000, Croat president Stipe Mesic warns, "We cannot speak of normal relations with Belgrade while those responsible for the bloodbaths of Vukovar and Srebrenica walk free in Serbia." [17] He hits this point again speaking to the summit's plenary session. Paul Garde, an expert on the Balkans, adds, "Imagine the reaction of Croat public opinion if today we tell them that in reality, nobody is going to try Milosevic, after we have forced Croatia to submit itself to the demands of the international court. In Zagreb, there would be an explosion." [18] The Croat authorities have, in fact, reason to find the European indulgence toward Vojislav Kostunica a bit much; since its ascension to power in January, 1999, the Mesic government has taken real risks in cooperating with the international court, to the point that the nationalists accuse their president of having betrayed the country by arresting and delivering Croat defendants to The Hague, as well as by collaborating with the investigators of the tribunal. A key witness, Milan Levar, is mysteriously assassinated on August 28, 2000. He had assisted in the executions of Serb civilians by Croat forces in October, 1991, in the village of Gospic and had risked testifying at The Hague against the generals of his country. Stipe Mesic also has received death threats. Faced with rumors of a coup d'etat in Zagreb, he dismisses seven army generals.

On January 23, 2001, Carla Del Ponte forces a meeting with Vojislav Kostunica in Belgrade. The president returns three times to the decision by the Office of the Prosecutor not to investigate the NATO bombing campaign, which is flagrant evidence, in his eyes, of the ICTY's partiality. Del Ponte replies that Belgrade did not furnish evidence to support a convincing charge, and she demands that Yugoslavia respect its international obligations and send Milosevic to her. As their exchange becomes increasingly acrimonious, Del Ponte puts an abrupt end to the meeting.[19]

American Checkbook Diplomacy

In contrast to the European Union, Washington hardens its tone in the spring of 2001 and pressures Belgrade to send Milosevic to his judges at The Hague. Somewhere within Washington's position is the arrogance of power that seeks to sanction the man who has mocked the United States for years. There is also the will to blend American power with an image of morality in the conduct of its foreign policy: the soldier's sword and the scales of justice. Finally, there is concern that Serbia, and even the Balkans as a whole, must progress toward normalization and stabilization. Hence, the initiation of checkbook diplomacy with Serbia on its knees: The United States conditions economic aid on Belgrade's arrest of Slobodan Milosevic and fixes March 31, 2001, as the deadline.

Should Serbia resist the American pressure on principle? Or should it give priority to reviving its drained economy? Six months after the fall of Milosevic, this choice divides the country to its very top. President Vojislav Kostunica and his prime minister, Zoran Djindjic, diverge radically. Hostile to Milosevic's arrest, Kostunica gives a speech on March 30 before the U.N. Human Rights Commission in Geneva. In the guise of a concession, he evokes cooperation with the tribunal but does not mention Milosevic's name. Instead, he emphasizes "what seems of particular importance for me . . . the establishment of the

Commission for Truth and Reconciliation [TRC]," without saying precisely how this would work. In short, he gives the privilege of installing the TRC to The Hague tribunal.[20] Djindjic, however, believes that Serbia cannot lift itself without Western aid and must accept the price: Milosevic.

This confrontation between the two men risks the political position of the new Serbia and climaxes on the night of Friday, March 30, and Saturday, March 31, the deadline fixed by the Americans. Units of the special police operating under the orders of Djindjic try twice to arrest Milosevic. They are deterred by a handful of militiamen and a detachment of the army, placed under the control of President Kostunica. Kostunica plays the card of Serb nationalism with a human face; he claims to be in favor of judging Milosevic, but in Serbia, and refuses to pass under the Caudine Forks of Washington; "national dignity is above a handful of dollars," he says.[21] Djindjic is more pragmatic; he anticipates, in exchange for the arrest of Milosevic, a massive financial infusion that only the West can offer. In the eyes of Djindjic, Milosevic is an indispensable source of export currency. At a donors' conference set for the end of June, he hopes to get $1 billion to aid the reconstruction of Serbia.

This argument wins. An extraordinary meeting between the two men allows them to refute what some observers are too quick to call "a miniature coup d'etat," and it leads to Milosevic's arrest. He resists briefly; his daughter Marija even fires three shots before her father surrenders to authorities following a brief negotiation.

The substance of this discussion between Milosevic and the police forces is confused. The Serb interior minister, Dusan Mihajlovic, asserts that Milosevic surrendered after obtaining assurance that he would not be transferred to the ICTY. On the other hand, the Serb justice minister declares that Milosevic's transfer to The Hague will be "a reality after the adoption of a law on cooperation with the Tribunal."[22] In any case, Washington appreciates the gesture and immediately releases $50 million while announcing that it will no longer oppose the grant of credits to Serbia by international financial institutions. Secretary of State Colin Powell notes, however, that financial support is conditioned on "total cooperation" with the ICTY.[23] State Department spokesman Richard Boucher is explicit: "It remains our goal to see him face justice in The Hague. We should be absolutely clear that we want that to take place sooner rather than later."[24]

On Monday, April 2, the Serbian press headlines "the first night of Milosevic in prison." The dailies *Blic* and *Vecernje Novosti* publish a sketch of cell 1121, on a floor of the central prison derisively nicknamed the "Hyatt" in reference to the luxury hotel chain. The cell contains a bed, a table with two chairs, and a shower. The Serb press details Milosevic's networks that looted the country and scoffs at the former president's inability to comprehend the accusations. Readers learn that the most famous prisoner in the world, prisoner number 101980, is accused of corruption, abuse of power, and embezzlement. Milosevic is not, however, accused of war crimes. The objective of the new authorities is to de-legitimize the former president, who retains the support of the ultrana-tionalists in the eyes of public opinion. A trial in Belgrade for embezzlement? Del Ponte, who feels Milosevic is escaping her, is not hostile to this idea "if the trial begins quickly and only lasts a few weeks," explains her spokeswoman, Florence Hartmann.[25]

In the somewhat deleterious climate of transition in Serbia, the Office of the Prosecutor makes the best of its narrow margin of maneuver. Carla Del Ponte has already proposed to give Belgrade information on the embezzlement of funds by Milosevic and his close associates, hoping that in exchange Kostu-nica will arrest Milosevic and eventually transfer him to The Hague after he has been tried in Belgrade. In fact, her deputy, Graham Blewitt, floats the idea of a series of trials, starting in Yugoslavia and ending up in The Hague, during re-marks to the International Institute for Strategic Studies in London, publicly signaling some flexibility.[26]

Other, less optimistic scenarios circulate, however. One possibility is that NATO forces could capture Radovan Karadzic—if he is not killed first—for judgment at The Hague. This move would allow the West and the ICTY to save face by forgetting about Milosevic temporarily.

The tribunal has, in effect, enough to worry about. On April 3, in an interview with the *New York Times,* Kostunica reaffirms his refusal to turn Milosevic over to The Hague: "It should never happen. I think that it's pos-sible to do everything so that it should never happen." Following that, "Other presidents are not being sent to The Hague. I must make some compro-mises, but there is a line I cannot cross. Even among those people in the Ser-bian and Yugoslav government who don't think about legitimacy, but only about what might be politically useful, the prevailing view is that it would be unacceptable."[27]

On April 6, the ICTY still refuses to admit defeat. It hastens its court clerk, Hans Holthuis, to the Serb authorities in Belgrade, so that they can "no-tify Slobodan Milosevic of the arrest warrant of January 23, 2001, in conjunc-tion with its indictment of May 24, 1999."[28] Politically fragile, the tribunal's position is legally solid: Article 9 of the statute that established the tribunal stipulates that "the International Tribunal shall have primacy over national courts. At any stage of the procedure, the International Tribunal may formally request national courts to defer to [its jurisdiction]."[29] These statutes have been passed by the U.N. General Assembly. They impose themselves, thus, on all states, even though Yugoslavia asserts that its own domestic law blocks the extradition of its nationals. Belgrade, in fact, dreads the reaction of public opinion and, worse, of its army.

Three months after the arrest of Milosevic, Serbia is more than ever at the edge of financial bankruptcy. The country desperately needs a massive injection of foreign capital that only international aid can provide. Washington conditions its participation in the donors' meeting on June 29 on the reinforcement of cooperation between Belgrade and the ICTY. In addition, if Belgrade intends to participate fully in international society, it can no longer extricate itself from the resolutions of the Security Council that oblige cooperation with the ICTY. After intense discussion among the ministers representing the governmental coalition, the decree of cooperation with the tribunal is signed on June 23, opening the way to transfer former Serb president Slobodan Milosevic to The Hague. At the same time, it provides a way around parliament, which opposes cooperation with the U.N. tribunal because of the opposition by deputies of the Popular Socialist Party (SNP, an old Montenegrin ally of Milosevic). "A ticket to The Hague!" heralds the Belgrade newspaper *Vecernje Novosti* on Sunday, June 24. The Yugoslav vice prime minister, Miroljub Labus, signer of the decree, confirms that the former strong man of the Balkans will taste, after a "very short delay," the pleasures of the cells at The Hague.[30]

At the tribunal and in the Western capitals, satisfaction reigns. "We are ready to receive Slobodan Milosevic at any moment," declares a member of the Office of the Prosecutor.[31] The former strong man sees the number of his partisans fall dramatically. A mere twenty assemble to denounce the fact that the government has ceded to Washington's *diktat*. The affirmations of one of his defenders, Veselin Crerovic, judging the governmental decree "unconstitutional," seem merely like a failed rearguard action. As for Milosevic, according to his declarations, he is proud to have led the nation against NATO aggression on the territorial integrity and the sovereignty of Yugoslavia. But his words no longer echo in the heart of a population that aspires to get out of the material difficulties and isolation into which this nationalist warrior has taken them.

The new power in Belgrade devotes itself to defusing resistance. For several weeks, state television prepares the public. It is fortuitous that the mass graves of Kosovars, distributed across the entire territory of the country and known to be near Belgrade, come to light at this precise moment. Serb society takes— perhaps for the first time—full measure of the violence with which Milosevic drove and lost his wars. Unthinkable earlier, Serb television now broadcasts a poignant BBC documentary on the massacres of Srebrenica, "A Cry from the Graves."

Milosevic's Line of Defense

PRESIDENT MAY: Do you want to have the indictment read out or not?
MILOSEVIC: That's your problem.[32]

The tribunal had feared that its famous defendant would show his scorn for
the court by remaining silent, as did the former Gestapo officer Klaus Barbie,
who sat out his hearings in Lyon in the quiet of his cell. On this point, and only
on this point, the tribunal can feel reassured about Milosevic. On July 3, 2001,
during his initial appearance before the judges, Milosevic does not play the
role of a defeated man, nor that of an absentee, like Barbie, nor of an Eichmann
portraying himself as a modest bureaucrat, nor of a Goering, who scoffed at the
tribunal of conquerors that was Nuremberg. Slobodan Milosevic has not lost
his taste for theatrics. He maintains his haughtiness, defiant and scornful, to
the point that his two guards in blue U.N. uniforms are taken for his body-
guards. Milosevic answers the accusations point by point. But behind his
haughty appearance, Milosevic is obviously a little disoriented when he enters
for his initial hearing—to the point of going directly to the witness stand, certain of holding center stage in this drama starring himself.

The judge-president, Richard May, sixty-three, a graduate of Cambridge,
sees no relief. He is known for his scrupulous respect for the rules of procedure, as well as his brief political career; as a Labor Party candidate, he had his
hour of glory when beaten in Finchley in 1979 by Margaret Thatcher, who
would go on to become prime minister of Great Britain. When Richard May
asks Milosevic if he pleads guilty, the former strong man launches into a long
diatribe: "I consider this Tribunal a false Tribunal and the indictment a false
indictment. It is illegal being not appointed by the U.N. General Assembly, so
I have no need to appoint counsel to an illegal organ."[33]

The president of the court ends this rant by cutting off Milosevic's micro-
phone and entering a plea of "not guilty" on his behalf. At 10:12 A.M., Milosevic's first appearance is over after only a few minutes and he is returned to his
cell at Scheveningen. The tone is set and it will not vary: To the trial created to
judge crimes for which he is presumed responsible, Milosevic counters with a
political trial against the "the masters of NATO."

On the first day of the trial, February 12, 2002, Carla Del Ponte begins her
opening statement solemnly:

The Chamber will now begin the trial of this man for the wrongs he is said to
have done to the people of his own country and to his neighbors. . . . [H]ow

remarkable it is that I am able to speak [these words] here. Today, as never before, we see international justice in action. Let us take a moment at the start of this trial to reflect upon the establishment of the Tribunal and its purpose. We should just pause to recall the daily scenes of grief and suffering that came to define armed conflict in the former Yugoslavia. The events themselves were notorious and a new term, "ethnic cleansing," came into common use in our language. Some of the incidents reveal an almost medieval savagery and the calculated cruelty that went far beyond the bounds of legitimate warfare.[34]

Impassive, Slobodan Milosevic says nothing, waiting for his moment. The former president's strategy is simple: to shift the focus of the confrontation step by step. He has no intention of answering the specific accusations of the crimes for which he is blamed. He refuses to enter into the penal logic of the trial. Infringing systematically on the rules of procedure, having nothing more to lose, he uses the tribunal as a political podium. He addresses himself beyond the three judges who confront him to the "jury" that is the Serb people and even more, the judgment of history, the only jury, no doubt, that counts in his eyes.

The accused turns himself into the prosecutor of "this false tribunal" of The Hague: "This trial's aim is to produce false justification for the war crimes of NATO committed in Yugoslavia," he thunders.[35] The fact that he does not have a lawyer gives him the speaking time to work at this inversion of roles. He presents himself as a lone man, confronting the unjust wrath of the American superpower, expiatory victim of the West and "of this Prosecutor," who directs "a parallel trial through the media which, along with this unlawful Tribunal, are there to play the role of a parallel lynch process."[36] For procedural reasons, the judges have begun the Milosevic trial with an inverse chronology of the wars, first Kosovo, then Bosnia and Croatia. This procedure gives Milosevic the advantage of denouncing NATO's campaign immediately. He shows shocking photographs of victims of NATO's bombing to advance his thesis: that the exodus of Albanians is explained by NATO's intervention and not by Serb forces, profoundly respectful of the Geneva Conventions.

Mastering the symbols of power, the accused refuses to call the president of the chamber by his honorific title "Mr. President," preferring to call him "Mr. May"—intending, no doubt, to indicate that if there is one president in this chamber, it is Slobodan Milosevic. As for the prosecution, represented by Carla Del Ponte and by her deputy, Geoffrey Nice (a famous former president of the London Bar, Shakespearean actor, and tourist guide in the Dalmatians during his youth), Milosevic sends them back to their NATO "chiefs" and "bosses."

By disqualifying the tribunal, Milosevic tries to free himself from its rules. He refuses to wear earphones. Fearing that someone will accuse them of directing an unfair trial, the judges install a loudspeaker for Milosevic, thereby making him an "exception." Antoine Garapon, secretary general of the Institute of Justice in Paris, explains Milosevic's strategy not of disruption, but of perversion: "Instead of disruption, that rejects all the rules of the trial, Milosevic's strategy consists of selecting certain rules to which he submits with relatively good grace to better contest the others. In short, he uses the court's own rules to better distort its legal foundation."[37] The history that Milosevic pleads is that of a Serb people still standing against American "neocolonialism": "The whole world should listen to this alarm bell because the whole world is the target of neo-colonialism, including the rather tired and sleepy Europe."[38] His view of history is that of a plot that makes his people the eternal victim: "[A]ll the former socialist countries of a multi-ethnic composition were to be destroyed by causing national tensions."[39] Parodying the prosecutor's indictment against him, Milosevic inverts the accusations against the instigators of the war—NATO, the United States, and Germany—who manipulate the complicit media all the better "to destroy the Serb people":

> Nobody will be able to conceal or justify the monstrous crimes committed by NATO in the Yugoslav part of the European continent at the threshold of the new millennium in spite of ten years of media demonization of Serbia, the Serb people, the intensified production of a factory of lies in a media war in which the global networks were misused. And even today, prior to this hearing, to this trial, there were a series of stories, and when they told me about them, I said they have to work hard to cover up the truth. The truth cannot be covered up easily. They have to work hard, but still they won't be able to cover up the truth. However, by deceiving one's own public through a systematic manufacturing of lies, they have actually abolished democracy for their own public precisely to the extent to which they have withdrawn their right to truthful information.[40]

Milosevic has a response to everything. The terrible camps of Bosnia? He himself was told nothing about them. The Bosnian Serb chiefs Radovan Karadzic and Momcilo Krajisnik told him that there were no such camps. The massacres of Srebrenica, on which the accusation of genocide against him is based? He knew nothing about them; it was the European negotiator, Carl Bildt, who informed him of them. As for the rest, his relations with Karadzic were not good. The other crimes in Croatia and Bosnia? He does not deny

them, but normalizes them, attributing them to the work of a handful of agi-
tators: "[T]hey started out the statement in a malicious way, using examples of
tragedies that occurred in Croatia and Bosnia. I don't know whether they did
occur. Maybe they did. And certainly they are major tragedies. And all of this
is tragic, and no one can deny that, but surely aren't there horrific crimes in
your own countries? Don't your courts have anyone to try in England when
somebody commits a murder or sets fire to a house? Do you attribute this to
the British Prime Minister by saying that he knew or ought to have reason to
know?"[41] The forty-five dead in the village of Racak that would trigger NATO
air strikes after the failure of the Rambouillet Conference? "A manipulation" of
the UÇK, designed to provoke the intervention of the West. The hundreds of
thousands of Albanians chased from Kosovo in 1999? "They were fleeing the
NATO bombing, not Serb forces."[42]

In his own view, Milosevic is the innocent victim of a conspiracy by the
"masters of the world" doing their utmost to bring him down so as to enslave
Serbia. The motive? Vengeance: "[T]he informed part of the world knew that
the bombing of Yugoslavia was retaliation for the policy of independence that
Yugoslavia was waging."[43]

In order to maintain influence over a part of the Serb population, Milosevic takes on the role of patriot and denounces the "puppet" government of Belgrade. Faced with the enterprise of "destruction" by NATO, "they have actually abolished democracy":

[B]y deceiving one's own public through a systematic manufacturing of lies,
they have actually abolished democracy for their own public precisely to the
extent to which they have withdrawn their right to truthful information. You
can have the best possible mechanism, but if you feed it with lies, it cannot produce results that are humane, honest, progressive and justified in civilizational
terms. Those are the means of war, what the media have done to destroy states
and peoples which they wish to place under their control. That is why it is the
task of this farce of a trial to legalize the crime, the propositions of which I have
only partially been able to outline.[44]

A man of peace, that is Milosevic, one who can sleep the slumber of
the just:

We did everything we could to put an end to the war. And that is why these accusations are simply proof that in fact you have no evidence for your real objectives. At the beginning, you said you would not talk about politics, but your-
selves [sic] kept talking about politics only for a whole day. On the other hand,

the crimes that were committed, and I spoke about them, and they were committed all over Yugoslavia, and I admire those that can sleep after all that. My advantage is that I can look anyone in the eye. I defended my country honorably and chivalrously, and I can say that the Yugoslav army and the police also defended their country honorably and chivalrously and that they did not stain their honour in any way.[45]

A witness says that Milosevic suffers from a Peter Pan complex: "My impression was that I was dealing with a person who felt that when he said something, that it made it true."[46]

Behind the NATO threat, Milosevic lays out the eternal struggle of the Serbs for their independence: the war against the fascist "ustasha" Croat regimes, the Kosovar Nazi collaborators, the Third Reich, and now the West allied "[with] the Albanian terrorists [who] have continued their policies [in] Kosovo, and with their puppet government in Belgrade they continued with the selling of Yugoslavia. Hitler had to occupy Yugoslavia first, too, in order to launch his attack again Russia, and again the Albanians were his allies. However, we had returned, and we shall return again. Therefore, their employers should not think that they will be successful with this farce. This will only increase the shame in the crime itself."[47]

The conclusion that Milosevic reaches in this Manichean world view is simple, and Milosevic strengthens himself by asserting it: "[T]here are many books of history, and what you are telling me in this pitiful indictment was gathered from mere journalistic pamphlets. And the wind will blow them away. They were written in order to serve the purposes of propaganda and a purpose of committing a crime against the Serbian people."[48] A few days later he states,

Responsibility for the war is being sought on that side that had advocated peace. Before the eyes of the entire world, there is an inversion. The instigators of war are accusing the protagonists of peace for [sic] war, and thanks to their powerful international positions, they are playing the roles of both Prosecutor and Judge. As for me personally, they are accusing me and condemning me in advance precisely of their own warmongering policies and the consequences of these policies that they had been pursuing themselves and that I had opposed to the best of my ability by advocating peace. This simple truth can be overlooked nowadays only by those who have an interest not to see this. And of course, those who are bombed by lies and who are exposed to such media manipulations that they have accepted lies as the truth and the other way around.[49]

But Milosevic is confident that "once this truth is heard . . . nobody will be able to deny it"; the public "is the jury, because this Tribunal does not have one," he concludes, isolating himself in his world where he is the victim rather than the perpetrator.[50]

Milosevic, Cross-Examiner

It is a strange sensation, the effect produced by this antiseptic court, laid out like a television studio, installed in the Dutch capital, as clean as it is sleepy. Classes of students come to the Milosevic trial as they might go to see a curious animal in a zoo reserved for deaf-mute visitors. The occasional noise made by the sparse public is deadened, neutralized by the wall-to-wall carpeting and the half-tinted lighting, under the surveillance of guards who suppress their yawns with difficulty. It is difficult in this context to feel the breath of history. Difficult, too, to make the link between the bloody dislocation of the former Yugoslavia accompanied by its procession of crimes and the muffled atmosphere that prevails here. It is a decor without memory to evoke a region, the Balkans, which Winston Churchill said has produced more history than it can consume.

Sometimes slumped, sometimes attentive, Milosevic makes the court pay heavily for his presence. Some bring up the suicides of his parents, worrying that he may do the same once imprisoned. At first, he is put under twenty-four-hour observation to make sure that he does no harm to himself. But the man refuses to admit defeat. He wants to force the appearance of the Western political leaders responsible for "the NATO aggression" against Serbia: former president Bill Clinton and former secretary of state Madeleine Albright of the United States, President Jacques Chirac of France, Prime Minister Tony Blair of Great Britain, Chancellor Gerhard Schroeder of Germany and his predecessor Helmut Kohl, as well as U.N. head Kofi Annan. "When Chirac comes here," declares Slobodan Milosevic during his opening statement, "I will have to ask him why he did not veto the killing of so many civilians, women, children."[51] In reality, Milosevic is playing to the gallery, because he does not have the power to subpoena them. The court must first evaluate the necessity of the appearance of his potential witnesses, and it is then up to the defense to convince these adverse witnesses to testify. But the propaganda victory, again, goes to Milosevic.

At one moment, Milosevic's health falters and Richard May expresses concern. Milosevic retorts, "That's your problem." He does not hide his contempt for the tribunal and those who incarnate it. The hostility between him and Carla Del Ponte is palpable. Against Milosevic's physical self-control, the continued force that emanates from this man is the prosecutor's need to be in contact with the victims as well as the accused. Nothing holds her back; at the start of each trial, she always goes to speak with the accused, and she makes no exception for Milosevic. She meets the accused in a little room adjoining the court at the beginning of the trial. "I need personal contact with the victims as with the accused," Del Ponte says. "They have heard of me, I prefer that they know me. Slobodan was angry when they brought him to me. I explained to him his rights, told him that he could cooperate, but he didn't want to wait, he didn't even look at me; he stared at his shoes like a sulking and grumbling child, then he began to insult me in Serb. I gave myself the little pleasure of calling the guards and saying, 'Go, take the accused back to his cell! This man still takes himself for a president!'"[52] The arm wrestling had only begun. Seeking to block Milosevic from transforming the trial into a political tribunal, Del Ponte asks the court—in vain—to provide the accused with a defense attorney. Milosevic does not appreciate this request and demands that the judges "disqualify the prosecutor."

Milosevic's combative and defiant attitude pays off during the first weeks of the trial dedicated to Kosovo. Not that his theories on NATO's responsibility are the least bit confirmed, nor that he has in any way shaken the judges. But his capacity to intimidate weak witnesses, even to threaten them, by indirectly revealing the identity of "protected witnesses," amuses a part of the Serb population, which talks of "The Milosevic Show" in The Hague.

The logical conclusion, with perverse effects, is that Milosevic himself, defender of his own case, directs the cross-examination. The judges, trying to save time, have limited the number of prosecution witnesses and instructed the prosecutor to depose written testimony, in accordance with Article 92 *bis* of the Rules of Procedure. But the defense retains the right to cross-examine the witnesses, however they testify, so the conjunction of multiple written depositions and the fact that Milosevic is his own defense attorney produces a stupefying result: Modest, semiliterate Albanian peasants from Kosovo come to the tribunal thinking they will be able to recount how their family members have been killed or deported by Serb forces. But they are terribly wrong. Instead of being heard by the tribunal, the deputy prosecutor summarizes in three minutes their written testimony, after which they are delivered directly into Milosevic's hands for forty-five minutes of withering cross-examination. These poor, unfortunate people find themselves thrown before the man who is in their eyes the incarnation of evil, without having been able to make themselves heard beforehand.

Once more, the reversal of roles. The accused, Milosevic, momentarily becomes the prosecutor. Against these weak witnesses—disoriented at finding

SLOBODAN MILOSEVIC—The ultimate quarry. His fall, arrest, and transfer to The Hague electrified the world, but his flamboyant behavior during the interminable trial—nicknamed "The Milosevic Show" at home—diminished the impact of the first war crimes proceedings against a sitting president. (OSCE)

themselves confronted with the man who was for so long the master of the Balkans—Milosevic intimidates and even threatens. Whenever he can, he throws them off. An Albanian from Kosovo come to recount his expulsion by Serb forces is asked if he is not "the cousin of that trafficker intercepted at the Bulgarian border with 200 kg of drugs." Another witness, "K25," a former member of the special police, is thought to be a protected witness. Milosevic does everything to pierce K25's identity, affirming that he was "'a deputy police chief in a large town' in Serbia, that he had received a medal for displaying courage in the 'NATO aggression' and had been promoted from corporal, his rank in 1999, to lieutenant and then captain."[53] So much for the protection of witness identity. While a professional lawyer would have been harshly sanctioned or indicted for contempt of court, Milosevic is not even reprimanded by the judges.

Disoriented, not wanting to give any advantage to this accused-prosecutor, some witnesses refuse to acknowledge the presence of the UÇK in their villages in spite of the evidence. This reaction changes nothing regarding the reality of the massacres perpetrated, which Milosevic tries to put into "context" rather than simply deny. But before the tribunal of public opinion, particularly in Serbia, Milosevic wins points. Del Ponte can only deplore his success:

In the Rules of the Tribunal, Article 92(b) is without doubt the one that bothers me the most. Because of it, the victims cannot make themselves civilian parties. Their voice is missing from this trial. I respect the procedure, but it is bad. The judges impose on us a very tight schedule. This compression of time is unhealthy. We are constrained to depose written testimony to save time. They are valid evidence, but the defense has the right to cross-examine the witnesses. The fact that it is Milosevic himself who proceeds with the cross-examination is a new aggression for the victims.[54]

Milosevic has another attitude with those whom he considers his equals. He speaks on equal terms with the diplomats and superior officers of NATO who testify against him, an echo of times not so long ago when these men had to ask for an appointment to talk with him. Faced with a "client" so formidable, the judge-president, Richard May, appears slightly outclassed, so obsessed is he with directing a "fair trial" and leaving an appreciable margin of maneuver for Milosevic. This practice of giving so much initiative to the accused infuriates Zoran Djindjic, the head of the Serbian government. He calls this trial of the former Yugoslav president a "circus": "The Tribunal permits Milosevic to deploy his demagoguery and to direct the trial. . . . This circus puts me, as well as my government, in a difficult position," he declares, affirming that he refuses from now on to arrest Ratko Mladic and to transfer him to the ICTY. After "the Milosevic experience," so unsatisfying in his eyes, Djindjic has no desire to pay the political price for new arrests of still-powerful personalities.[55]

Far from the image of a solitary hero that he seeks to project, Milosevic is, in reality, anything but a man alone. To protect his rights, the judges have accorded him a college of three "friends of the court" (*amici curiae*) and two legal counselors who take turns following all the hearings.[56] Installed in the public chamber, one of them candidly confesses to "making dozens of telephone calls to Belgrade during the breaks," in order "to activate a very effective network," reports *Le Monde*. The Serb press confirms that the former president has the support of the secret services, the army, and the police in preparing his cross-examinations and for throwing off balance those who testify against him.[57]

Under such treatment, some witnesses finish by collapsing at the bar, like Hazbi Loku. He recounts how on March 18, 1999, he fished his brother's body out of a river, how he heard the cries of twenty-two young men thrown into two wells, into which Serb police then tossed explosives, while he watched from a wooded hill. Milosevic counterattacks. "Is it correct what I'm going to state right now: that fighting was taking place in that area, that the KLA was emptying villages, using empty houses as fortified positions, which necessarily led to the fact that they were shooting at the police from there, and this therefore made the Serb forces react to that? Is that correct? ... That it retook refugees as hostages?" demands Milosevic. "This has been made up. No villagers were kept hostage by anyone," responds Hazbi Loku, who refused against the evidence to admit the presence of the UÇK in the village.[58]

Confronted with Ibrahim Rugova, the Kosovar leader nicknamed "the Gandhi of the Balkans" for his pacifism, Milosevic ends his cross-examination with a veiled threat of retribution: "When you were threatened that you and your family, you fled to Italy. Have you thought about where you would be fleeing now once the occupation of Kosovo comes to an end?"[59]

Terrorized, the protected witness "K12," testifying on May 3 and 4, 2002, as a witness of the prosecution, leaves without saying a word. After taking the oath to "speak the whole truth and nothing but the truth" masked from the public by a screen, his image veiled on television, his name hidden behind an enigmatic code, K12 cracks out of the fear of reprisals. The judge's threat of criminal contempt actually reassures him: "If this is the only solution, throw me in prison, if you want it. I will be more secure there than free if I testify here."[60]

The difficulty for the prosecution is not to establish the veracity of the crimes in Kosovo, for it is not evidence that is lacking. Rather, it is to demonstrate that the chain of command leads to Milosevic. Because Belgrade refuses to transmit compromising evidence, the prosecution needs to produce "initiated" witnesses, meaning people who had belonged to the circles of power during the Milosevic era and who carry the evidence that he exercised his hierarchical responsibility over the executors of the crime. Geoffrey Nice, the chief deputy prosecutor, explains his difficulty to the judges: "Cases like this would be easy to prove in a short time if there was one member of the accused's inner circle who was able to give a fully accurate and acceptable testimony of everything that happened. Maybe the case could almost be proved by a single witness. Unfortunately, life isn't like that. As regards the witnesses, the closer they were to the accused, the more difficult they are to approach and to use."[61]

Geoffrey Nice certainly thinks he has a "big fish" in Radomir Markovic, former head of state security. At the beginning of his testimony, July 25, 2002, Markovic explains that Milosevic is responsible for the repression in Kosovo. The next day, confronted with his old master, who refers to him familiarly (calling him by his given name, evoking common memories, and treating him like unruly child), Markovic immediately retracts, as illustrated in the following scene:

JUDGE MAY: Yes, Mr. Milosevic.
(Cross-examined by Mr. Milosevic:)

M. MILOSEVIC [Interpretation]: Radomir, you read countless reports which, along a variety of lines, were submitted by members of the state security sector and which, through respective administrations, were all funneled to the central headquarters; is that correct?

M. MARKOVIC: Yes.

M. MILOSEVIC: Since heads of state security services of every country are usually the best-informed people in that country, and especially in view of all those reports, did you ever get any kind of report or have you ever heard of an order to forcibly expel Albanians from Kosovo?

M. MARKOVIC: No, I never heard of such an order, nor have I seen such an order, nor was it contained in the reports I received. Nobody, therefore, ever ordered for Albanians from Kosovo to be expelled.[62]

But Milosevic also confronts personalities who do not give in. Agron Berisha miraculously survived after Serb forces used machine guns and grenades to murder forty-four of his family members at Suva Reka. Some of these bodies are found in a mass grave in Serbia, not far from Belgrade. Agron Berisha recounts that he saw the Serb police kill two of his cousins, two of their sons, and their grandson. He saw the tanks that arrived and the houses that burned.

Witness "K32" was a driver in the Yugoslav army. He served during 1998 and 1999 in Kosovo and relates that his commander at the time, Colonel Bozidar Delic, ordered his soldiers "not to leave any survivors." He recounts that when the police and the army entered a village, they joined forces in carrying out the "cleansing operations," killing everyone, most often women and children.[63]

Milosevic tries to make this witness say that the cleansing operations are targeted against "the terrorists" and not against civilians. K32 replies, "The cleansing, Mr. Milosevic, happens when the army starts killing civilians. It was something that went without saying over there. When the army moved in, the soldiers were not looking to see who is a terrorist and who is not, but [cleansed] everybody in sight. I know, because I was there. You were not there. You should have come to see."[64]

In July, 2002, Captain Dragan Karleusa recounts how eighty-six bodies of Albanians had been sent by refrigerated truck to the Danube to be thrown in, before being secretly fished out and buried in a common grave in the compound of a police training post at Batanjica, near Belgrade. Put on the defensive, not wanting to contest the facts, Milosevic takes another tactic, accusing Captain Karleusa of working for the "lackey authorities" in Belgrade.[65]

Sometimes Slobodan Milosevic confronts personalities as strong as his own. In these cases, the confrontation turns clearly to his disadvantage. This occurs with the British politician Paddy Ashdown during two days of testimony, when he describes warning Milosevic that indiscriminate military operations could put him before the international court: "I told you in specific terms that if you went on acting in this fashion, the international community would have to act, and at the end they did have to act. And I warned you that you would end up in this court. And here you are!"[66]

> MILOSEVIC: [Y]ou knew your position, that you strove for the bombing of Yugoslavia. You advocated that; is that correct?
> ASHDOWN: Absolutely not, Mr. Milosevic, as you know well. I told you—
> MILOSEVIC: All right. You said no. You say no.
> ASHDOWN: My interview with you, Mr. Milosevic, was to warn you that if you continued, the intervention of NATO was inevitable. I sought to avoid that intervention. That was the purpose of our interview.[67]

To Milosevic's questioning the evidence of crimes furnished by Paddy Ashdown, the latter responds,

> ASHDOWN: Mr. Milosevic, the evidence that I present this Court is the evidence in toto. It is the evidence of your guns, your artillery, your tanks bombarding from a distance of ten kilometers indiscriminately villages, driving out the civilian population, burning their houses, looting them. That's the evidence in toto.
> MILOSEVIC: What you saw in those two days; is that it? [Ashdown made a brief trip in 1999 to Kosovo and Belgrade.]
> ASHDOWN: What I saw over the period that I've given evidence before this Court, the evidence that I warned you about, and the evidence which supports the position which I said to you, if you continued, you would make it impossible for the international community not to intervene.[68]

The First Lessons of the Milosevic Trial

On September 11, 2002, exactly one year after the terrorist attacks by al Qaeda that killed some three thousand people in the United States, the Western countries are absorbed with the anniversary of that event. The closure of the first part of the Milosevic trial, the Kosovo phase, is totally overshadowed by this omnipresent commemoration. At the same time both symbol and laboratory of international justice, after more than ninety-five hours of testimony, the trial ends in a feeling of ambivalence: The momentous historic encounter has not taken place. At least not yet.

The first phase of the trial sought to prove that Milosevic, as commander in chief, undoubtedly knew that his troops were committing atrocities in Kosovo. The prosecution has not found the "smoking gun." Neither the dozens of witnesses nor the supporting convictions have brought direct proof that the former strong man of Belgrade ordered the massacres or mass expulsions. Milosevic only rarely gave his orders in writing, and when he did, the documents had long been destroyed or were out of reach of the tribunal, remaining in safe hands in Yugoslavia. In contrast to the Nuremberg trials, where the prosecutor had all the written evidence at his disposal, the ICTY has recourse only to the testimony of the "initiated," the few people who had assisted Milosevic during those years. But as the trial amply demonstrated, many people are too frightened to testify. Even the protected witnesses fear for their security. The attitude of Zoran Lilic, Yugoslavia's president from 1993 to 1997, is symptomatic of the capacity for intimidation by the nationalists in Belgrade: The ICTY issued a subpoena to oblige him to appear, and the former president appeared before the judges at The Hague. Once there, however, he confined his remarks to explaining that he would remain silent about the bloody years in order to avoid being prosecuted at home: "Anyone in Yugoslavia can file a complaint against me. I could be accused of revealing state secrets and that is severely punishable. . . . I would not like my move to be understood as a contempt of court, but as an attempt to protect myself from any prosecution [in Yugoslavia]." [69]

Carla Del Ponte recognized these difficulties:

> We're not in a Hollywood movie, where the mystery is solved at the end of the film. We do not have the smoking gun, the one piece needed for conviction—even if it exists—that establishes the personal responsibility of Slobodan Milosevic for the crimes that we blame him for. We must thus patiently, minutely, demonstrate his responsibility. I have no doubt that we will achieve that. If I had access to the archives of the Yugoslav army, as I have asked, the case could be made much more quickly. The crimes in Kosovo, as in Croatia and in Bosnia, are attested and irrefutable. I determined that just as the curtain closes on Kosovo today, the prosecution made the link between the direct responsibility of Milosevic and the crimes that were committed. [70]

In fact, the extent of the crimes—deportations, murder, and the destruction of villages and cultural and religious monuments—and their systematic character support the prosecutor's thesis: that all these measures were planned, organized, and coordinated, even if the plan was put into execution only on the day the NATO campaign began. The overwhelming testimony of victims, of former soldiers, officers, and Serb leaders, as well as of the diplomats and experts, gives even more credence to the idea of a concerted plan to expel the Albanians. "If this does not resemble a prepared plan, then a horse does not resemble a horse," says Judith Armatta of the Coalition for International Justice.[71] The prosecutor and the majority of observers even believe the prosecution has demonstrated that Milosevic was not only aware of the atrocities but also that he had arranged their concealment. Assured of his impunity, he did not heed warnings, neither from Paddy Ashdown, nor from the German general Klaus Naumann nor from his American counterpart, Wesley Clark. To the point that Naumann and Clark were staggered to hear Milosevic say how he counted on reversing the demographic imbalance in Kosovo: "We'll do the same what [sic] we did in Drenica in '45 or '46. . . . We got them together and we shot them." These words were denied by the accused, but Naumann confirms them.[72]

Against such systematically established evidence, Milosevic's line of defense had, little by little, worn down over time. The addition of precise testimony detailing how the regular Yugoslav forces, operating under the direct command of Belgrade, had perpetuated and then sought to hide the atrocities is confounding: Milosevic can no longer totally deny the evidence. Put on the defensive, his weapon of last resort is to put these facts into "context," to compare them to the atrocities committed, according to him, by the "terrorists" of the UÇK and by NATO.

As for the Bosnian dossier, the evidence risks being far more overwhelming. Biljana Plavsic, the deputy of Radovan Karadzic between 1992 and 1995 and then president of the Bosnian Serbs (1996–98), has agreed to collaborate with the prosecutor in exchange for abandoning seven counts against her, among them the strongly symbolic charge of genocide. On October 2, 2002, addressing herself to the judges via video connection to Yugoslavia, Biljana Plavsic pleaded guilty to crimes against humanity, for having planned, instigated, or otherwise helped to prepare the persecution of Muslims and Croats in Bosnia in dozens of municipalities across Bosnia-Herzegovina. As for the issue of her personal recognition of culpability, her legal counsel, Eugene O'Sullivan, addressed the Hague: "I am here to make a brief statement on behalf of Mrs. Plavsic: by accepting responsibility and expressing her remorse fully and unconditionally, Mrs. Plavsic hopes to offer some consolation to the innocent victims—Muslim, Croat and Serb—of the war in Bosnia Herzegovina."[73] It is the first time that a member of the inner circle of "initiated" Serb leaders cooperates with the prosecution. Biljana Plavsic could furnish essential testimony since she had participated in all the important planning meetings of the Bosnian Serb leadership during the war. She justified ethnic cleansing at the time by saying "ethnic purification is an entirely natural phenomenon."[74]

In April, 1992, she had embraced the paramilitary leader Zeljko Raznotovic ("Arkan") in Bijelijna after his "Tigers" had taken control of the Bosnian town.[75] She was accused by Goran Jelisic, a Serb police officer, himself sentenced by the ICTY to forty years in prison for crimes against humanity and war crimes, of being one of the organizers of the crimes committed by Serb forces at Psavina and Semerija in the north and northeast of Bosnia.[76] Richard Dicker of Human Rights Watch states, "This is potentially an enormous breakthrough for the prosecution. [Plavsic] is uniquely positioned to provide potentially damaging evidence against senior indictees including Slobodan Milosevic."[77]

If the Milosevic trial is making progress, however, its failure as a media coup is incontestable. It is taking place, in effect, against an all but general indifference of the dailies and television networks. Did the three judges so worry of being accused of running a media circus? The fact is that they have gone overboard in the other direction. The hearings are often difficult to understand, technical and overly detailed, apparently to guarantee fairness. The trial is "too long, too slow, too confusing," notes *Le Monde*.[78] Moreover, the judges allow Milosevic to direct his cross-examinations as he likes, focusing on discrediting witnesses rather than questioning them on precise facts. In a general way, the court gives the impression of being disembodied. Neither the judges, nor the chief deputy prosecutor, seek—or want?—to elevate the debate to the level of historic political and legal stakes right now, to the point that the atrocities that created hundreds of thousands of victims during three wars have become, at the heart of the court at The Hague, a more and more distant abstraction.

This failure can be at least partly blamed on an international court cut off from the cultural and political reality in which these abominable crimes were committed.

Accused of everything and its opposite, staggered by the weight of trying innumerable crimes spread out over ten years, fearing being "influenced" by their environment, the judges have closed themselves off from all outside contact. Have the judges also psychologically cloistered themselves, to the point of losing sight of the fact that the very foundation of the international court is to be in step with the world? Thus, when, for once in agreement, the defense and prosecution allowed Biljana Plavsic, former president of the Bosnian Serbs, to plead guilty to crimes against humanity and then to explain her responsibility over three days, Judge Robinson wanted to limit her speaking to one and a half days, in order to save time! In short, the judges give the impression of being legal bureaucrats, determined to maintain the trial within strict legal lines, holding as tightly to this stake as Molière's miser holds his purse.

To their credit, the judges are under pressure from the U.N. Security Council, which does not want the trial to continue interminably. A marathon judiciary also risks harming the trials' image of fairness with an accused (Milosevic) formally handling his defense alone with hundreds of documents to read. His fragile health threatens constantly to slow the trial, even—who knows?—to put an end to it prematurely. According to his legal counsel, Dragoslav Ognjanovic, Milosevic "is exhausted by this very intensive trial."[79] On November 13, 2002, the judges order a psychiatric examination in order to determine if Milosevic suffers from "mental stress." A cardiologist must also determine if the accused is able to survive the trial under current conditions. This fear exasperates the prosecutor: "If the trial lasts three years or more, the judges are afraid that someone will say that the accused could not defend himself, because the charge was too heavy. Then let Milosevic get some lawyers. It is he who refuses to take his responsibilities. It is not for us to pay the consequences."[80] The prosecutor enumerates the statistics for the Kosovo dossier: It is Milosevic who monopolizes the speaking time of 159 hours (56 percent of the time), before the prosecution (110 hours, 38 percent) and 16 hours for the *amici*.[81]

In fact, Carla Del Ponte is not far from thinking that the judges' obsession with the clock itself endangers the trial's impartiality, to the benefit of the accused. "This time limit has consequences for our ability to prove certain facts," she says. "For example, the attacks on Sarajevo: I will need three to four weeks to establish incident by incident the responsibility of Milosevic, but the judges only give me ten hours, which is insufficient." The prosecutor even accuses the judges of abandoning the charge of genocide regarding the Croatian victims in Bosnia: "The judges simply did not leave us the time needed to present the evidence in our possession. To demonstrate a genocidal will in the case of the Croats in Bosnia, we would have to list all the municipalities where the massacres were perpetrated, but the judges asked us to select one example among them, to save time during the trial. The focus of this account is the *addition* of these crimes that proved the genocide, [but] we were no longer allowed to demonstrate this." But is it not shocking to abandon the charge of genocide, the gravest crime of all, to accelerate a trial that could last for years? "Ask the judges!" Del Ponte explains, before pushing on:

> I confess that I do not understand their decision. I put myself in the place of the victims. They were questioned by tribunal investigators. They were preparing themselves to testify and, believe me, it is not easy to testify. And then we tell them that, "For lack of time, the judges are not going to hear you." What are they going to think of this court? Their families were massacred and the tribunal destined to render justice does not even want to hear them? Even when the objective of this tribunal was to expose the crimes, to aid the victims, to soothe their sufferings and to encourage reconciliation?[82]

In spite of all these criticisms, the judges demonstrate that an international tribunal can render an equitable justice, something that was far from certain. On the other hand, the provisory outcome is, at least, mixed in terms of the exemplarity of the trial. Certainly, without the existence of the ICTY, one can reasonably bet that Radovan Karadzic would have remained for a long time the head of the Republika Srpska and that Slobodan Milosevic would perhaps have continued to lead Serbia, or that he would have achieved his transformation into the respected opposition, once again received by the entire world. But has the Milosevic trial returned dignity to the victims? Has it changed how the societies of the former Yugoslavia see the crimes that were perpetrated? Has it deterred other potential "ethnic purifiers"? These questions are, for now, difficult to answer. If some victims who testified before the ICTY have been handled roughly during the hearings, the fact that Milosevic is behind bars may still be an immense comfort for the great majority among them. The fact that the former president is incarcerated has also made it possible for Serb society to evolve.

It goes without saying that it is premature to ask about the pedagogical virtue of this trial. We are still too close to it, and only when the Milosevic trial is finally over will it take its sense as a whole. At the time of the Nuremberg tribunals, the German population was completely deaf to them. However, one or two generations later, who would question the capital importance that the work of those allied military tribunals, in spite of their weaknesses, had for the reconstruction of Germany, of Europe, and even beyond?

C h a p t e r **Nine**

"To be without being a murderer."
—Emmanuel Levinas, *Difficult Freedom: Essays on Judaism*

A Court Standing above It All

66"My grandson is three years old. If the murderers of twelve members of our family are not punished as they ought to be, it will be up to him, when he is twenty, to kill them. Justice will thus be done." Sakib Ahmic speaks steadily. His voice only breaks when he looks at the photographs of his other grandson, Elvis, about six years old when he was murdered. It is to recount this tragedy that, in the spring of 1999, Sakib Ahmic is before the International Criminal Tribunal for the Former Yugoslavia at The Hague. He speaks of that night of December 14, 1992, when his Croat neighbors, former friends turned extremists, killed his loved ones in the village of Ahmici. Hasan Nuhanovic lost his parents and his brother at Srebrenica. Lucidly, he wonders aloud if he will instill "hatred" of Serbs in his baby daughter. Sinisa, twenty, lost his father, Cedomir Avramovic, a Serb killed in the camp at Čelebici by the Bosnian army, eight hundred meters from his home. Sinisa dreams of a "de-nazification of all of Bosnia, like in Germany" so that, "in twenty years, the same cycle of hatred and violence will not perpetuate itself." [1] Justice? Everyone thinks about it. They know that their lives, like the future of Bosnia, are indissolubly linked to the crimes committed during this war that, between 1992 and 1995, left some 200,000 people dead.

The role of the ICTY, bearer of the "official discourse of the truth," has been from the beginning a central stake for all the local protagonists of the war. But around this stake a strange dialectic has been put in place. Despite the distance between the scene of the crime and the location of the tribunal, installed more than a thousand kilometers from the former Yugoslavia, the international

176

court has made punishment possible. Yet, by its remove, it has become an obstacle to the work of integration and memory for the concerned populations. Distance is simultaneously the tribunal's force and its weakness: It reconstitutes legal conditions missing in the former Yugoslavia but, at the same time, loses its resonance in the cultural setting where the atrocities were committed by dispossessing the successor countries of the former Yugoslavia of the capacity to judge.[2]

The "minorities" of the former Yugoslavia, tormented by persecution, can expect nothing from a local court. When the Serbian authorities considered judging Milosevic in Belgrade, it was only for financial wrongdoing and corruption. Despite the fact that the ICTY is the product of an international community that abandoned them, this supranational court remains the sole refuge against the criminals. The ICTY is essential to the victims; its failure would signify "the burying of all hope for justice for a long time for all those who did not have a sole and absolute national orientation," says Zarko Puhovski, a professor of philosophy in Zagreb.[3] Despite its distance, this public exposure of crimes "suffices as public acknowledgement of what happened. Without such acknowledgement, survivors feel invisible, erased, forgotten. . . . The legitimized, distant words of law open a door to remembrance for some, providing words with which to talk about personal suffering. The naming may help survivors redefine themselves 'as a collective self engaged in common struggle.'"[4] They are no longer shadows, and they have regained a part of their dignity as men. Sakib Ahmic looks at some photographs of his grandson, Elvis, killed at Ahmici, and, lost in thought, then says, "In testifying before the ICTY, I had a good feeling. I told the truth. Exactly what happened, so that the entire world would know."[5]

In a larger way, the work of the ICTY is essential for all those who have no place in the nationalism of the former Yugoslavia, be they Serbs, Croats, Bosnians, or Albanians from Kosovo. In fingering the crimes committed by all the belligerents, including those by members of their own camp, the tribunal provides an account in which those indicted by the ICTY no longer appear as invulnerable heroes but as criminals in flight. This account of the facts, an alternative to the ideology dominant in the Serbia of Milosevic and the Croatia of Tudjman, offers an antidote to exacerbated nationalism. Julia Bokeva, covering the ICTY trial for the Beta Agency of Belgrade, affirms, "The crimes committed in the former Yugoslavia have destroyed our past, destroyed our present, and will destroy the future of generations to come. Only the truth will allow our society to heal. It is a grave illusion to believe that democracy and the market economy can exist without truth. Because they only function on a factual basis, and if the denial and the lies perpetuate themselves, they will resolve nothing and the problems will continue to arise. How will we live in a democracy if the former heads of the militia continue to be living legends?"[6]

The authorities of the Republika Srpska and Yugoslavia, and, to a lesser degree, of Croatia, very quickly understand the danger the ICTY represents to them as a subversive force of speech beyond their control, breaking free of "ethnic" logic. In a very concrete way, the tribunal questions the ideological base that has served to justify the war. As Zarko Puhovski notes, the war's legitimacy is built on the fallacious idea of avenging "the just cause." " 'They are all guilty' is the slogan in the name of which we persecuted and murdered in the occupied regions of Croatia and Bosnia-Herzegovina," he says.[7] Fed by hate propaganda, each "ethnic" group gave to every other the mask of the executioner, making each member carry the collective guilt of his ethnic origin. By putting a "mask" on the Other, they could take vengeance on the "Turks" (Muslims) or the *ustashas* (Croats) or the *chetniks* (Serbs). Closed off in the airless logic of nationalism, the belligerents largely saw themselves as victims or as "correctors" of ancient crimes left unpunished.

Now, by the aridity of its procedures, by the administration of concrete proof that one can neither refute nor reinterpret, by the individualization of the crimes, the work of the tribunal undermines that propaganda, instills doubt in the executors of ethnic cleansing of their leaders' ability to protect them from penal pursuit. "Facts have always been the greatest challenge for nationalist regimes: they create an obligation to think," says Julia Bokeva.[8] It is this incitement to think that Slobodan Milosevic and, to a lesser degree, Franjo Tudjman dread. The testimonies and the confessions about precise events and circumstances have undermined their methods and thrown a shadow on the cause that the nationalists claimed to defend. Testimony about collective rapes of Muslims at Foca, about murders of Serb civilians at Celebici and of Croat victims in Bosnian Serb camps raises questions: Why this bloodbath? Who committed these atrocities? Who organized and planned them? How far does the responsibility go? Who witnessed these crimes? What was his behavior? The societies where the crimes were committed will have to answer these questions.

It is because the tribunal threatens the nationalist regimes that it is a victim of attempts at sabotage and manipulation. The nationalist regimes seek to demonize it, to reduce it to one more example of American hegemony. "The thesis advanced and intelligently disseminated by Milosevic was to convince the Serb people that the ICTY was a monstrous creature that aimed to make all Serbs guilty for crimes they had not committed," Julia Bokeva says. "The government created the image of a collective culpability, while the entire work of the ICTY was precisely the opposite. Criminal law blames the individual, not groups. There is no such thing as collective guilt. But once again Milosevic knew how to use the Serb people as a shield."[9]

During his trial, Milosevic continues to follow this line of defense, although it has shown its limitations. The fact that soldiers and Serbian officers have testified against Milosevic, the fact also that Biljana Plavsic, a member of the tripartite presidency of the Republika Srpska during the war, is now pleading guilty, has shattered the idea of collective guilt. After having passionately defended Greater Serbia, Plavsic now admits to participating in "the persecution of the Muslims and Croats of Bosnia" in thirty-seven municipalities of the country, notably in the "killings" and "forced removals" carried out by the "Bosnian Serb forces and their political and governmental organs."[10] The fact that the Albanians of Kosovo will soon be indicted by the ICTY for having committed crimes against Serb civilians will help defuse attempts to demonize the tribunal.

Certainly, much will depend on the attitude of the Serb authorities. Although they have taken the risk of turning Milosevic over to The Hague, they remain profoundly reluctant to cooperate with the tribunal, whether because they support him or because they are intimidated by the Serbian secret service and the part of the political class and the army that have much to lose. The nationalists remain powerful.[11] Milan Milutinovic, although indicted with Slobodan Milosevic on May 22, 1999, remains acting president of Serbia as of December, 2002, more than a decade after the war started. And Zoran Djindjic declares that, given the capacity for trouble from the Red Berets (a secret police unit known for its crimes in Bosnia and Kosovo), he has no intention of turning any of their members over to the ICTY. "The majority of them are wanted by The Hague. I know definitely in some cases, because I have checked," Djindjic says. "Personally, I would rather leave politics and withdraw into private life than extradite them to The Hague."[12]

Faced with the lack of any real cooperation from Belgrade, Carla Del Ponte lays out the situation for the U.N. Security Council on October 30, 2002:

> Needless to say . . . sensitive information, archives and military sources of evidence remain beyond the reach of justice. Indeed, the [Federal Republic of Yugoslavia] does not show the slightest inclination to comply with any requests relating to the Yugoslav army. You will undoubtedly have heard and continue to hear the strongest assurances that Ratko Mladic is not in the FRY. While constantly denying that Mladic is in Serbia, the authorities have always conceded, in private meetings, that he had been in Serbia, "until recently." In July, authorities in Belgrade admitted he had been there in June, but was no longer in Serbia. In June, they admitted that, yes, he had been spotted in April,

but was now in Republika Srpska. We have had enough of this, and at my request [court] President [Claude] Jorda has now formally seized the Council of the failure of the FRY to meet its obligations under the Tribunal's Statute.[13]

In Croatia, the attack on the tribunal is done differently. A part of the media denounces the fact that the ICTY, by not preoccupying itself with whether the war was just or not, put the aggressors and the victims in the same bag and could thus not claim to render justice.[14] But since Stjepan Mesic's ascension to power, Zagreb has cooperated much more easily with the ICTY. On September 25, 2002, during a televised speech, President Mesic confirms Croatia's commitment to maintaining "complete cooperation, in all cases and at any time" with the tribunal.[15] Points of friction, however, remain, notably the arrest of the former Croatian army chief of staff, Janko Bobetko, accused on September 17, 2002, of crimes against humanity for the deaths of one hundred Serbs, including twenty-nine civilians, killed between September 9 and September 16, 1993, during the taking of Medak by Croatian forces. Zagreb wages a guerrilla legal war to avoid the transfer to and judgment of Bobetko at The Hague, to the fury of Carla Del Ponte, who explains the situation to the Security Council: "In May 2002, I provided the Croatian authorities with advance notice of an imminent indictment against General Bobetko, former Chief of Staff of the Croatian Army. . . . Instead of compliance with the Tribunal's order, the Croatian Government has taken upon itself to seek to challenge the warrant and the indictment itself. We next heard that the General's health does not permit his travel to The Hague. More delay and obstruction. The attitude of Croatia is unacceptable." [16]

But the Bosnians, the principal victims of the conflict, actively support the work of the ICTY to cement their identity as victims and to signify to the world the weight of the suffering they endured. Indeed, the authorities in Sarajevo are the first to hand over voluntarily citizens indicted by the international court. This goodwill sometimes even leads to bad faith. In the Dusko Tadic trial, the Bosnian government prepares a false witness, "L," to "accuse" the indicted. This trickery is discovered through the string of contradictions in "L's" deposition.

On September 12, 2001, the prosecutor indicts General Sefer Halilovic, commander of Bosnian forces during the war, for "responsibility by omission" in the war crimes committed by his subordinates in September, 1993, in two central Bosnian villages, Grabovica and Uzdol, where sixty-one Croatian civilians were executed.[17] Sefer Halilovic, who led Operation "Neretva-93," is accused by the ICTY of having done nothing to stop these crimes, nor of having taken any measures to identify and punish the perpetrators. Now minister of social affairs and refugees, Halilovic voluntarily surrenders to The Hague the same month as the indictment, announcing that he will plead "not guilty." Sarajevo's attitude to the ICTY is not changed by this indictment. The government of the Croatian-Muslim federation reaffirms its support of the ICTY: "The decision of Sefer Halilovic to surrender voluntarily to The Hague constitutes 'a sign of confidence and respect' for the tribunal."[18]

Other problems persist with the tribunal. In the Milan Simic trial, a Bosnian Serb lawyer uses death threats to force an opposing witness to go back on his deposition, making him rehearse the "new version" with the aid of a tape recorder. In December, 1999, SFOR soldiers raid a site in Mostar where the Croat secret service is spying on thirty ICTY investigators who are conducting research on war crimes at Livno, using electronic devices to monitor radio signals and telephone conversations. Each year, the Dutch authorities express concern about attempts by Bosnian, Croat, and Serb spies to infiltrate the tribunal. In this war of influence, one of the most absurd episodes is when Serbia protests the translation of ICTY documents on the grounds that they are being translated into Croat and not Serb, although, despite some regional variations, they are the same language. The ICTY decides to suspend temporarily the Serbo-Croat translations.

The court, caught in a political-legal arm-wrestling match, struggles to secure its victory—the stigmatization of crimes. At stake for the nationalists is their continuing domination of hearts and minds in Bosnia. And, for the moment, they appear to have achieved this objective. The fact is that no matter who committed the atrocities—whether Serb, Croat, Bosnian, or Albanian— denial of the crimes, repression, embarrassment, fear (both of testifying and of reprisals), and, for some, guilt all remain wrapped in heavy silence. It is a collective *omerta* that is only now beginning to crack. For years, a law of silence as heavy as a lead blanket has closed mouths and minds across Yugoslavia. At Prijedor, a city whose Muslims have been chased away and where now flies the flag of the Republika Srpska, Muharem Murselovic, a Muslim, sighs, "I have never heard the first word of remorse from a Serb, even from those who didn't do anything. . . . I was at Omarska for 73 days, from May 30 to August 6, 1992. My best friends all died there." Prijedor is the city with the highest number of citizens indicted for war crimes and crimes against humanity. It is in this town hall that the region's ethnic cleansing was conceived and planned. The native Muslims of the city, who no longer live there, participated in the local elections. They elected Murselovic vice mayor in 1999. The Serbs accept this official with difficulty. "Every day, I cross paths with people who arrested, interrogated, and detained me. Some still work for the police, others have gone back to their former professions, others have emigrated. There is even one,

Ratko, who works at the city hall as an engineer. When I bring up the subject, he does what everybody else here does: He buries his head in the sand. How can we construct a democratic society with such deniers?" Murselovic wonders after his election. "When 450 bodies of the victims of Omarska and Trnopolje were exhumed from common graves for reburial in 1999, not one Serb official was present. There was not one word in the local media. It is as if all these people who were murdered had never existed." [19] There is no acknowledgment of the crimes and thus no responsibility and no guilt. It is the reasoning of Dusko Tadic during his trial at The Hague: "I do not think that anybody is guilty." [20]

If the very essence of justice is the stigmatization of crimes, Srebrenica is the most symbolic case of the ICTY's difficulty in getting its message across. Four years, day for day, after the beginning of the crimes, the truth of the facts still has difficulty imposing itself. According to a sixty-year-old man, "Nothing happened here in July 1995. . . . I never heard of any massacres of Muslims. On January 7, 1993, around the Orthodox Christmas, Serb civilians were murdered by Bosnian soldiers. In 1995, I was absent two months. No, a year, I no longer remember, I know nothing." [21] Visibly ill at ease, the man returns to sawing wood. His house faces the vast warehouse of Kravica, a few kilometers from Srebrenica. According to the ICTY, it was in this building, today blackened and partially destroyed, that "Bosnian Serb soldiers under the command of Radislav Krstic [the right hand of General Mladic] summarily executed hundreds of Muslim men. . . . They used automatic weapons, hand grenades and other weapons to kill the Bosnian Muslims inside the warehouse," the Krstic indictment reads. [22] At the former U.N. base in Potocari, in an old workshop for assembling batteries, three workers eat their snacks. For them, as for the immense Serb majority at Srebrenica, nothing happened here: "Propaganda, all of it." [23] The majority of the Bosnian Serbs who live in Srebrenica believe that the whole world is in league against them, and so they disqualify this foreign court. The vice mayor, Dragan Yevtic, of Serb origin, concedes that if any crimes occurred here, "it was no doubt the paramilitaries that committed them. . . . Anyway," he adds, "their extent has been exaggerated." As for Radislav Krstic, "He's a good general," Yevtic says. [24]

The ICTY will later sentence Krstic to forty-six years in prison for the crime of genocide—for having "planned, incited to commit, [and] ordered the mass execution, in the course of which perished some thousands of Bosnian Muslim men captured in the Safe Area of Srebrenica." [25] As if to add to this denial, the Muslims deported from Srebrenica have seen few concrete effects from this international court. Certainly, General Krstic and a young death squad member, Drazen Erdemovic, have been convicted at The Hague, but the most responsible, Mladic and Karadzic, remain free men. The survivors cannot even return to their own homes. As Julie Mertus puts it, "There is no bill of indictment for the destruction of souls, the privation of childhood, the breaking of dreams, nor is there a bill of indictment for having been forced to watch, impotent, the suffering inflicted on a loved one—which according to the survivors is the worst pain one can inflict."[26] Sulejma Pezer lost nineteen members of his family at Ahmici, including his parents, aged ninety and eighty-five, a mentally handicapped brother, his cousins. He wrote, he says, "a poem for his parents": "My soul is prisoner in the ice and nothing will ever be able to warm it."[27] The court, obviously, cannot respond to such pain.

Even at The Hague, one perceives that the victims often remain unsatisfied with the pronounced sentences. ICTY spokesman Christian Chartier takes a cold view of this gap: "We have a problem of marketing. Most often, the people who lost their loved ones think that only the death penalty is adequate punishment for war criminals. We know that the most serious punishment we can dispose of—life in prison—is in any case going to disappoint them. They want to see their own conception of justice at work, and we can only offer them our interpretation of law."[28] In the village of Vosica, sixty kilometers from Tuzla in central Bosnia, live three thousand women and children originally from Srebrenica. For them, often but not always, the death penalty is considered the only adequate punishment. Many are shocked by the "leniency" of the ICTY that condemns Erdemovic to five years in prison. They have done the arithmetic; Erdemovic will spend twenty-five days in prison for each person he killed. "It is possible to live again with the Serbs, but all the criminals must pay first. They must be tortured as they tortured our husbands and children, and this, I would like to see with my own eyes," says Harrija, who is in her thirties. "All the criminals must at least be punished. It is not a question of numbers. From the smallest to the greatest. It is a question of justice," adds Develeta Omerovic, thirty-five years old. She lost her father, her brother, and her cousins in July, 1995.[29]

Hasan Nuhanovic knows only too well the limits of the action of the international court. This former translator for UNPROFOR at Srebrenica went in the spring of 1999 to The Hague to meet the assistant prosecutor of the ICTY. He left there vexed: "The problem at the base is that the International Tribunal wants to judge only the four or five political and military figures responsible for Srebrenica. But there are many hundreds of murderers who are free. It is not realistic to expect that they will be judged here. And they are the ones blocking any democratic process. It is necessary to indict them, otherwise the return of the refugees will be impossible. How can you expect me to return if I know that my neighbor killed my father, my mother and my brother?"[30]

The frustration and the deception of the victims feed on other causes the ICTY can do nothing about. The court cannot remedy the failure of politics. It cannot exist without some notion of common good. As long as there is not even a minimal consensus between the former belligerents, justice can have little effect at the heart of society. And even when, under intense pressure, this consensus is reached, it remains difficult to apply. The question of the war's twenty thousand missing persons demonstrates that. These bodies, anonymously buried, by their very silence perpetuate the memory of the crimes and deepen the sadness of their families. Under immense pressure from these families, the respective authorities have implemented an agreement to exhume the bodies from common graves: "Sometimes, it's enough to find a single bone to soothe the families. They can then begin their work of mourning," notes Milan Bogdanic, a member of the Bosnian-Serb missing persons delegation.[31] But, out of fear of being pursued by the ICTY, those who are in possession of information about the common graves—soldiers, former members of the militia, and police officers—sometimes prefer to conceal them. As Zeljko Karan, a forensic scientist for the Republika Srpska, puts it, "They are afraid of being themselves accused of crimes and pursued by the Tribunal."[32]

Bosnia-Herzegovina pays the price of ambiguity born of the Dayton Accords. For now, Bosnia-Herzegovina is an unhealthy institutional no-man's-land; the nature of this state, multiethnic or not, has not been made clear. The war has stopped, but the roots of the conflict live on. In this unresolved context, the ICTY has become, against its will, a factor of tension, while the exhumations are in themselves sources of appeasement.

In this vacuum in which Bosnia exists, the current paralysis can only encourage the lassitude of international donors and the despair of the young, who are prisoners without a future. At Kozarac, one kilometer from the Trnopolje camp where the majority of the Muslims were imprisoned, the divided communities are on alert. Mladen Tadic, brother of Dusko, runs a bistro called the Senzei. He is one of the rare Serbs of Kozarac to affirm openly, "The camps at Omarska, at Trnopolje, at Manjaca are the shame of our people." He points to a man. "That one, he got rid of the Muslims' bodies. There is no will to punish the criminals," he regrets. But he also fears the mounting violence: "The young Muslims threaten us. I fear that their thirst for vengeance, alcohol and unemployment will render them uncontrollable and dangerous."[33]

At Celebici, where some dozens of Serb civilians were murdered by Bosnians, Sinisa Avramovic dreams of breaking the cycle of violence. A computer science student in Stuttgart, he notes, "The young Germans are again proud of their Fatherland, because they have assumed not only the glory, but also the dark past of their country."[34] Deprived of the possibility of envisioning a future and living in an uncertain present, Bosnia has to this day never benefited from a framework that would allow the construction of a national identity. As a result, the impact of justice can only be marginal in a country with such vague foundations.

Faced with this dereliction, the disappointment and frustration of some victims lead them to accuse the creators of the ICTY, Boutros Boutros-Ghali and Kofi Annan, of being accomplices in crimes against humanity for not having carried out their responsibilities to protect them. On February 4, 2000, an association calling itself Mothers of Srebrenica and Podrinje lodges a criminal complaint at the ICTY against fifteen U.N. officials, diplomats, and mediators for "the role they played in the fall [of these towns] and the genocidal massacre" on July 15 at these two sites.[35] Figuring notably on their list are the former secretary-general of the United Nations, Boutros Boutros-Ghali; the current secretary-general, Kofi Annan, then special envoy of the United Nations in Bosnia; the commander of UNPROFOR, General Bernard Janvier; Lieutenant Colonel Thomas Karremans; and European negotiators Thorvald Stoltenberg, Carl Bildt, and David Owen. The lawyer for Mothers of Srebrenica and Podrinje, Francis Boyle, specifies, "We are here at The Hague to say that these men, these officials of the United Nations, may have committed no crime, but that without their decisions [the massacre] of Srebrenica would never have occurred."[36] Graham Blewitt rejected the accusation for the ICTY, explaining that "a little common sense must be exercised here: to suggest that the United Nations, in its role as peacekeeper in Bosnia, behaved in any way similar to a criminal is absurd."[37]

Some signs of hope exist, however. The choice of a new Croat president, Stjepan Mesic, in January, 2000, and the municipal elections in Sarajevo in April, 2000, demonstrate the retreat of the nationalists. Until then, the ICTY could see that its work of "stigmatizing the criminals" was being destroyed by the policy of President Franjo Tudjman. The fact that Zlatko Aleksovski, after two and a half years in prison, received a hero's welcome home in Zagreb demonstrates the limits of the ICTY's action. "When a war criminal has served his punishment at The Hague and returns to his own country as a hero, how do you expect our job to mean anything?" the tribunal members say.[38] President Mesic himself incarnates the evolution of his country. He was a (badly) protected witness at the tribunal, and contrary to the immense majority of witnesses of the ICTY he testified against one of his fellow citizens, General Tihomir Blaskic, for atrocities committed in central Bosnia in 1993.

Without the consent of the local political figures who control most of the Balkan media, however, the tribunal's message simply cannot get to its destination. On the contrary, it is particularly striking how Belgrade is preparing public opinion in May and June, 2001, for the transfer of Milosevic to The Hague, showing for the first time proof of crimes committed by Serbian forces. Yugoslavs are receptive, but this policy of communication is of short duration. The stakes are high: a regional time bomb. Jacob Finci, president of the Jewish community in Sarajevo, warns, "We are engaged in a race against time. There is no future for Bosnia-Herzegovina without reconciliation. And, contrary to the Americans and the Japanese, we do not have fifty years in which to build a peace worthy of this name."[39]

The Responsibility of the ICTY

Despite the propaganda and maneuvers to sabotage its work, the ICTY also carries a part of the responsibility for its failure to stigmatize crimes. Withdrawn into itself, the tribunal of The Hague has never really set up a communications strategy. Closed inside their legal world, their hopes turned toward the institution of an international criminal court for which the ICTY is only a laboratory, the judges have never put an emphasis on transmitting their message to the peoples of the former Yugoslavia. Paul Stuebner notes,

> In 1995, we received some requests from Sarajevo, from Banja Luka, from Belgrade, from the different faculties of law in the former Yugoslavia. They asked us to give them courses on the tribunal, to explain its statutes and functioning, but the prosecutor was never interested. A lot of material was never even translated into local languages. When the Tadic judgment was finally translated two and a half years after the verdict, it was already at the point of being obsolete, since the Chamber of Appeal was also in the process of making its ruling. There was an inexplicable lack of interest in getting our message across.[40]

This absence of will to explain the ICTY's work to the people most concerned by it is one of the most important failures of the tribunal at The Hague. It can be taken as a sign, perhaps, that the tribunal's essential audience was primarily in the West rather than in Bosnia.

Given the lack of resources during its establishment phase, the International Criminal Tribunal for the Former Yugoslavia did have some excuses. "For a long time, the question of stigmatization did not preoccupy us," one judge admits. "We had other, more vital priorities. This tribunal, was it truly going to exist? Was it really going to judge war criminals?"[41] But later, as it became operational, the ICTY would commit several errors that would limit its efficacy and ensure that its work would meet all but total indifference.

The ICTY rapidly showed its pedagogical limits. Crushed by the lead weight of a strict legal system borrowed from the American model, its procedures were complex, too long, and almost incomprehensible. It was not intentional; it was simply the fruit of the judges' will to create an irreproachable legal system by synthesizing two great juridical traditions—common law and continental law. Caught in their own logic as lawyers, they did not weigh the heaviness of the procedures created. The result: From appeal to appeal, the Tadic case lasts five years; that of General Blaskic, two years with periods of interruption that give the ICTY a sense of judicial self-absorption. It goes on and on. If it goes to the end, the Milosevic trial will last four years. "It is a system of justice as annoying and interminable as the Tour de France," complains Jacob Finci. The functionaries of the international court have lost sight of what the judges of the Jerusalem tribunal, charged with judging Adolf Eichmann, understood perfectly from the start. During their first deliberation, one month before the start of Eichmann's trial, those judges noted, "'Where there is no publicity, there is no justice. . . . Publicity is the soul of justice.'"[42] On this point, the ICTY is not very effective, despite the judges' acceptance of filming inside the hearing rooms. Other than a handful of exceptions, no media in the world can afford the luxury of following the trial at The Hague. Generally, they only cover the first few days of the hearings and the sentencing. But at the beginning, the media were more than receptive, even to the point of overkill. For the Tadic trial, the twenty-four-hour legal news network, Court TV, had placarded New York City buses with aggressive advertisements ("The first war crimes trial since Nuremberg"), hawked some merchandise, and opened a website. Some associations wanted to rebroadcast the trial live to the Balkans. But boredom rapidly triumphs. Even the Milosevic trial, after the first few days, does not capture the media. Court TV broadcasts rare excerpts of the trial during its first year. With the exception of the weekly twenty-minute program by Balkan journalist Mirko Klarin for the various media in Yugoslavia, there is no televised follow-up of the ICTY's work.

This boredom and disinterest are, in part, the heritage of the Goldstone era, when, according to Judge Jorda, the tribunal carried out an erratic policy of indictments, "[s]ince it could just as well pursue Hitler as [it could] the conductor of the locomotive that rolled to Auschwitz."[43] At the time, the ICTY faced an impossible mission; although deprived of resources, it had to be seen in action in order to exist in the eyes of the world and to satisfy its bosses in the Security Council. Hence, the multiplication of indictments of "small fry." This agitation, which responded to a political necessity, was without real consequence until the day the arrests and voluntary surrenders began.

In addition to interminable procedures, the three criminal chambers continue to accumulate delays. The most worrying: Under this avalanche of indictments of secondary personalities, the effect of exemplarity of punishment is, in part, lost. "We are not here to 'fill quotas'!" Judge Jorda exclaims. He adds, "We must take this bull by the horns. Our prison is full, notably of the 'second guns' indicted during the initial period of the tribunal, while we ought to be concentrating on the higher echelons."[44] At the ICTY, the question is how to get the message across: "The problem is the following. How to reduce the number of indictments of the 'small fry' without hurting the image of the tribunal that is beginning to improve? How to sell that to the witnesses and to the victims? No, thank you, Madame, your testimony is useless and your executioner will not be pursued? . . . All the more in that the tribunal has always said that justice brings some relief to the victims, by the recognition of their suffering. With the question at the base: so, if we are not here to tend the wounds, what are we here for?" says Christian Chartier.[45] Louise Arbour may well cancel a third of the indictments, but that would not change things much.[46] This strategy of rough-draft indictment, added to the weight of the procedures, has the effect not only of "threatening to paralyze" the tribunal but, worse, of blurring the perception of its work from the outside.[47]

The judges' trial-and-error process in setting penalties does not help either. Initially sentenced to ten years in prison, Drazen Erdemovic sees his sentence reduced by half on appeal, because the judges decide that he "is reformable and must have the possibility of restarting his life while he is still young, after having purged his penalty."[48] Zlatko Aleksovski, accused of "inhuman treatment" toward many hundreds of Muslim detainees near Mostar, is first condemned to two and a half years of detention before the court of appeal, on March 24, 2000, changes the sentence to seven years, on the grounds that "Trial Chamber erred in not having sufficient regard to the gravity of the conduct of the Appellant. His offences were not trivial. . . . [H]is superior responsibility as a warden seriously aggravated the Appellant's offences. Instead of preventing it, he involved himself in violence against those whom he should have been protecting."[49] This considerable variation in the scale of punishment underlines the innovative character of the international court, where precedents were lacking. But it did not contribute to improving the legitimacy of the tribunal's action.

To these difficulties is added the inability of the ICTY to transmit its message to the former Yugoslavia. The obstacles put in place by the local actors have already been mentioned. But there is also a cultural dimension to the political problems. Not only the judges but also a substantial number of ICTY personnel are lacking in knowledge about the former Yugoslavia. This situation was abysmal in 1993, even if today the ICTY has created some of the best military experts on the Balkans. This conglomeration of factors probably explains why the ICTY only belatedly invested in communicating its message in Yugoslavia. The tribunal was, in effect, turned almost naturally toward the Western audience, which was also its principal funding source, its political support, and its cultural origin. It is one of the perverse effects of this international court. Belatedly, certain judges did travel to Sarajevo for a few days. Others practically never set foot in the Balkans. Louise Arbour notes, "The judges had one incurable fault. They did not know Bosnia, except for two or three days outside a plenary session. There was something at the level of emotive engagement that was missing; they had no human contact with this reality, and that is something that cannot be found among the papers in a file." She recognizes that "[i]f there was one thing to redo, and if we were sure of the tribunal's growth, I would have had my staff learn Serbo-Croatian, so that they could better understand the documents, so that the people would no longer be such strangers. It is very frustrating to work in a language that you do not master. There is something of the culture, of the history, of the emotion that is necessary to us."[50]

At the same time, the tribunal has no permanent presence in Bosnia, which was understandable as long as the war continued but which is less so after the Dayton Accords, when the tribunal has still not named a spokesperson in the Balkans. In the summer of 1999, a foreign journalist in Sarajevo desiring to know more about the work of the ICTY was ejected politely from tribunal offices in the barracks of Lukavica. What then can be said for the civilian populations, which are even less informed except by media that are mostly controlled by interested parties across Bosnia-Herzegovina?

Essentially, the question of exemplarity of punishment preoccupies the judges and the prosecutor of the ICTY only in an abstract and legalistic manner. By nature, the judges little desire throwing themselves into a "spectacle of justice," of which Minister of Defense Alain Richard of France has nevertheless accused them. However, the judges did not totally ignore the question of the tribunal's deep-rooted culture when they were writing the ICTY's rules. Article 4 foresaw in effect the possibility of relocating the tribunal to the former Yugoslavia to read an indictment or pronounce a judgment. Such a move would have been a strong symbol: the tribunal anchored finally on the land of the former Yugoslavia to address the affected populations and to take them directly as witnesses. One may dream of the impact that such a process could have had in the ultranationalist fiefdoms of Foca or Prijedor. One can imagine the reach of an international court rendering justice, in turn, at Sarajevo, Mostar, and Banja Luka, and which, deeply rooted in the local soil, would have a profound impact on the work of international justice.

In fact, two attempts at this change of venue were sketched out, even if they were hardly made public. In the spring of 1996, the idea burst forth to conduct another Rule 61 hearing in the village of Tuzla, but SFOR opposed it there for "reasons of security." In the autumn of 1998, the second Trial Chamber considered sending the judges to central Bosnia, in Ahmici, a steep and spread-out village, to better understand the unfolding of a massacre there of a hundred Muslim civilians by Croats. But again SFOR refused to guarantee the judges' safety. Louise Arbour had herself expressed reservations, fearing the spectacle of a court under siege: "Already, at The Hague, we meet behind bullet-proof screens. Over there, we would have no doubt needed tanks for protection, because the political authority of the territory where we would have found ourselves would have exaggerated our security needs to demonstrate the bad faith of its former enemies. This is not the best image of justice that we could give, besides the fact that I was not convinced of the power to guarantee anonymity, and thus the security, of threatened witnesses." [51] Claude Jorda, the president of the ICTY, would re-launch the idea of holding a trial in Bosnia, in order to alleviate the number of cases for the ICTY. But this project has so far never materialized because of the difficulties involved, notably the lack of an adequate legal system free of political constraints. [52]

Caught between the impossibility of countering the propaganda of the local governments and the necessity of getting the ICTY's message across, the tribunal charges one of its employees, Liam McDowell, with finding a solution. His idea, the "Outreach" program, is launched in 1999. "Through seminars, publications in local languages, and no doubt eventually with CD-ROMs and electronic communications, we are going to explain to all those in the Balkans who want to hear it that the Tribunal is neither an abstract instrument nor an organ charged for organizing vengeance, but an instrument with a role in the reestablishment of the rule of law and which contributes to the reconciliation, and thus, in the end, to peace and stability," says McDowell. Outreach's intended audiences include victims' associations, lawyers, the media, and the "curious." "The objective," he continues, "is for people to at last acknowledge that the ICTY is theirs, even if it is geographically in The Hague." [53]

To what degree might Outreach be capable of changing the perception of the international court? Even inside the ICTY, some feel that it is not the role of the tribunal to "do public relations." At the least, they feel, the exercise is doomed to failure. "'Outreach' was launched ten days after Jelisic's acquittal for genocide," says one insider. "It would take millions of dollars to offset this simple bit of news. How can we explain this verdict to the people of Brcko?"[54] Perhaps this analysis is too quick. The people's frustration is probably due more to the fact that the leaders of ethnic cleansing—Karadzic and Mladic— remain free men and that even the rare stooges who are convicted escape the most severe punishment. It is less Jelisic's acquittal than the victims' sense of the ICTY's general ineffectiveness that is in question. In reality, the international court has never been at the heart of the plan put in place by the international community to manage the postwar situation in Bosnia-Herzegovina after Dayton. The diplomats and the soldiers did not want a supplementary constraint in a mandate that already appeared perilous enough. As for the ICTY, it feared that its autonomy, won progressively and with difficulty, would again be put into question. Richard Goldstone recognized the result of this marginalization: "The people of the former Yugoslavia did not see much out of the Tribunal."[55]

The Duplicity of the Security Council

The most profound roots of the ICTY's failure to get its message across extend elsewhere: to its creation. "Politics" warped what should have been a judiciary instrument by depriving it of the means to live, and worse, by loading it with unrealistic objectives. Unless one lives in an ideal universe, governed by human rights, a tribunal alone cannot "dissuade, contribute to reestablishing peace, and reconciliation." The ICTY paid in the long run for its original sin, for having been born of the Security Council, a purely political organ of the United Nations. It was the Security Council that had established on its own initiative such as dubious mandate. As the jurist Olivier Russbach notes, "Formally, these tribunals are subsidiary organs of the Security Council, which is *a priori* incompatible with the work of justice. They were created with the objective of 'pacifying,' to reestablish peace and security. (Article VII of the U.N. Charter), and in this specific mission are doomed to failure."[56]

As for dissuasion from conflict, reestablishment of peace and reconciliation belong to the field of politics. Antoine Garapon has pointed out that it is not by creating a tribunal that one stops a war: "There was a deliberate confusion of roles, when the Security Council, in the middle of the war in Bosnia, decided to judge the principal war criminals. It was not the tribunal of Nuremberg that liberated the camps at Auschwitz and at Mathausen, it was the Red Army and the Americans."[57] It is a truism: Peace is obtained by capitulation or negotiation, never by the decision of a court. On the Richter scale of cynicism in politics, the creation of the ICTY is quite remarkable: The court served as an alibi for nonintervention. This fraud—too obvious—could not hold the illusion forever. It was at Srebrenica, two years after the creation of the ICTY, that the veil was torn away.

Beyond this initial trickery, the Western states largely contributed to the discrediting of this first attempt at international justice. In the beginning, they did not give it the means to operate. Then, for years, they did not pass on information they alone held to indict the highest political and military leaders of ethnic cleansing. Finally, they balked at proceeding with arrests. How are we to understand that the most powerful armies in the world are incapable of arresting Radovan Karadzic in a territory the size of a pocket handkerchief? Profoundly irritated, Carla Del Ponte asks the NATO forces deployed in Bosnia "to really work on arresting Karadzic instead of making public relations": "I am sick of reading in the press that they are making attempts to arrest him. The day they arrest him, they can talk about it. Until then, they should keep quiet," she advises SFOR.[58] For a long time, neither the Americans nor the French have wanted to risk reprisals in arresting the former Bosnian Serb leader. The notoriously bad relations between the French and American soldiers in Bosnia do not make things any easier.

In reality, whatever their differences, the states never abandoned an approach dictated by their own interests; they were allergic to the idea of punishing political leaders. Despite the rhetoric, peace, however iniquitous, always took precedence over justice. And, if the particular chain of events in Kosovo had not happened, the man most responsible for ethnic cleansing would no doubt never have been indicted, nor arrested.

In spite of these obstacles, the tribunal would perhaps have been able to play some dissuasive role. Again, it would have been necessary to use the tribunal correctly. Instead, the politicians used it as a sword of Damocles, and so they violated the very principle of dissuasion, which is based on its exemplarity. They wanted to instrumentalize the international court, to use it as a means of pressure, in the same way they use threats of sanctions or air strikes. This strategy politicized the tribunal and inevitably damaged its image. During his trial, Milosevic makes the politicization of the tribunal one of his principal arguments in attacking its legitimacy. Even more, this strategy of the Western nations revealed an ambiguous behavior. The Great Powers had a true legal strike force but voluntarily checked it to leave open the road to negotiation, to the point that even Richard Goldstone was furious to learn that Richard Holbrooke—seeking to put Arkan (Zeljko Raznatovic) out of the game—had shown the CIA's file on that militia chief to Milosevic, while not passing it on to the ICTY. What dissuasive impact could one hope for after that?

As for the goal of "reconciliation," applied with bewitching rhetoric, the Security Council also made a mistake of tone; even the word "reconciliation" is improper. The word evokes the religious rite in which one seeks a pardon for crimes committed. In reality, the one thing needed to create a livable post–civil war environment is political order. That is the case for many communities; they must be able to live together without recourse to violence. It means enacting a civil pact, not absolving people for any crimes they may have committed. But in moving the stakes to the field of pardon and reconciliation, the international community reveals more about itself than about the situation that it pretends to address: It signifies its will to turn, as quickly as possible, the page on a disturbing reality from which it attempts in vain to escape. When an international administration was put in place in Bosnia, the ICTY was plainly never integrated into it. The tribunal remains a peripheral element in the international community's planning and execution of the reconstruction of Bosnia.

It could have been otherwise. Without becoming blindly utopian, the tribunal could have more rapidly indicted the principal instigators and engineers of ethnic cleansing. Neither Richard Goldstone nor Louise Arbour, except during the war in Kosovo, put much effort into rapid-fire indictments. Nobody doubts the complexity of putting together files of charges backed up with evidence, with the war raging and the Western governments only collaborating when their interests command them to do so. The ICTY's head of investigation has pointed out that the attack on the federal building in Oklahoma City mobilized hundreds of investigators, while the tribunal has to this day only one hundred personnel to detail not one but dozens of even more complex crimes. Despite everything, the ICTY could have used its meager resources to target the "warlords" more rapidly. It must be said in its defense that the tribunal, starting from nothing in 1993, needed to establish basic procedures on how to function before throwing itself into the most ambitious tasks. Without doubt, the Security Council, and particularly the governments that had troops in the former Yugoslavia, would have wanted to curb any indictment that would have weakened the slightest diplomatic hope. Would they have succeeded if the prosecutor had been determined to move forward? No one knows. In other words, the tribunal could have and should have indicted the warlords much sooner, forcing the Security Council to end its ambiguous policy of either negotiating with war criminals or judging them. In retrospect, one perceives that the indictment of Karadzic and Mladic, as well as that of President Milosevic, had a profound effect, even if it was not immediate. The first two men have been progressively marginalized and the latter was put in "quarantine" by the international community until he was arrested in April, 2001, in Belgrade and transferred to The Hague for his historic trial, now scheduled through 2005.

The Difficult Death of the ICTY

After a difficult start, the tribunal has progressively achieved power and efficacy. Its budget has soared from $276,000 in 1993 to level off at $100 million in
1999, and in May, 2002, it employed 1,248 civil servants from 82 countries. By
June, 2000, it had overtaken, in administrative terms, the Nuremberg tribunals
at their peak.

While increasing in power and expertise, the tribunal has suffered several
negative side effects from its growth. One of the accused, Zoran Zigic, sentenced to twenty-five years in prison for "crimes against humanity for persecution and the war crimes of murder, torture and cruel treatment," gets rich
during his provisory detention in The Hague.[59] By declaring himself "indi-
gent," he is able to call on a team of up to ten people paid by the tribunal according to the highest international standards, and he gets a cut of their fees.
Zoran Zigic and his family receive at least $175,000. In addition, two of the in-
vestigators on his team, although paid by the ICTY, never provide the slightest
work for the defense of their client, except to share his gains. Among the accused, Zigic's case is no doubt not unique.

Beyond such minor although shocking dysfunction, seventy-eight defendants appear before the ICTY by the end of 2002 and eighteen are acquitted,
have served, or are still serving their time. At the end of 2002, forty-two defendants are in provisional detention, eleven have provisional liberty, and twenty-
four are still at large. From now on, the ICTY is confronting its last major challenge: to leave its mark, before proceeding with its dissolution.

Despite multiple obstacles, the tribunal of The Hague has managed to justify its principal reason for being. It began by judging the principal instigators
and executors of the worst atrocities committed in the former Yugoslavia. Responsible for ethnic cleansing in the valley of Lasva in Bosnia between April
and June, 1993, the Croat general Tihomir Blaskic has been convicted and sentenced in the first instance to forty-five years in prison. In August, 2001, the
Bosnian Serb general Radislav Krstic, the second in command of General
Ratko Mladic during the massacres at Srebrenica, has been sentenced to forty-
six years in prison. Other superior officers and camp commanders, including
those of Omarska, have been apprehended. Besides Slobodan Milosevic and
Biljana Plavsic, former president of Republika Srpska, the most spectacular
arrest has been that of Momcilo Krajisnik. This former right-hand man of
Radovan Karadzic has been charged on nine counts, including genocide, crimes
against humanity, murder, persecution, and deportation for political, racial, or
religious reasons. He is accused of having planned and directed ethnic cleans-

ing in some twenty towns in Bosnia in 1992, causing the deaths of thousands of people and the persecution of hundreds of thousands of others. Indicted secretly on February 21, 2000, only six weeks passed before Krajisnik was arrested. During the night of Sunday, April 2 and early morning hours of Monday, April 3, 2000, French commandos entered his house in Pale and seized him, without a single shot fired.

The ICTY has never had so many important defendants behind bars, and there is the prospect of detaining, in the near future, the principal masterminds of ethnic cleansing. The cells of the U.N.'s penitentiary quarter at Scheveningen Prison will be full from now on. The three Trial Chambers are completely booked by the fifty-five defendants now before the tribunal. The judicial process has reached the point that presumed war criminals have been released into provisory liberty pending their trial.

It is in this context that Claude Jorda presented an ambitious project of reform to the Security Council on June 20, 2000. The project's goal is to accelerate the trials so that the tribunal's ultimate success will not be lost on a public weary of trials that have dragged on for fifteen to twenty years. If the tribunal dragged on like that, one of the essential objectives of the international court—the stigmatization of crimes—would then be doomed to failure. The projections of the tribunal were worrisome: With some two hundred accused still to be judged, at its current pace the ICTY would finish the trials of first instance only in 2016, and much later when appeals are taken into account.

Created initially with a mandate of four years in 1993, and extended in 1997 and 2001, the tribunal has never been thought of as a permanent institution. "[S]hould no remedy be found immediately, the institution's very credibility will be put into question," Claude Jorda warns.[60] The president of the ICTY has proposed a series of measures that would permit the tribunal to finish up its inquiries in 2004 and terminate its work in 2008, at least for the trials of the first instance. Among these measures are the acceleration of the trials' preparatory phases and an increase in the number of ad hoc judges. In January, 2002, nine judges *ad hoc* arrived in The Hague. Now, every day in the three chambers, six trials are under way simultaneously, instead of three as was previously the case.[61] To meet the deadline for finishing the ICTY's work, one idea was to turn over some of the less important cases to the national courts in the former Yugoslavia.[62] But Claude Jorda reports to the Security Council the difficulties, "political, legal, and financial," involved in relocating the trial: "We cannot relocate these trials without the certitude that the defendants will be judged according to the minimal norms of protection of human rights."[63]

Before the time of its self-programmed death arrives, the ICTY must undertake its last challenge: to anchor as strongly as possible, in the heart of civil society, the necessity of punishing those responsible for the most abominable crimes. The ICTY must accomplish this feat so that, as the first international criminal tribunal ever created, it can replace the Nuremberg "victor's justice" in the collective conscience and bring some sense of morality to the global community.

Conclusion

Leontius, the son of Aglaion, as he was walking up from the
Piraeus and approaching the northern wall from the outside,
observed some dead bodies on the ground, and the executioner
standing by them. He immediately felt a desire to look at them,
but at the same time loathing the thought he tried to divert
himself from it. For some time he struggled with himself, and
covered his eyes, till at length, over-mastered by the desire, he
opened his eyes wide with his fingers, and running up to the
bodies, exclaimed, "There! You wretches! Gaze your fill at the
beautiful spectacle!"
—Plato, *The Republic*

In 1969, Charles de Gaulle dismissed the ban on French television of
Marcel Ophul's documentary, *The Sorrow and the Pity*, about French
collaboration with the Nazis, by saying, "Our country does not need
truth. What we must give it is hope, cohesion and a goal."[1] Mere decades
later, that prism has been inverted. From now on, the quest for truth appears
to be a precondition for the installation of a durable peace. From Africa to the
Balkans to Latin America, the cry for justice and truth is making itself heard as
dislocated, torn societies find the path toward dialogue and away from revenge, in order to break the cycle of violence. A Chinese saying warns of the alternative: "If you want to avenge yourself, prepare two tombs." From South
Africa's Truth and Reconciliation Commission to the International Criminal
Tribunal for the Former Yugoslavia, there is the same will to refuse to forget so
that impunity does not lead, in time, only to new bloodbaths.

The international court is beginning to take root; it is a new utopia containing the world's violence in the space of a trial chamber. How can we not congratulate ourselves that impunity for the most abominable crimes today revolts human conscience? This idea forms the base of the International Criminal Court, officially created on July 1, 2002. If the ICTY has had only one merit, it is to make evident the necessity of an international criminal court.

The ICTY's legacy is already ensured by the rapid development of international jurisprudence following its creation. The ICTY opened the road to the establishment of the International Criminal Tribunal for Rwanda (ICTR) in 1994. On May 1, 1998, Jean Kambanda, the former prime minister, pleaded guilty to genocide and crimes against humanity, and he was sentenced to life in prison on September 4, 1998. Also in 1998, a British court, at the demand of a Spanish judge, rejected immunity for the former Chilean dictator Augusto Pinochet. His eventual release by British authorities for "reasons of illness" changed nothing; a precedent had been established. Strengthened by this evolving international jurisprudence, in 1999 a Senegalese magistrate decided to indict the former dictator of Chad, Hissène Habré, exiled in Dakar, for war crimes. This decision was later reversed on appeal, but the fact remains that national sovereignty is no longer a barrier to universal jurisdiction when confronted by the most serious crimes. On August 14, 2000, the U.N. Security Council, in agreement with the government of Sierra Leone, approved a resolution to establish a semi-international tribunal to "judge those most responsible" for horrific crimes committed during the ten years of civil war in that country. This tribunal is unique in that it is composed of both local and international judges. The new court has the mandate to try not only Foday Sankoh and other rebel leaders but also some commanders of the pro-government civil defense army. The frontier between national and international affairs is becoming blurred. In Belgium, in Switzerland, and elsewhere, presumed war criminals from Yugoslavia, Rwanda, and other countries have also been arrested and put on trial. To cite only one example, on April 30, 1999, a Swiss military tribunal sentenced Fulgence Nyontese, former mayor of the Rwandan village of Mushubati, to life in prison for his participation in genocide. The law is experiencing a revolution: an escape from its traditional foundation in national sovereignty.

But in this new international reality, a balance must be found between "the will to direct an active and voluntary policy for the promotion of human rights" and simple realism.[2] Belgium, which had devoted itself to the most progressive law in matters of universal jurisdiction, recognized the growing interference and burden of burgeoning complaints and curtailed the statute. From Cuban dictator Fidel Castro to his Iraqi counterpart Saddam Hussein, to

Israeli prime minister Ariel Sharon, Palestinian Authority president Yasser Arafat, the Khmer Rouge, Rwandan president Paul Kagame, Ivory Coast president Laurent Gbagbo . . . more than thirty high-ranking political figures were sued in Belgian courts, which were quickly crushed under a heavy case load.[3]

Still, the ICTY demonstrated that a tribunal created as an alibi can progressively escape from its creator to generate new initiatives, cracking the lid of established certitudes. It showed that Anglo-American common law and continental law can be unified, something that was much in doubt. It has given a decisive push to international criminal law. It has incorporated rape among the crimes against humanity. It has judged war criminals of all stripes in the former Yugoslavia. It has returned dignity to victims by publicly recognizing their suffering. It has indicted, for the first time, a sitting head of state. These contributions are important because in the long run they create a common narrative in societies divided by war and crimes committed on a massive scale. By doing so, and by indicting individuals, it weakens the perception of collective responsibility and opens the door for hope in these once war-torn societies.

Obviously, this march forward for international justice has been marked by reversals, obstacles, and the constant risk of derailment. The history of the ICTY has revealed, *ad nauseam,* the contradictions between *raison d'état* and a culture of human rights that is still being formed. There is no doubt that all justice is born in ambiguity and blood, and the ICTY is no exception. On the contrary, it has bluntly demonstrated the cynicism of politicians who used the creation of the tribunal to camouflage their lack of political will to put an end to the atrocities. The Security Council installed the International Criminal Tribunal for Rwanda after blocking intervention to stop the genocide. Out of its own guilty conscience, it has confined the mandate of the ICTR to 1994, limiting the action of the international court to the genocide itself and not its chaotic aftermath. Thus, the ICTR has no jurisdiction over the murders of 180,000 to 200,000 Hutu refugees in the former Zaire in 1996, for which the current Rwandan government bears a share of the responsibility. And when prosecutor Carla Del Ponte wanted to advance her investigation into the crimes committed by the Armée Populaire Rwandaise (APR) in 1994, whose intervention put an end to the genocide in that country, she collided with not only noncooperation from Kigali but also the desire of the Rwandan government (largely made up of former APR leaders) to have her dismissed. The influence of the International Criminal Tribunal for Rwanda was mitigated when its work became the focus of a devastating audit by U.N. inspectors in 1996.[4] Moreover, nothing indicates that impunity is in retreat anywhere. In Cambodia, discussions between the government and the United Nations to create a tribunal charged to judge the Khmer Rouge, responsible for killing more than one million fellow citizens, went nowhere. After four and a half years of negotiation, the United Nations has put a time limit on discussions with the Cambodian government, refusing to threaten what would only be a parody of justice in judging the crimes committed by the Khmer Rouge. In Afghanistan, it is unlikely that members of the Northern Alliance will be tried for the deaths of one thousand Taliban prisoners, asphyxiated in container trucks between November 28 and November 30, 2001.[5] In Russia, again, nothing indicates that the authorities wish to punish those responsible for massive atrocities in Chechnya.

The road is still long, and, wherever it leads, the international court must guard itself against multiple dangers. Foremost is the risk of losing its soul in exercising jurisdiction only in the weakest states. If the most powerful states appropriate the idea of universality of law to administer justice on a selective basis, any hope of a true international court is lost. The risk of a political double standard is not slim, judging by Washington's attitude toward the future International Criminal Court (ICC). At the Conference of Rome on July 17, 1998, 160 countries signed the treaty to create the ICC; the United States was one of seven that opposed it. From the perspective of the Clinton administration, the ICC statute had serious deficiencies: undefined jurisdiction over aggression, inadequate limits on the initiation of prosecutions, and a last-minute provision related to Israel's policy toward settlements in occupied territories. Above all, the United States wanted to strengthen guarantees that American military personnel would not be prosecuted internationally without U.S. concurrence. That is why the American delegation even fought—fortunately, without success—to refuse any autonomous initiative for the prosecutor. Moreover, the American delegation submitted an amendment (rejected in large part) whose objective was to shield American citizens pursued by the court. As for France, it managed to introduce into the statutes the possibility that any state could avoid the treaty's obligations regarding war crimes (Article 124) for seven years—until the next conference to review and extend the agreement establishing the ICC, effectively granting perpetual immunity to the signers. It is no doubt unique in the annals of international law that a treaty is written simultaneously with the handbook on how to evade it. "It is a license to kill for seven years," many nongovernmental organizations noted.[6] This disposition weakens the entire range of the ICC, as well as its dissuasive and punitive functions.

The attacks of September 11, 2001, only reinforced the determination of President George W. Bush's administration to free itself from the court's jurisdiction, execrated before even being born. In an act unprecedented in international relations, on May 6, 2002, the Americans immediately withdrew their signature from the statutes of the ICC, putting an end to the ambiguity of U.S.

policy.[7] The Clinton administration had reluctantly signed the ICC treaty on the last possible day, December 31, 2000, in order to influence the choice of the judges and the prosecutor, but with no real intention of becoming a party to the ICC. Later, under the George W. Bush administration, the American authorities also directed a veritable guerrilla diplomatic war in the Security Council, not hesitating to resort to blackmail by threatening SFOR's mandate if they did not get immunity from ICC prosecution for American soldiers. They organized a global campaign—described as a "jihad" by Human Rights Watch—to dissuade countries tempted to ratify the ICC's constituting treaty. Lastly, the United States exercised economic and political pressure to conclude bilateral treaties with other states, agreeing not to extradite American nationals to the ICC.[8] All of this amply demonstrates that, in the dialectic between morality and politics, the Great Powers balk at submitting themselves to the same rules they have written for the ICTY.

The extraordinary reversal of roles must be noted in this dialectic between law and power: The United States no longer wants an international court of which it was the principal creator during the twentieth century, when the European powers were profoundly skeptical toward the concept. The Old World was the last to cross this new democratic horizon. This permutation of roles is explained in part by the weakness of the Europeans on the international scene—must law be the weapon of the weak?—while the United States assumes its role as planetary gendarme and opposes a court it cannot master, and which could potentially turn against it.[9]

The International Criminal Court has become today one of the principal fault lines between Europe and the United States. If the countries of the European Union have largely given birth to and carried the ICC, it is because criminal law has become the new civilizing mission of the Union, whose initial objective was to eliminate war among its members. "Now Europeans have become evangelists for their 'postmodern' gospel of international relations," notes Robert Kagan, a policy expert at the Carnegie Endowment for International Peace in Washington.[10] From now on, however, the Europeans must demonstrate that they have the capability to ensure that the ICC survives.

But between this legal evangelism and fundamentalist realism, between the fantasy of eternal peace and the return of classic international law (of which unassailable sovereignty would be the central element), the destiny of the ICC is profoundly uncertain. But reason for hope exists. The ICC reflects the new architecture of the international system, where states coexist next to supranational institutions. Antoine Garapon notes that, in substance, "political relations are not destroyed by the idea of an international criminal court, but, on the contrary, they are stimulated."[11] The statutes of the ICC in fact give primary jurisdiction to the states to prosecute authors of mass crimes. In other words, international justice is no substitute for states, but rather makes them more responsible.

Another difficulty is that this "transplanted" justice must manage, in spite of everything, to implant itself in the populations concerned. From this point of view, the Milosevic trial has demonstrated its limits. Without the support of the political leadership, the message of international justice is very difficult to transmit to the population of Serbia. As a result, the examination of conscience in these torn societies will be delayed, at the risk of fanning new flames of violence. The former Yugoslavia demonstrates how difficult this task is.

The international court must not get carried away with its new power. A penal vision cannot replace a cohesive political vision of the world. The international court's mission is to erect a boundary between barbarism and civilization. It is not to reestablish peace or to seal the reconciliation between former enemies.

Finally, the tragedy evoked in the tribunal's hearing rooms must not anesthetize the global community to crimes against humanity. It must, on the contrary, raise awareness of the different mechanisms of crime and of the individual responsibility of its authors and their supporters.

Unprecedented links are being made between law and war, and between justice and diplomacy. The contours of this new geography remain uncertain. But civil society holds one profound aspiration today, which is not to let die the hope contained in the preamble of the Universal Declaration of Human Rights: "Disregard and contempt for human rights have resulted in barbarous acts which have outraged the conscience of mankind, and the advent of a world in which human beings shall enjoy freedom of speech and belief and freedom from fear and want has been proclaimed as the highest aspiration of the common people." [12] This will to moralize public life is essential; it is only through the constant pressure of civil society that international justice can truly emerge.

The globalization of justice will become the ultimate safety net for a decaying international system incapable of controlling murderous conflicts. It incarnates a desperate quest for a bulwark against awakening national demons and the crimes that the world believed would never be repeated after the cataclysm of World War II. Before the reemerging specter of barbarism, the international court constitutes a frail hope. Alone, it is insufficient. But in any case it is indispensable.

APPENDIX

Amended Statute of the International Tribunal

(ADOPTED 25 MAY 1993 by Resolution 827)
(AS AMENDED 13 MAY 1998 by Resolution 1166)
(AS AMENDED 30 NOVEMBER 2000 by Resolution 1329)
(AS AMENDED 17 MAY 2002 by Resolution 1411)

Having been established by the Security Council acting under Chapter VII of the Charter of the United Nations, the International Tribunal for the Prosecution of Persons Responsible for Serious Violations of International Humanitarian Law Committed in the Territory of the Former Yugoslavia since 1991 (hereinafter referred to as "the International Tribunal") shall function in accordance with the provisions of the present Statute.

ARTICLE 1
Competence of the International Tribunal

The International Tribunal shall have the power to prosecute persons responsible for serious violations of international humanitarian law committed in the territory of the former Yugoslavia since 1991 in accordance with the provisions of the present Statute.

ARTICLE 2
Grave breaches of the Geneva Conventions of 1949

The International Tribunal shall have the power to prosecute persons committing or ordering to be committed grave breaches of the Geneva Conventions of 12 August 1949, namely the following acts against persons or property protected under the provisions of the relevant Geneva Convention:
  (a) wilful killing;
  (b) torture or inhuman treatment, including biological experiments;
  (c) wilfully causing great suffering or serious injury to body or health;
  (d) extensive destruction and appropriation of property, not justified by military necessity and carried out unlawfully and wantonly;

(e) compelling a prisoner of war or a civilian to serve in the forces of a hostile power;

(f) wilfully depriving a prisoner of war or a civilian of the rights of fair and regular trial;

(g) unlawful deportation or transfer or unlawful confinement of a civilian;

(h) taking civilians as hostages.

ARTICLE 3
Violations of the laws or customs of war

The International Tribunal shall have the power to prosecute persons violating the laws or customs of war. Such violations shall include, but not be limited to:

(a) employment of poisonous weapons or other weapons calculated to cause unnecessary suffering;

(b) wanton destruction of cities, towns or villages, or devastation not justified by military necessity;

(c) attack, or bombardment, by whatever means, of undefended towns, villages, dwellings, or buildings;

(d) seizure of, destruction or wilful damage done to institutions dedicated to religion, charity and education, the arts and sciences, historic monuments and works of art and science;

(e) plunder of public or private property.

ARTICLE 4
Genocide

1. The International Tribunal shall have the power to prosecute persons committing genocide as defined in paragraph 2 of this article or of committing any of the other acts enumerated in paragraph 3 of this article.

2. Genocide means any of the following acts committed with intent to destroy, in whole or in part, a national, ethnical, racial or religious group, as such:
   (a) killing members of the group;
   (b) causing serious bodily or mental harm to members of the group;
   (c) deliberately inflicting on the group conditions of life calculated to bring about its physical destruction in whole or in part;
   (d) imposing measures intended to prevent births within the group;
   (e) forcibly transferring children of the group to another group.

3. The following acts shall be punishable:
   (a) genocide;
   (b) conspiracy to commit genocide;
   (c) direct and public incitement to commit genocide;
   (d) attempt to commit genocide;
   (e) complicity in genocide.

ARTICLE 5
Crimes against humanity

The International Tribunal shall have the power to prosecute persons responsible for the following crimes when committed in armed conflict, whether international or internal in character, and directed against any civilian population:
- (a) murder;
- (b) extermination;
- (c) enslavement;
- (d) deportation;
- (e) imprisonment;
- (f) torture;
- (g) rape;
- (h) persecutions on political, racial and religious grounds;
- (i) other inhumane acts.

ARTICLE 6
Personal jurisdiction

The International Tribunal shall have jurisdiction over natural persons pursuant to the provisions of the present Statute.

ARTICLE 7
Individual criminal responsibility

1. A person who planned, instigated, ordered, committed or otherwise aided and abetted in the planning, preparation or execution of a crime referred to in articles 2 to 5 of the present Statute, shall be individually responsible for the crime.
2. The official position of any accused person, whether as Head of State or Government or as a responsible Government official, shall not relieve such person of criminal responsibility nor mitigate punishment.
3. The fact that any of the acts referred to in articles 2 to 5 of the present Statute was committed by a subordinate does not relieve his superior of criminal responsibility if he knew or had reason to know that the subordinate was about to commit such acts or had done so and the superior failed to take the necessary and reasonable measures to prevent such acts or to punish the perpetrators thereof.
4. The fact that an accused person acted pursuant to an order of a Government or of a superior shall not relieve him of criminal responsibility, but may be considered in mitigation of punishment if the International Tribunal determines that justice so requires.

ARTICLE 8
Territorial and temporal jurisdiction

The territorial jurisdiction of the International Tribunal shall extend to the territory of the former Socialist Federal Republic of Yugoslavia, including its land surface, airspace and territorial waters. The temporal jurisdiction of the International Tribunal shall extend to a period beginning on 1 January 1991.

ARTICLE 9
Concurrent jurisdiction

1. The International Tribunal and national courts shall have concurrent jurisdiction to prosecute persons for serious violations of international humanitarian law committed in the territory of the former Yugoslavia since 1 January 1991.
2. The International Tribunal shall have primacy over national courts. At any stage of the procedure, the International Tribunal may formally request national courts to defer to the competence of the International Tribunal in accordance with the present Statute and the Rules of Procedure and Evidence of the International Tribunal.

ARTICLE 10
Non-bis-in-idem

1. No person shall be tried before a national court for acts constituting serious violations of international humanitarian law under the present Statute, for which he or she has already been tried by the International Tribunal.
2. A person who has been tried by a national court for acts constituting serious violations of international humanitarian law may be subsequently tried by the International Tribunal only if:
   (a) the act for which he or she was tried was characterized as an ordinary crime; or
   (b) the national court proceedings were not impartial or independent, were designed to shield the accused from international criminal responsibility, or the case was not diligently prosecuted.
3. In considering the penalty to be imposed on a person convicted of a crime under the present Statute, the International Tribunal shall take into account the extent to which any penalty imposed by a national court on the same person for the same act has already been served.

ARTICLE 11
Organization of the International Tribunal

The International Tribunal shall consist of the following organs:
   (a) the Chambers, comprising three Trial Chambers and an Appeals Chamber;

(b) the Prosecutor; and

(c) a Registry, servicing both the Chambers and the Prosecutor.

ARTICLE 12
Composition of the Chambers

1. The Chambers shall be composed of sixteen permanent independent judges, no two of whom may be nationals of the same State, and a maximum at any one time of nine ad litem independent judges appointed in accordance with article 13 ter, paragraph 2, of the Statute, no two of whom may be nationals of the same State.
2. Three permanent judges and a maximum at any one time of six ad litem judges shall be members of each Trial Chamber. Each Trial Chamber to which ad litem judges are assigned may be divided into sections of three judges each, composed of both permanent and ad litem judges. A section of a Trial Chamber shall have the same powers and responsibilities as a Trial Chamber under the Statute and shall render judgement in accordance with the same rules.
3. Seven of the permanent judges shall be members of the Appeals Chamber. The Appeals Chamber shall, for each appeal, be composed of five of its members.
4. A person who for the purposes of membership of the Chambers of the International Tribunal could be regarded as a national of more than one State shall be deemed to be a national of the State in which that person ordinarily exercises civil and political rights.

ARTICLE 13
Qualifications of judges

The permanent and ad litem judges shall be persons of high moral character, impartiality and integrity who possess the qualifications required in their respective countries for appointment to the highest judicial offices. In the overall composition of the Chambers and sections of the Trial Chambers, due account shall be taken of the experience of the judges in criminal law, international law, including international humanitarian law and human rights law.

ARTICLE 13 BIS
Election of permanent judges

1. Fourteen of the permanent judges of the International Tribunal shall be elected by the General Assembly from a list submitted by the Security Council, in the following manner:
   (a) The Secretary-General shall invite nominations for judges of the International Tribunal from States Members of the United Nations and non-member States maintaining permanent observer missions at United Nations Headquarters.
   (b) Within sixty days of the date of the invitation of the Secretary-General, each State may nominate up to two candidates meeting the qualifications set out in

article 13 of the Statute, no two of whom shall be of the same nationality and neither of whom shall be of the same nationality as any judge who is a member of the Appeals Chamber and who was elected or appointed a judge of the International Criminal Tribunal for the Prosecution of Persons Responsible for Genocide and Other Serious Violations of International Humanitarian Law Committed in the Territory of Rwanda and Rwandan Citizens Responsible for Genocide and Other Such Violations Committed in the Territory of Neighbouring States, between 1 January 1994 and 31 December 1994 (hereinafter referred to as "The International Tribunal for Rwanda") in accordance with article 12 of the Statute of that Tribunal.

(c) The Secretary-General shall forward the nominations received to the Security Council. From the nominations received the Security Council shall establish a list of not less than twenty-eight and not more than forty-two candidates, taking due account of the adequate representation of the principal legal systems of the world.

(d) The President of the Security Council shall transmit the list of candidates to the President of the General Assembly. From that list the General Assembly shall elect fourteen permanent judges of the International Tribunal. The candidates who receive an absolute majority of the votes of the States Members of the United Nations and of the non-member States maintaining permanent observer missions at United Nations Headquarters, shall be declared elected. Should two candidates of the same nationality obtain the required majority vote, the one who received the higher number of votes shall be considered elected.

2. In the event of a vacancy in the Chambers amongst the permanent judges elected or appointed in accordance with this article, after consultation with the Presidents of the Security Council and of the General Assembly, the Secretary-General shall appoint a person meeting the qualifications of article 13 of the Statute, for the remainder of the term of office concerned.

3. The permanent judges elected in accordance with this article shall be elected for a term of four years. The terms and conditions of service shall be those of the judges of the International Court of Justice. They shall be eligible for re-election.

ARTICLE 13 TER
Election and appointment of ad litem judges

1. The ad litem judges of the International Tribunal shall be elected by the General Assembly from a list submitted by the Security Council, in the following manner:

(a) The Secretary-General shall invite nominations for ad litem judges of the International Tribunal from States Members of the United Nations and non-member States maintaining permanent observer missions at United Nations Headquarters.

(b) Within sixty days of the date of the invitation of the Secretary-General, each State may nominate up to four candidates meeting the qualifications set out in

article 13 of the Statute, taking into account the importance of a fair representation of female and male candidates.

(c) The Secretary-General shall forward the nominations received to the Security
Council. From the nominations received the Security Council shall establish a
list of not less than fifty-four candidates, taking due account of the adequate
representation of the principal legal systems of the world and bearing in mind
the importance of equitable geographical distribution.

(d) The President of the Security Council shall transmit the list of candidates to
the President of the General Assembly. From that list the General Assembly
shall elect the twenty-seven ad litem judges of the International Tribunal. The
candidates who receive an absolute majority of the votes of the States Members
of the United Nations and of the non-member States maintaining permanent
observer missions at United Nations Headquarters shall be declared elected.

(e) The ad litem judges shall be elected for a term of four years. They shall not be
eligible for re-election.

2. During their term, ad litem judges will be appointed by the Secretary-General,
upon request of the President of the International Tribunal, to serve in the Trial
Chambers for one or more trials, for a cumulative period of up to, but not including, three years. When requesting the appointment of any particular ad litem judge,
the President of the International Tribunal shall bear in mind the criteria set out in
article 13 of the Statute regarding the composition of the Chambers and sections of
the Trial Chambers, the considerations set out in paragraphs 1 (b) and (c) above
and the number of votes the ad litem judge received in the General Assembly.

ARTICLE 13 QUATER
Status of ad litem judges

1. During the period in which they are appointed to serve in the International
Tribunal, ad litem judges shall:
   (a) benefit from the same terms and conditions of service mutatis mutandis as the
   permanent judges of the International Tribunal;
   (b) enjoy, subject to paragraph 2 below, the same powers as the permanent judges
   of the International Tribunal;
   (c) enjoy the privileges and immunities, exemptions and facilities of a judge of the
   International Tribunal.

2. During the period in which they are appointed to serve in the International
Tribunal, ad litem judges shall not:
   (a) be eligible for election as, or to vote in the election of, the President of the Tribunal or the Presiding Judge of a Trial Chamber pursuant to article 14 of the
   Statute;
   (b) have power:
      (i) to adopt rules of procedure and evidence pursuant to article 15 of the
      Statute. They shall, however, be consulted before the adoption of those
      rules;

(ii) to review an indictment pursuant to article 19 of the Statute;

(iii) to consult with the President in relation to the assignment of judges pursuant to article 14 of the Statute or in relation to a pardon or commutation of sentence pursuant to article 28 of the Statute;

(iv) to adjudicate in pre-trial proceedings.

ARTICLE 14
Officers and members of the Chambers

1. The permanent judges of the International Tribunal shall elect a President from amongst their number.
2. The President of the International Tribunal shall be a member of the Appeals Chamber and shall preside over its proceedings.
3. After consultation with the permanent judges of the International Tribunal, the President shall assign four of the permanent judges elected or appointed in accordance with Article 13 bis of the Statute to the Appeals Chamber and nine to the Trial Chambers.
4. Two of the judges elected or appointed in accordance with article 12 of the Statute of the International Tribunal for Rwanda shall be assigned by the President of that Tribunal, in consultation with the President of the International Tribunal, to be members of the Appeals Chamber and permanent judges of the International Tribunal.
5. After consultation with the permanent judges of the International Tribunal, the President shall assign such ad litem judges as may from time to time be appointed to serve in the International Tribunal to the Trial Chambers.
6. A judge shall serve only in the Chamber to which he or she was assigned.
7. The permanent judges of each Trial Chamber shall elect a Presiding Judge from amongst their number, who shall oversee the work of the Trial Chamber as a whole.

ARTICLE 15
Rules of procedure and evidence

The judges of the International Tribunal shall adopt rules of procedure and evidence for the conduct of the pre-trial phase of the proceedings, trials and appeals, the admission of evidence, the protection of victims and witnesses and other appropriate matters.

ARTICLE 16
The Prosecutor

1. The Prosecutor shall be responsible for the investigation and prosecution of persons responsible for serious violations of international humanitarian law committed in the territory of the former Yugoslavia since 1 January 1991.

2. The Prosecutor shall act independently as a separate organ of the International Tribunal. He or she shall not seek or receive instructions from any Government or from any other source.
3. The Office of the Prosecutor shall be composed of a Prosecutor and such other qualified staff as may be required.
4. The Prosecutor shall be appointed by the Security Council on nomination by the Secretary-General. He or she shall be of high moral character and possess the highest level of competence and experience in the conduct of investigations and prosecutions of criminal cases. The Prosecutor shall serve for a four-year term and be eligible for reappointment. The terms and conditions of service of the Prosecutor shall be those of an Under-Secretary-General of the United Nations.
5. The staff of the Office of the Prosecutor shall be appointed by the Secretary-General on the recommendation of the Prosecutor.

ARTICLE 17
The Registry

1. The Registry shall be responsible for the administration and servicing of the International Tribunal.
2. The Registry shall consist of a Registrar and such other staff as may be required.
3. The Registrar shall be appointed by the Secretary-General after consultation with the President of the International Tribunal. He or she shall serve for a four-year term and be eligible for reappointment. The terms and conditions of service of the Registrar shall be those of an Assistant Secretary-General of the United Nations.
4. The staff of the Registry shall be appointed by the Secretary-General on the recommendation of the Registrar.

ARTICLE 18
Investigation and preparation of indictment

1. The Prosecutor shall initiate investigations ex-officio or on the basis of information obtained from any source, particularly from Governments, United Nations organs, intergovernmental and non-governmental organisations. The Prosecutor shall assess the information received or obtained and decide whether there is sufficient basis to proceed.
2. The Prosecutor shall have the power to question suspects, victims and witnesses, to collect evidence and to conduct on-site investigations. In carrying out these tasks, the Prosecutor may, as appropriate, seek the assistance of the State authorities concerned.
3. If questioned, the suspect shall be entitled to be assisted by counsel of his own choice, including the right to have legal assistance assigned to him without payment by him in any such case if he does not have sufficient means to pay for it, as well as to necessary translation into and from a language he speaks and understands.
4. Upon a determination that a prima facie case exists, the Prosecutor shall prepare an indictment containing a concise statement of the facts and the crime or crimes with

which the accused is charged under the Statute. The indictment shall be transmitted to a judge of the Trial Chamber.

ARTICLE 19
Review of the indictment

1. The judge of the Trial Chamber to whom the indictment has been transmitted shall review it. If satisfied that a prima facie case has been established by the Prosecutor, he shall confirm the indictment. If not so satisfied, the indictment shall be dismissed.
2. Upon confirmation of an indictment, the judge may, at the request of the Prosecutor, issue such orders and warrants for the arrest, detention, surrender or transfer of persons, and any other orders as may be required for the conduct of the trial.

ARTICLE 20
Commencement and conduct of trial proceedings

1. The Trial Chambers shall ensure that a trial is fair and expeditious and that proceedings are conducted in accordance with the rules of procedure and evidence, with full respect for the rights of the accused and due regard for the protection of victims and witnesses.
2. A person against whom an indictment has been confirmed shall, pursuant to an order or an arrest warrant of the International Tribunal, be taken into custody, immediately informed of the charges against him and transferred to the International Tribunal.
3. The Trial Chamber shall read the indictment, satisfy itself that the rights of the accused are respected, confirm that the accused understands the indictment, and instruct the accused to enter a plea. The Trial Chamber shall then set the date for trial.
4. The hearings shall be public unless the Trial Chamber decides to close the proceedings in accordance with its rules of procedure and evidence.

ARTICLE 21
Rights of the accused

1. All persons shall be equal before the International Tribunal.
2. In the determination of charges against him, the accused shall be entitled to a fair and public hearing, subject to article 22 of the Statute.
3. The accused shall be presumed innocent until proved guilty according to the provisions of the present Statute.
4. In the determination of any charge against the accused pursuant to the present Statute, the accused shall be entitled to the following minimum guarantees, in full equality:
   (a) to be informed promptly and in detail in a language which he understands of the nature and cause of the charge against him;

(b) to have adequate time and facilities for the preparation of his defence and to communicate with counsel of his own choosing;

(c) to be tried without undue delay;

(d) to be tried in his presence, and to defend himself in person or through legal assistance of his own choosing; to be informed, if he does not have legal assistance, of this right; and to have legal assistance assigned to him, in any case where the interests of justice so require, and without payment by him in any such case if he does not have sufficient means to pay for it;

(e) to examine, or have examined, the witnesses against him and to obtain the attendance and examination of witnesses on his behalf under the same conditions as witnesses against him;

(f) to have the free assistance of an interpreter if he cannot understand or speak the language used in the International Tribunal;

(g) not to be compelled to testify against himself or to confess guilt.

ARTICLE 22
Protection of victims and witnesses

The International Tribunal shall provide in its rules of procedure and evidence for the protection of victims and witnesses. Such protection measures shall include, but shall not be limited to, the conduct of in camera proceedings and the protection of the victim's identity.

ARTICLE 23
Judgement

1. The Trial Chambers shall pronounce judgements and impose sentences and penalties on persons convicted of serious violations of international humanitarian law.

2. The judgement shall be rendered by a majority of the judges of the Trial Chamber, and shall be delivered by the Trial Chamber in public. It shall be accompanied by a reasoned opinion in writing, to which separate or dissenting opinions may be appended.

ARTICLE 24
Penalties

1. The penalty imposed by the Trial Chamber shall be limited to imprisonment. In determining the terms of imprisonment, the Trial Chambers shall have recourse to the general practice regarding prison sentences in the courts of the former Yugoslavia.

2. In imposing the sentences, the Trial Chambers should take into account such factors as the gravity of the offence and the individual circumstances of the convicted person.

3. In addition to imprisonment, the Trial Chambers may order the return of any property and proceeds acquired by criminal conduct, including by means of duress, to their rightful owners.

ARTICLE 25
Appellate proceedings

1. The Appeals Chamber shall hear appeals from persons convicted by the Trial Chambers or from the Prosecutor on the following grounds:
   (a) an error on a question of law invalidating the decision; or
   (b) an error of fact which has occasioned a miscarriage of justice.
2. The Appeals Chamber may affirm, reverse or revise the decisions taken by the Trial Chambers.

ARTICLE 26
Review proceedings

Where a new fact has been discovered which was not known at the time of the proceedings before the Trial Chambers or the Appeals Chamber and which could have been a decisive factor in reaching the decision, the convicted person or the Prosecutor may submit to the International Tribunal an application for review of the judgement.

ARTICLE 27
Enforcement of sentences

Imprisonment shall be served in a State designated by the International Tribunal from a list of States which have indicated to the Security Council their willingness to accept convicted persons. Such imprisonment shall be in accordance with the applicable law of the State concerned, subject to the supervision of the International Tribunal.

ARTICLE 28
Pardon or commutation of sentences

If, pursuant to the applicable law of the State in which the convicted person is imprisoned, he or she is eligible for pardon or commutation of sentence, the State concerned shall notify the International Tribunal accordingly. The President of the International Tribunal, in consultation with the judges, shall decide the matter on the basis of the interests of justice and the general principles of law.

ARTICLE 29
Co-operation and judicial assistance

1. States shall co-operate with the International Tribunal in the investigation and prosecution of persons accused of committing serious violations of international humanitarian law.
2. States shall comply without undue delay with any request for assistance or an order
issued by a Trial Chamber, including, but not limited to:
   (a) the identification and location of persons;
   (b) the taking of testimony and the production of evidence;
   (c) the service of documents;
   (d) the arrest or detention of persons;
   (e) the surrender or the transfer of the accused to the International Tribunal.

ARTICLE 30
The status, privileges and immunities of the International Tribunal

1. The Convention on the Privileges and Immunities of the United Nations of 13 February 1946 shall apply to the International Tribunal, the judges, the Prosecutor and
his staff, and the Registrar and his staff.
2. The judges, the Prosecutor and the Registrar shall enjoy the privileges and immunities, exemptions and facilities accorded to diplomatic envoys, in accordance with
international law.
3. The staff of the Prosecutor and of the Registrar shall enjoy the privileges and immunities accorded to officials of the United Nations under articles V and VII of the
Convention referred to in paragraph 1 of this article.
4. Other persons, including the accused, required at the seat of the International Tribunal shall be accorded such treatment as is necessary for the proper functioning of
the International Tribunal.

ARTICLE 31
Seat of the International Tribunal

The International Tribunal shall have its seat at The Hague.

ARTICLE 32
Expenses of the International Tribunal

The expenses of the International Tribunal shall be borne by the regular budget of the
United Nations in accordance with Article 17 of the Charter of the United Nations.

ARTICLE 33
Working languages

The working languages of the International Tribunal shall be English and French.

ARTICLE 34
Annual report

The President of the International Tribunal shall submit an annual report of the International Tribunal to the Security Council and to the General Assembly.

NOTES

PREFACE

1. Abbé Modeste Mungwareba, interview with the author, Kigali, November, 1996. The biblical passage is: "You veiled yourself in wrath and pursued us, you slew us and took no pity; You wrapped yourself in a cloud which prayer could not pierce. You have made us offscouring and refuse among the nations" (Lamentations 3:43–45).

2. Mungwareba interview.

INTRODUCTION

1. Milan Vujin, former attorney for Dusko Tadic, was fined fifteen thousand guilders (about five thousand dollars) and barred from the tribunal by the Court of Appeal until January, 2000.

2. Elements of JSO had arrested Slobodan Milosevic in Belgrade in April, 2001, and organized his June 28 transfer to The Hague. This cooperation with the tribunal would have a price: The Red Berets later engaged in arm wrestling with the new regime, notably on the question of arrests insistently demanded by prosecutor Carla Del Ponte. Some Red Berets feared that they themselves would appear in secret tribunal indictments because of crimes they had committed.

3. The quotation is from Antoine Garapon, secretary-general of the Institut des Hautes Études sur la Justice, Paris, interview with the author published in "Antoine Garapon: 'Nous voulons contenir la barbarie du monde,'" *Le Temps* (Geneva), Dec. 6, 1999.

4. Ibid.

5. The investigator's interview with the author in The Hague on March 7, 1996, was organized by the Office of the Prosecutor on the condition that the investigator's identity not be disclosed.

CHAPTER 1

1. Boutros Boutros-Ghali quoted in Afsané Bassir Pour, "En espérant qu'il aura un effet dissuasif en Bosnie-Herzégovine L'ONU a décidé la création d'un tribunal pénal international pour juger les responsables de crimes de guerre dans l'ex-Yougoslavie," *Le Monde* (Paris), Apr. 24, 1993.

2. Ahmed Snoussi quoted in ibid.

3. Jean-Bernard Mérimée quoted in ibid.

4. Zlatko Dizdarevic and Gigi Riva, *J'accuse l'ONU* (Paris: Calmann-Lévy, 1995), 14.

5. Patrick Sabatier, "L'Impossible Nuremberg yougoslave," *Libération* (Paris), Feb. 23, 1993.

6. The expression "crimes against humanity" was born after the Armenian massacres in Turkey in 1915. In 1920, the Consultative Committee of Jurists had proposed that the High Court of International Justice, which the League of Nations was in the process of creating, was equally competent to "judge crimes that constitute a violation of the international public order or the universal laws of nations." But the Assembly of the League of Nations rejected this idea, judging it "premature." The resulting Permanent Court of International Justice, which lasted from 1920 to 1945, heard cases between nations, not against individuals.

7. Alain Pellet, note on the responsibility of Saddam Hussein, Apr. 16, 1991, quoting Hans-Dietrich Genscher, in ICTY, *The Path to the Hague,* Document 2 (an official publication of the ICTY, available at <www.un.org/icty>).

8. Mr. Jacques Poos, President-in-Office of the Council of Ministers of the European Communities, to the Secretary-General of the United Nations (not dated), in ICTY, *The Path to The Hague,* Document 1.

9. Baker quoted in David Halberstam, *War in a Time of Peace* (New York: Simon & Schuster, 2002), 46.

10. Poos quoted in Joel Havemann, "EC Urges End to Yugoslav Violence, Threatens Aid Cut," *Los Angeles Times,* June 24, 1991, A11.

11. Claire Nullis, "Red Cross Still Barred from Camps, Despite Security Council Backing," Associated Press, Aug. 6, 1992.

12. The ICTY investigators reconstructed the events in the camp at Luka. Goran Jelisic, alias "Adolf," was an executioner (IT-95-10, July 21, 1995, available at <www.un.org/icty>).

13. On July 14, 1997, the ICTY sentenced Dusko Tadic to twenty years (including seven years for the beatings of Hase Icic and other prisoners). Hase Icic quoted in Prosecutor *v.* Dusko Tadic, Sentencing Judgment of the Trial Chamber, IT-94-1, July 14, 1997, para. 31.

14. Roy Gutman, "Bosnia's Camps of Death," *Newsday,* Aug. 2, 1992.

15. Roy Gutman, *Tortures et mort, récits de témoins, une furie meurtière de six semaines qui a fait au moins 3000 tués en Bosnie: témoins d'une génocide* (Paris: Desclée de Brouwer, 1994), 122.

16. George H. W. Bush quoted in Michael Scharf, *Balkan Justice: The Story behind the First International War Crimes Trial since Nuremberg* (Durham, N.C.: Carolina Academic Press, 1997), 33.

17. The ICTY definition of genocide appears in the appendix.

18. *War Crimes in Bosnia-Herzegovina,* report issued by Human Rights Watch, 1992, 6–7.

19. Helsinki Watch, *War Crimes in Bosnia-Herzegovina,* report issued August, 1992, 17. Helsinki Watch is a nongovernmental organization that is part of Human Rights Watch.

20. Ibid., 18.

21. Robert Badinter, interview with the author, Paris, Oct. 26, 1999.

22. Swiss diplomat Lucius Caflisch was also present at the meeting and recounted the scene in an interview with the author, Geneva, Dec. 6, 1999.

23. Roland Dumas, interview with the author, Paris, Oct. 27, 1999.

24. Ibid.

25. Ibid.

26. Mirko Klarin, "Nuremberg Now," *Borba* (Belgrade), May 16, 1991, in ICTY, *The Path to The Hague,* Document 7.

27. The military-humanitarian intervention in Somalia, which began in December, 1992, with a landing under the dramatic lights of news cameras, will, however, be a dramatic fiasco.

28. Dr. Klaus Kinkel, German minister of foreign affairs, speech delivered at the London Conference in general debate, Sept. 9, 1992, in ICTY, *The Path to The Hague,* Document 8.

29. Roland Dumas, French minister of foreign affairs, speech delivered at the London Conference, Aug. 26, 1992, in ICTY, *The Path to The Hague,* Document 9.

30. François Mauriac, preface to *Night,* by Elie Wiesel (New York: Bantam Books, 1986), ix. This passage was translated by Stella Rodway.

31. Dumas speech delivered at the London Conference, Aug. 26, 1992.

32. Elie Wiesel, telephone interview with the author, Feb. 2, 2000.

33. Finkielkraut quoted in Pierre Hazan, "Regards croisés sur les espoirs et les dangers de la justice pénale internationale," *Le Temps* (Geneva), Dec. 6, 1999.

34. Rony Brauman, "L'Humanitaire, nom moderne de la lâcheté," *Libération* (Paris), Sept. 9, 1992.

35. Interview with the author, Banja Luka, Apr. 5, 1993.

36. Tadeusz Mazowiecki, letter to U.N. Secretary-General Boutros Boutros-Ghali, U.N. doc. 5/1995/626, July 27, 1995.

37. Interview with the author, Washington, D.C., Nov. 30, 1999.

38. Roland Dumas, French minister of foreign affairs, statement following the vote by the Security Council on Resolution 780, June 10, 1992, in ICTY, *The Path to The Hague,* Document 11.

CHAPTER 2

1. M. Cherif Bassiouni, interview with the author, New York, Dec. 2–3, 1999.

2. Ralph Zacklin, interview with the author, New York, Dec. 2, 1999.

3. Bassiouni interview, Dec. 2–3, 1999.

4. M. Cherif Bassiouni, interview with the author, New York, Dec. 12, 1999.

5. Zacklin interview, Dec. 2, 1999; Bassiouni interview, Dec. 2–3, 1999.

6. Bassiouni interview, Dec. 2–3, 1999; Zacklin interview, Dec. 2, 1999.

7. Bassiouni interview, Dec. 12, 1999.

8. Carla Anne Robbins, "World Again Confronts Moral Issues Involved in War Crimes Trials," *Wall Street Journal,* July 13, 1993.

9. Lawrence Eagleburger, U.S. secretary of state, statement, "The need to respond to war crimes in the former Yugoslavia," Dec. 16, 1992, in ICTY, *The Path to The Hague,* Document 12.

10. Ibid.

11. Ibid.

12. Lawrence Eagleburger quoted in Scharf, *Balkan Justice,* 44.

13. Confidential interview with the author.

14. Confidential interview with the author. *Harkis* were Algerians who fought with the French army during the Algerian war of independence.

15. John Fox, telephone interview with the author, Dec. 1, 1999.

16. Lawrence Eagleburger, letter to Antonio Cassese, May 8, 1996, in ICTY, *The Path to The Hague,* Document 17.

17. Scharf, *Balkan Justice,* 44.

18. Elie Wiesel, letter to Antonio Cassese, June 28, 1996, in ICTY, *The Path to The Hague,* Document 18.

19. The peace plan intends to save the unity and territorial integrity of Bosnia-Herzegovina at the price of very strong decentralization. Cut up into ten provinces, this plan of cantonization arouses sharp criticism. It is accused of ratifying parts of the territorial conquests by Serb and Croat militias and of legitimizing the brutal policy of ethnic cleansing.

20. European Community investigative mission into the treatment of Muslim women in the former Yugoslavia, report to European Community Foreign Ministers, U.N. doc. S/25240, Feb. 3, 1993.

21. Dumas interview, Oct. 27, 1999.

22. Roland Dumas, French minister of foreign affairs, letter to the prosecutor, Pierre Truche, concerning the establishment of a Committee of Jurists to consider questions raised by the establishment of an international criminal tribunal, Paris, Jan. 16, 1993, in ICTY, *The Path to The Hague,* Document 13.

23. Declaration of François Mitterrand, President of the Republic, and Chancellor Helmut Kohl, Palace of Schaumburg, Bonn, Jan. 21, 1993, in *Le Magazine de l'actualité presidentielle* (available at <www.elysee.fr>).

24. Scharf, *Balkan Justice,* 52.

25. French casualties in Bosnia grew to sixty-eight dead between 1992 and 1997.

26. Dumas interview, Oct. 27, 1999.

27. Ibid.

28. Ibid.

29. Article 7-3 of the draft Yugoslav war crimes tribunal statute, quoted in Scharf, *Balkan Justice,* 59.

30. Dumas interview, Oct. 27, 1999.

31. Interim Report of the Commission of Experts, U.N. doc. S/25274, Jan. 26, 1993, 16.

32. Press office of the French presidency, speech distributed to the media, The Hague, May 18, 1999.

33. Scharf, *Balkan Justice,* 56.

34. Ibid.

35. Confidential interview with the author.

36. Zacklin interview, Dec. 2, 1999.

37. U.N. Security Council Resolution 808, Feb. 22, 1993, para. 1.

38. Communication of the U.N. Secretary-General to the Assembly General and the Security Council, U.N. doc. A/49/342/S/1994/1007, Aug. 29, 1994, para. 11−14 (citing U.N. Security Council Resolutions 808 and 827).

39. Ibid., para. 10.

40. Confidential interview with the author.

41. Communication of the U.N. Secretary-General to the Assembly General and the Security Council, A/49/342/S/1994/1007, Aug. 29, 1994, para. 13–15.

CHAPTER 3

1. Confidential interview with the author.

2. Georges Abi-Saab, interview with the author, Geneva, Jan. 13, 2000.

3. Confidential interview with the author.

4. Members of the Security Council made many uncompromising comments after voting for Resolutions 780, 808, and 827.

5. Confidential interview with the author.

6. Confidential interview with the author.

7. Mohamed Sacirbey quoted in "U.N. Panel Picked to Hear Bosnian War Crimes," United Press International, Sept. 17, 1993.

8. M. Cherif Bassiouni quoted in Scharf, *Balkan Justice*, 49.

9. Frits Kahlsoven quoted Scharf, *Balkan Justice*, 46.

10. Bassiouni interview, Dec. 2–3, 1999.

11. Antonio Cassese, interview with the author, The Hague, Nov. 3–4, 1999.

12. Luigi Condorelli quoted in Pierre Hazan, "Un juge révolté luttant pour une justice capable de brider la barbarie," *Le Temps* (Geneva), June 19, 1999.

13. Antonio Cassese, *Inhuman States: Imprisonment, Detention, and Torture in Europe Today* (Cambridge: Polity Press, 1996).

14. Cassese interview, Nov. 3–4, 1999.

15. Confidential interview with the author.

16. Cassese interview, Nov. 3–4, 1999.

17. Confidential interview with the author.

18. Confidential interview with the author.

19. Cassese interview, Nov. 3–4, 1999.

20. Ibid.

21. Confidential interview with the author.

22. Confidential interview with the author.

23. Confidential interview with the author.

24. There are two great, though very different, systems of law. The broad tradition in continental Europe is derived from the Roman code and characterized by an "inquisitory" method of investigation. In this system, the judge is both the prosecutor and arbiter of fact and law. By contrast, Anglo-American common law subscribes to the "adversarial" tradition, where the judge is the impartial arbiter of law, a jury is the determiner of fact, and the state prosecutes the accused. The two systems are coherent within themselves, and lawyers considered them to be impossible to harmonize just prior to the creation of the ICTY.

25. Contumacy refers to the refusal of the defendant to appear before the tribunal when summoned.

26. Communication of the U.N. Secretary-General to the Assembly General and the Security Council, A/49/342/S/1994/1007, Aug. 29, 1994, para. 144.

27. The American government had already provided free personnel to the U.N. division that it considered strategic—the Department of Peace-Keeping Operations (DPKO). The Americans had also furnished to the DPKO materials and information technology provided by the Pentagon.

28. Christian Chartier, interview with the author, The Hague, Nov. 3, 1998.

29. Cassese interview, Nov. 3–4, 1999.

30. Ibid.

31. Madeleine Albright quoted in Stanley Meisler, "U.N. Names South African Judge as Balkans War Crimes Prosecutor," *Los Angeles Times,* July 9, 1994, A5.

32. Cassese interview, Nov. 3–4, 1999.

33. Richard Goldstone, "Juger les criminels," in *Des choix difficiles: les dilemmes moraux de l'humanitaire,* edited by Jonathan Moore (Paris: Gallimard, 1999).

34. Confidential interview with the author.

35. Confidential interview with the author.

36. Confidential interview with the author.

37. General Tomoyuki Yamashita was the architect of the Japanese victory over Singapore in 1942. On October 9, 1944, he had taken command of the Japanese forces in the Philippines, nine days before the invasion of that archipelago by soldiers under General Douglas MacArthur. Although actually cut off from his troops, Yamashita was later convicted and sentenced to death by virtue of his command responsibility; the judges had determined that he had permitted the assault and bloodbath of Manila, although there was no proof that he had ever given an order in that regard. But as the commander of Japanese soldiers in the Philippines, he had assumed responsibility for them. After an appeal to the U.S. Supreme Court, a controversial opinion confirmed that General Yamashita was guilty because of his responsibility for the criminal behavior of his troops, even if he had given no instruction to his solders to commit the atrocities.

38. Paul Stuebner, telephone interview with the author, June 13, 2000.

39. Confidential interview with the author.

40. Confidential interview with the author.

41. Goldstone quoted in, for example, Clare Dyer, "Judge of Our Inactions," *Guardian* (London), Oct. 1, 1994, 29. Goldstone is quoted in the article, saying, "There is a lot of material. There are a lot of witnesses, and we're not going to leave anything undone."

42. Cassese interview, Nov. 3–4, 1999.

43. Richard Goldstone quoted in confidential interview with the author.

44. Cassese interview, Nov. 3–4, 1999.

45. "The Judges of the Tribunal for the former Yugoslavia express their concern regarding the substance of their programme of judicial work for 1995," ICTY press release, CC/PIO/003-E, Feb. 1, 1995.

46. Christian Chartier, interview with the author, The Hague, June 15, 1999.

47. Richard Goldstone, interview with the author, Geneva, Nov. 16, 1999.

48. Confidential interview with the author.

49. Lord David Owen, interview with the author, London, Nov. 8, 1999.

50. M. Cherif Bassiouni, interview with the author, New York, Feb. 12, 1999.

51. Quoted in Goldstone, "Juger les criminels," 261.

52. Goldstone, "Juger les criminels," 262.

CHAPTER 4

1. Goldstone quoted in ICTY press release, CC/PIO/006-E, Apr. 24, 1995.

2. Confidential interview with the author.

3. Lord David Owen, interview with the author, London, Nov. 3–4, 1999.

4. In November, 1995, an indictment for Srebrenica completes the indictment of July 24, 1995 (IT-95-18 and IT-95-5, respectively).

5. Prosecutor *v.* Radovan Karadzic and Ratko Mladic, IT-95-5, July 24, 1995, para. 19.

6. Stuebner telephone interview, June 13, 2000.

7. Abi-Saab interview, Jan. 13, 2000.

8. Stuebner telephone interview, June 13, 2000.

9. Cassese interview, Nov. 3–4, 1999.

10. U.N. Security Council Resolution 827, May 25, 1993, para. 2.

11. Cassese interview, Nov. 3–4, 1999.

12. ICTY press release CC/PIO/023-E, Oct. 9, 1995.

13. Ibid.

14. Pauline Neville-Jones, interview with the author, London, Nov. 9, 1999.

15. The United States sent troops to Somalia on a purported humanitarian mission. When they tried to arrest Somali warlord Mohamed Farrah Aidid, the mission turned into a disaster. Several American soldiers were killed without Aidid being captured.

16. Richard Holbrooke, *To End a War* (New York: Random House 1999), 221.

17. Ibid., 226.

18. Ibid., 222.

19. Neville-Jones interview, Nov. 9, 1999.

20. Ibid.

21. Holbrooke, *To End a War,* 338.

22. Ibid., 339–40.

23. Both quotations recollected in Cassese interview, Nov. 3–4, 1999.

24. Cassese interview, Nov. 3–4, 1999.

25. Ibid.

26. Anglo-American law does not recognize contumacy—the active refusal of an accused to appear in court—and does not allow trials without the defendant's presence. Rule 61 is the compromise reached after a long battle lost by the continental judges. The common law judges consider that a trial in the absence of the accused does not respect the rights of the defense and would transform the tribunal into a "legal circus." This culture clash between the judges goes back to a fundamental question, that of the conception of the ICTY. For the continental judges, the question of stigmatization—making examples of the accused—and the instructive effect of the trial are essential and justify the recourse to contumacy.

27. Note of the Secretary-General of the United Nations General Assembly and the Security Council, A/52/375/S/1997/729, 1997, 47.

28. Primo Levi, *The Drowned and the Saved,* translated by Raymond Rosenthal (New York: Summit Books, 1988), 11–12.

CHAPTER 5

1. Report of the Secretary-General Pursuant to General Assembly Resolution 53/35 ("Srebrenica Report"), 1998, para. 2 (citing remarks of Fouad Riad during confirmation of the indictment, Nov. 16, 1995).

2. English transcript of testimony of Jean-René Ruez, Prosecutor *v.* Karadzic and Mladic, IT-95-18-R61/IT-95-5-R61, July 3, 1996, 550–51 (available on ICTY website, <www .un.org/icty>).

3. Ibid., 537, 539, 545.

4. Ibid., 587.

5. Ibid., 548–49.

6. Testimony of Witness "A," Prosecutor *v.* Karadzic and Mladic, IT-95-18-R61/IT-95-5-R61, July 5, 1996, 787–90.

7. Ibid., 792–93.

8. Testimony of Colonel Thomas Karremans, Prosecutor *v.* Karadzic and Mladic, IT-95-18-R61/IT-95-5-R61, July 4, 1996, 672.

9. Thomas Karremans's recollection of Mladic's statement quoted in Anna Pukas, "There Were No Secret Horrors, They Were All Captured on Camcorder," *The Express* (London), Nov. 25, 1999.

10. Corporal Paul Groenewegen quoted in Pierre Hazan, "Au tribunal onusien de la Haye, les soldats de l'ONU en accusation," *Le Nouveau Quotidien* (Lausanne), July 5, 1996, 5.

11. Testimony of Lieutenant Koster, Prosecutor *v.* Karadzic and Mladic, IT-95-18-R61/IT-95-5-R61, 703.

12. Testimony of Colonel Karremans, July 4, 1996, 643, 681.

13. Ibid., 659–60.

14. Ibid., 663.

15. Testimony of Drazen Erdemovic, Prosecutor *v.* Karadzic and Mladic, IT-95-18-R61/IT-95-5-R61, 842–54.

16. Ibid., 854.

17. Marlise Simons, "Broader Warrants Issued for 2 Bosnian Serbs," *New York Times,* July 12, 1996, A10.

18. ICTY press release, CC/PIO/026-E, The Hague, Nov. 16, 1995.

19. Christian Chartier quoted in Pierre Hazan, "Karadzic et Mladic recherchés, mais qui les arrêtera?" *Le Soir* (Brussels), July 9, 1996.

20. Tadeusz Mazowiecki, letter to Chairman of Commission on Human Rights, July 27, 1995, in Final Periodic Report, Part Four, E/CN.4/1996/9, Aug. 22, 1995.

21. Report of the Secretary-General Pursuant to General Assembly Resolution 53/35: The Fall of Srebrenica, A/54/549, Nov. 15, 1999, 106. All further excerpts are from this report unless otherwise noted.

22. Petition for Arrest Warrants by Prosecutor Mark Harmon, IT-95-18-R61/IT-95-5-R61, 960708IT, July 8, 1996, 916.

CHAPTER 6

1. Louise Arbour, interview with Mirko Klarin, Tribunal Update 13, Jan. 27, 2001, Institute for War and Peace Reporting (IWPR, <www.iwpr.net>, hereafter cited by update number and date).

2. Louise Arbour quoted in Marc Semo, "Un Tribunal de plus en plus crédible," *Libération* (Paris), Sept. 9, 1999.

3. Louise Arbour quoted in Marc Semo, "Toute à traque," *Libération* (Paris), Jan. 29, 1999.

4. Antonio Cassese quoted in Tribunal Update 1, Oct. 28, 1996.

5. Louise Arbour quoted in Tribunal Update 11, Jan. 29, 1997.

6. Quote recalled in Cassese interview, Nov. 3–4, 1999.

7. Resolution 922 adopted by unanimous vote of the judges of the ICTY, twelfth plenary meeting, Dec. 2–3, 1996; ICTY press release, CC/PIO/136-E, Dec. 3, 1996.

8. Louise Arbour quoted in Zlatko Dizarevic, "The Tribunal Has Come a Long Way: Interview with Mirko Klarin," *Dani* (Sarajevo), Dec. 1, 2000, translated and republished in Tribunal Update 218, May 1, 2001.

9. Arbour quoted in Semo, "Toute à traque."

10. Louise Arbour, interview with the author, Paris, Nov. 26, 1999.

11. Ibid. Bosnia-Herzegovina was divided into different military sectors under the responsibility of different NATO countries.

12. Stuebner telephone interview, June 13, 2000.

13. Louise Arbour, interview with the author, Paris, Jan. 26, 1999.

14. Ibid.

15. Arbour interview, Nov. 26, 1999.

16. Cassese interview, Nov. 3–4, 1999.

17. Arbour interview, Nov. 26, 1999.

18. Ibid.

19. Igor Ivanov quoted in Tribunal Update 106, Dec. 18, 1998.

20. Arbour interview, Nov. 26, 1999.

21. Cassese interview, Nov. 3–4, 1999.

22. Ibid.

23. Slavko Dokmanovic hangs himself in the tribunal prison at Scheveningen after his trial and one week before the verdict is announced (Case IT-95-13a).

24. Arbour interview, Nov. 26, 1999.

25. Ibid.

26. Ibid.

27. Alain Richard quoted in "Bosnie: aucun officier français ne témoignera devant le TPI," *Le Monde* (Paris), Dec. 10, 1997.

28. Henri Rochereau, "Crimes de guerre, faut-il créer une justice pénale international?" *Revue armées d'aujord'hui* 207 (February 1996): 60–62.

29. Arbour interview, Nov. 26, 1999.

30. Louise Arbour, interview with Remy Ourdan, published in "En Bosnie, 'les criminels de guerre se sentent en sécurité absolue dans le secteur français,'" *Le Monde* (Paris), Dec. 14, 1997.

31. Hubert Védrine quoted in "Bosnie: la France se defend de protéger des criminels de guerre," *Libération* (Paris), Dec. 17, 1997, 7.

32. Lionel Jospin quoted in Remy Ourdan, "La France est 'résolue à agir' contre les criminels de guerre en Bosnie," *Le Monde* (Paris), Dec. 18, 1997.

33. Sylvaine Pasquier, "A Foca, de très tranquilles tortionnaires serbes," *L'Express* (Paris), Feb. 12, 1998.

34. Confidential interview with the author.

35. David Scheffer quoted in Boris Cambreleng, "US asks France to Arrest Bosnian Serb War Crimes Suspect Karadzic," Agence France-Presse, June 24, 1999; and in Ray Moseley, "U.S. Envoy Vows a Trial for Milosevic," *Chicago Tribune,* June 25, 1999, 3.

36. Anne Gazeau-Secret, French foreign ministry spokeswoman, quoted in "France Hits Back in Spat with US over Bosnia War Criminals," Agence France-Presse, June 25, 1999.

37. This statement was made by a French army officer who was acquainted with the local press (confidential interview with the author, Sarajevo, June, 1996).

38. Arbour interview, Nov. 26, 1999.

39. Kris Janowski quoted in Holbrooke, *To End a War,* 337.

40. Jacques Klein, interview with the author, Sarajevo, July 14, 1999.

41. Ibid.

42. Ibid.

43. Holbrooke, *To End a War,* 338.

44. Stuebner telephone interview, June 13, 2000.

45. Antonio Cassese, interview with the author, The Hague, June 17, 2000.

46. Counselor's quote recollected in Stuebner telephone interview, June 13, 2000.

47. Holbrooke, *To End a War,* 351.

48. Note of the Secretary-General of the United Nations to the General Assembly and the Security Council, A/51/292/S/1996/665, Aug. 16, 1996, para. 168–69, 171.

49. Note of the Secretary-General of the United Nations to the General Assembly and the Security Council, A/52/375/S/1997/729, Sept. 18, 1997, para. 134.

50. Quoted in ibid., para. 185.

51. Ibid., para. 189-90.

52. Gabrielle Kirk McDonald quoted in Tribunal Update 106, Dec. 19, 1998.

CHAPTER 7

1. Slobodan Milosevic, speech in Kosovo Field, June 28, 1989 (translated by the National Technical Information Service, U.S. Department of Commerce, available at <www.slobodan-milosevic.org/spch-kosovo1989.htm>).

2. Louise Arbour, prosecutor's statement regarding the tribunal's jurisdiction over Kosovo, ICTY press release CC/PIO/302-E, The Hague, Mar. 10, 1998.

3. Morton Abramowitz quoted in Neil King, Jr., "Hague Panel May Indict Milosevic, Kosovo Killings Could Prompt Charges," *Wall Street Journal Europe,* Mar. 16, 1998, 2.

4. Robert Gelbard quoted in Laura Myers, "Envoy: Bosnia Indictments Too Weak," Associated Press, Feb. 25, 1998.

5. "Justice Arbour Reprimands Ambassador Gelbard," Tribunal Update 65, Feb. 23–28, 1998.

6. Communication from the prosecutor to the contact group members, ICTY press release, CC/PIU/329-E, July 7, 1998.

7. John Fox, telephone interview with the author, Nov. 29, 1999.

8. Both quotations recollected in ibid.

9. James R. Hooper, "War Crimes Tribunal U.N. Prosecutor Must Go to Kosovo," *Toronto Star,* Oct. 16, 1998, A20.

10. Confidential interview with the author.

11. Arbour interview, Nov. 26, 1999.

12. Nicolo Figa-Talamanca, interview with the author, New York, Dec. 3, 1999.

13. Nicolo Figa-Talamanca, interview with the author, New York, Dec. 6, 1999.

14. Aryeh Neier, interview with the author, New York, Dec. 2, 1999.

15. Ibid.

16. Arbour interview, Nov. 26, 1999.

17. Confidential interview with the author.

18. Gabrielle Kirk McDonald, president of the ICTY, statement on the agreements on Kosovo, ICTY press release CC/PIU/352-E, Oct. 14, 1998.

19. "Prosecutor seeks assurance from President Milosevic regarding Kosovo investigations," ICTY press release CC/PIU/353-E, Dec. 15, 1998.

20. Zoran Knezevic elaborates his analysis to Tanjug (Croatian official state news agency), Nov. 15, 1998 (available in summary form in English in the Yugoslav Daily Survey, Nov. 16, 1998, <www.hri.org/news/balkans/yds/1998/98-11-16.yds.html>).

21. "The president urges the Security Council 'to provide the support necessary to enable the Tribunal to discharge its mandate,'" ICTY press release, CC/PIU/362-e, Nov. 11, 1998.

22. Madeleine Albright, *Madam Secretary* (New York: Miramax Books, 2003), 392.

23. Jean-Arnault Dérens, *Balkans: la crise* (Paris: Gallimard, Folio, 2000), 261.

24. The author was present at Racak and personally interviewed the individuals who are quoted.

25. Emine Bekiri, interview with the author, Racak, Jan. 16, 1999.

26. Rame quoted in Pierre Hazan, "Nous étions sûr de tous mourir," *Libération* (Paris), Jan. 18, 1999, 4–5.

27. Indictment of Slobodan Milosevic et al., IT-99-37-I, May 22, 1999, para. 98(a).

28. Quotations from Hazan, "Nous étions sûr de tous mourir," 4–5.

29. Notes of the author from General Walker's press conference, Pristina, Jan. 16, 1999.

30. "Massacre of Civilians in Racak," special report, OSCE-KVM/HQ, Jan. 17, 1998.

31. Quotations are from the author's interviews in the vicinity of Racak.

32. Ibid.

33. Quoted in Guy Dinmore, "Villagers Slaughtered in Kosovo 'Atrocity,'" *Washington Post,* Jan. 17, 1999, A01.

34. Arbour interview, Nov. 26, 1999.

35. Ibid.

36. Ibid.

37. Madeleine Albright quoted in Thomas W. Lippman, "Deadline Set for Kosovo Accord," *Washington Post,* Jan. 30, 1999, A16.

38. Arbour interview, Nov. 26, 1999.

39. Ibid.

40. George J. Tenet, testimony at Hearing of the Senate Armed Services Committee, Feb. 2, 1999.

41. Gabrielle Kirk McDonald quoted extensively in Mirko Klarin, "Role of the Tribunal in Rambouillet," Tribunal Update 114, Feb. 22–27, 1999.

42. Louise Arbour quoted in Mirko Klarin, "The Prosecutor's Letter to Ministers Vedrine and Cook," in Tribunal Update 116, Mar. 8–14, 1999.

43. Christopher Hill quoted in Kosovo chronology, *PBS Frontline,* <www.pbs.org/wgbh/pages/frontline/shows/kosovo/etc/cron.html>.

44. Nicolas Levrat, "The good usage of 'legality' in international relations in light of the recent Balkan crisis," unpublished article shared with the author.

45. The description of this massacre figures in the indictment against Slobodan Milosevic, IT-99-37-I, May 24, 1999.

46. "Lawyers Charge NATO Leaders before War Crimes Tribunal and NATO Leaders Named in War Crimes Complaint," <www.counterpunch.org/serbia>, May 7, 1999.

47. "Is War Crimes Prosecutor Louise Arbour Becoming a Pawn of NATO?" (unsigned editorial), *The Globe and Mail* (Toronto), May 22, 2000, A13.

48. Louise Arbour quoted in "ICTY's Kosovo Investigation: Suspicions of Manipulation," Tribunal Update 122, Apr. 19–24, 1999.

49. Confidential interview with the author.

50. Arbour quoted in Tribunal Update 122, Apr. 19–24, 1999.

51. Graham Blewitt, interview with the author, The Hague, June 16, 1999.

52. "James Rubin Holds State Department News Briefing," Federal Document Clearinghouse (FDCH/Nexis) Political Transcripts, Dec. 1, 1998.

53. Louise Arbour and Harold Koh quoted in Tribunal Update 121, Apr. 12, 1999.

54. Graham Blewitt quoted in Tribunal Update 122, Apr. 19-24, 1999.

55. Robin Cook quoted in ibid.

56. Arbour interview, Nov. 26, 1999.

57. Ibid.

58. Ibid.

59. Louise Arbour, quoted in Péter Kovács, "Intervention armée des forces de l'OTAN au Kosovo," *Revue internationale de l'Croix-Rouge,* Mar. 31, 2000 (<www.icrc.org/Web/fre/sitefreo.nsf/>).

60. Transcript of press conference by Jamie Shea and Major General W. Jertz, Brussels, M2 Presswire, May 17, 1999.

61. Carla Del Ponte quoted in Tribunal Update 158, Dec. 27, 1999.

62. Louis Freeh quoted in John Tagliabue, "Breaking the Swiss Banking Silence," *New York Times,* June 4, 1996, 1.

63. Carla Del Ponte quoted in transcript of the 4150th meeting of the U.N. Security Council, U.N. doc. S/PV.4150, June 2, 2000.

64. Final Report to the Prosecutor by the Committee established to review the NATO Bombing Campaign against the Federal Republic of Yugoslavia, June 13, 2000 (available at <www.un.org/icty>) (hereafter cited as Final Report on the NATO Bombing Campaign).

65. Georges Abi-Saab quoted in Pierre Hazan, "Kosovo, la paix sans la droit?" *Le Temps* (Geneva), June 9, 2000.

66. Confidential internal report of the International Committee of the Red Cross (ICRC), 1999 (unpublished).

67. Protocol I to the Geneva Conventions of 1949 (1979), Art. 57.

68. Confidential internal ICRC report, 1999.

69. Final Report on the NATO Bombing Campaign, para. 62.

70. Confidential internal ICRC report, 1999.

71. Ibid.

72. Ibid.

73. Ibid.

74. Final Report on the NATO Bombing Campaign, para. 90.

75. Confidential internal ICRC report, 1999.

76. Full text of the U.N. draft resolution on Kosovo published in the *New York Times*, June 8, 1999 (available at <www.globalpolicy.org/security/issues/kosovo70.htm>).

77. "Justice Arbour Discusses Charging Slobodan Milosevic with War Crimes," *Meet the Press*, NBC News Transcripts, May 30, 1999.

78. Foreign ministry spokesman quoted in "Group of Eight Try to Hammer Out Kosovo Peace Plan," Agence France-Presse, May 19, 1999.

79. Lamberto Dini, minister for foreign affairs, interview with F. Rav, *Il Giornale* (Milan), May 20, 1999 (translation courtesy of the Italian Foreign Affairs Ministry, available at <www.esteri.it/eng/archives/arch_press/interviews/may99/in20may99e.htm>).

80. Graham Blewitt, Christian Chartier, and Paul Risley, interview with the author, The Hague, June 6, 1999; Arbour interview, Nov. 26, 1999.

81. Arbour interview, Nov. 26, 1999.

82. Ibid.

83. Ibid.

84. Presentation of an Indictment for Review and Application for Warrants of Arrest and for Related Orders, Indictment of Slobodan Milosevic, IT-99-37-I, May 23, 1999.

85. Arbour interview, Nov. 26, 1999.

86. Ibid.

87. Ibid.

88. Confidential interview with the author.

89. Arbour interview, Nov. 26, 1999.

90. Louise Arbour, statement in ICTY press release, JL/PIU/404-E, May 27, 1999.

91. First Amended Indictment of Slobodan Milosevic et al., IT-99-37-I, May 27, 1999, para. 16, 94, 96–97, 99.

92. Louise Arbour quoted in "Louise Arbour holds news conference on indictment of

Milosevic by war crimes tribunal," FDCH Political Transcripts, May 27, 1999; last quoted line from *NBC Nightly News,* NBC News Transcripts, May 27, 1999.

93. *Libération* (Paris), May 28, 1999, 1; *Financial Times* (London), May 28, 1999, 1; *Le Figaro* (Paris), May 28, 1999, 1; *Wall Street Journal,* May 28, 1999, 1; *Le Monde* (Paris), May 28, 1999.

94. Jean-Pierre Chevènement statement, broadcast on LCI Television, May 27, 1999.

95. Quoted in "Fischer Reacts Cautiously to Milosevic War Crimes Indictment," Associated Press, May 27, 1999.

96. "Milosevic Indictment Makes History," CNN, May 27, 1999, <www.cnn.com/WORLD/europe/9905/27/kosovo.milosevic.04>.

97. President Jacques Chirac of France, televised speech at the Palais de l'Elysée, May 27, 1999 (French transcript available at <www.elysee.fr>).

98. Prime Minister Lionel Jospin of France, address before the National Assembly, June 1, 1999 (available in French at <www.archives.premier-ministre.gouv.fr/jospin>).

99. Statement of President Bill Clinton quoted in Federal News Service, May 27, 1999.

100. Ambassador Branko Brankovic quoted in "Yugoslavia Official: Milosevic Indictment Excuse to Continue Bombing," Associated Press, May 27, 1999.

101. Prosecutor *v.* Slobodan Milosevic et al., Initial Indictment, IT-99-37 ("Kosovo"), May 24, 1999.

CHAPTER 8

1. Carla Del Ponte, interview with the author, The Hague, Oct. 17, 2002.

2. Initial Indictment for Croatia, Prosecutor *v.* Slobodan Milosevic, IT-01-50-I, Oct. 8, 2001.

3. Initial Indictment for Bosnia, Prosecutor *v.* Slobodan Milosevic, IT-01-51-I, Nov. 22, 2001.

4. The International Criminal Court was officially created July 3, 2002, when more than sixty states ratified its statutes.

5. Florence Aubenas, "Belgrade plan de chute," *Libération* (Paris), Oct. 16, 2001.

6. Carla Del Ponte quoted in "Carla Del Ponte Tells Kostunica the Tribunal Is Ready for Milosevic 'at Any Time,'" Tribunal Update 193, Oct. 2–7, 2000.

7. President Vojislav Kostunica quoted in David Williams, "West Struggles over End-Game for War Crimes Suspect Milosevic," Associated Press, Oct. 6, 2000.

8. Slobodan Milosevic quoted in "Socialists Re-Elect Milosevic," BBC, Nov. 25, 2000, <news.bbc.co.uk/1/hi/world/europe/1040562.stm>.

9. Vojislav Kostunica quoted in Misha Savic, "Kostunica Lays Out Yugoslavia Plans," Associated Press, Sept. 25, 2000.

10. "Vojislav Kostunica, President of Yugoslavia," Agence France-Presse, Oct. 7, 2000.

11. Hubert Védrine and Jacques Chirac quoted in Nathalie Dubois and Jean Quartremer, "L'Europe couve Kostunica," *Libération* (Paris), Oct. 16, 2000, 13. The original idiom is: "L'esprit de la communauté n'est pas du tout: je te donne la rhubarbe, passe-moi la séné."

12. Unsigned editorial, "L'Europe et la Serbie," *Le Monde* (Paris), Oct. 12, 2000.

13. Jiri Dienstbier quoted in Jolyon Naegele, "Yugoslavia: U.N. Envoy Dienstbier Advocates Deal for Milosevic," Radio Free Europe/Radio Liberty, Oct. 4, 2001, <www.rferl.org/nca/features/2000/10/04102000163613.asp>.

14. Carla Del Ponte, prosecutor of the ICTY and the ICTR, address to the U.N. Security Council, U.N. doc. JL/PIS/542-e, The Hague, Nov. 24, 2000.

15. Claude Jorda, president of the ICTY, address to the U.N. General Assembly, U.N. doc. JD/SIP/54-e, The Hague, Nov. 20, 2000.

16. Informal discussion with members of the ICTY on the condition of anonymity.

17. Stipe Mesic quoted in "Croatian presses Yugoslavia over war criminals, damages," Agence France-Presse, Oct. 18, 2000.

18. Paul Garde, "Ex-Yugoslavia: deux poids, deux measures," *Le Monde* (Paris), Nov. 24, 2000.

19. Del Ponte interview, Oct. 17, 2002.

20. Vojislav Kostunica, statement at the fifty-seventh session of the U.N. Commission on Human Rights, Mar. 30, 2001.

21. Kostunica quoted in "Court Tries to Deliver Milosevic Warrant," BBC News, Apr. 5, 2001 (available at <news.bbc.co.uk/2/hi/europe/1259369.stm>).

22. "Milosevic est poursuivi pour corruption et abus de pouvoir par la justice serbe," *Le Monde* (Internet edition), Apr. 3, 2002, <www.lemonde.fr/article/0,5987,3230-5447-168030,00.html>.

23. Jane Perlez, "As Expected, Belgrade Wins 'Cooperative' Seal from U.S.," *New York Times,* Apr. 3, 2001, 3.

24. Richard Boucher quoted in ibid.

25. Florence Hartmann quoted in Pierre Hazan, "La Longue route vers La Haye a commencé dans la prison centrale de Belgrade," *Le Temps* (Geneva), Apr. 2, 2001, 2.

26. Tribunal Update 221, Mar. 5–10, 2001.

27. Vojislav Kostunica quoted in Steven Erlanger, "Yugoslavia Chief Says Milosevic Shouldn't Be Sent to The Hague," *New York Times,* Apr. 3, 2001, A3.

28. Justice Minister of the Federal Republic of Yugoslavia gives commitment to serve ICTY arrest warrant on Slobodan Milosevic, J.L./PIS/585-E, Apr. 6, 2001.

29. See the appendix to this volume for the text of the statute.

30. Miroljub Labus quoted in Pierre Hazan, "Les Pressions américaines ont eu raison de Belgrade: Milosevic sera livré au TPI," *Le Temps* (Geneva), June 25, 2001.

31. Confidential interview with the author.

32. Prosecutor *v.* Milosevic, Transcript 010703IA, July 3, 2001, 2.

33. Ibid.

34. Carla Del Ponte, Prosecutor *v.* Milosevic, Transcript 020212IT, Feb. 12, 2002, 2–3.

35. Slobodan Milosevic, Prosecutor *v.* Milosevic, Transcript 010703IA, July 3, 2001, 5.

36. Slobodan Milosevic, Prosecutor *v.* Milosevic, Transcript 020213IT, Feb. 12, 2002, 219.

37. Antoine Garapon and Joël Hubrecht, "La Justice pénale internationale entre la balance et le sablier," *Revue esprit,* July, 2002, 34.

38. Slobodan Milosevic, Prosecutor *v.* Milosevic, Transcript 020215IT, Feb. 15, 2002, 412.

39. Slobodan Milosevic, Prosecutor *v.* Milosevic, Transcript 020218IT, Feb. 18, 2002, 428.

40. Slobodan Milosevic, Prosecutor v. Milosevic, Transcript 020215IT, Feb. 15, 2002, 413.

41. Ibid., 414.

42. Slobodan Milosevic, quoted in Garapon and Hubrecht, "La Justice pénale internationale," 34.

43. Slobodan Milosevic, Prosecutor v. Milosevic, Transcript 020218IT, Feb. 18, 2002, 469.

44. Slobodan Milosevic, Prosecutor v. Milosevic, Transcript 020215IT, Feb. 15, 2002, 413.

45. Ibid., 415.

46. William Walker testimony in Mirko Klarin, "Milosevic Creates His Own Reality," Tribunal Update 270, June 10–16, 2002.

47. Slobodan Milosevic, Prosecutor v. Milosevic, Transcript 020215IT, Feb. 15, 2002, 419–20.

48. Ibid., 425.

49. Slobodan Milosevic, Prosecutor v. Milosevic, Transcript 020218IT, Feb. 18, 2002, 459–60.

50. Ibid., 508.

51. Slobodan Milosevic, in "Milosevic Trial: Potential Witnesses," BBC, Feb. 19, 2002 (available at <news.bbc.co.uk/2/low/europe/1830219.stm>).

52. Del Ponte interview, Oct. 17, 2002.

53. Slobodan Milosevic quoted in Tribunal Update 274, July 8–13, 2002.

54. Del Ponte interview, Oct. 17, 2002.

55. Zoran Djindjic quoted in "Serbie: Zoran Djindjic qualifie de 'cirque' le procès Milosevic," Le Monde (Paris), Feb. 27, 2002.

56. The three amici curiae are Steven Kay (London barrister), Branislav Tapuskovic (Belgrade barrister), and Michaïl Wladimiroff (Amsterdam barrister), who will be revoked October 10, 2002. Wladimiroff is accused of having betrayed the confidence of three judges, when in two interviews, one on September 7, in the Dutch daily Haasche Courrant, and the other in the Bulgarian magazine Kultura, he estimated that if the judgment had to be rendered during the trial, Milosevic would be found guilty. On November 16, 2001, two legal counselors, former U.S. attorney general Ramsey Clark and British attorney John Livingston, were designated to the benefit of the accused. On April 19, 2002, Zdenco Tomanovic and Dragoslav Ognjanovic replaced Clark and Livingston.

57. Christophe Châtelot, "A La Haye, l'avocat Milosevic," Le Monde (Paris), Mar. 29, 2002.

58. Slobodan Milosevic and Hazbi Loku, Prosecution v. Milosevic, Transcript 020312IT, Mar. 12, 2002, 1998–2002.

59. Slobodan Milosevic, Prosecutor v. Milosevic, Transcript 020506IT, May 6, 2002, 4347.

60. Witness "K12" quoted in Christophe Châtelot, "'K12,' le témoin qui préfère aller en prison que déposer devant le TPIY," Le Monde (Paris), June 8, 2002.

61. Geoffrey Nice quoted in Mirko Klarin, "Former Yugoslav Federal President Zoran Lili Is Forced to Travel to The Hague as Prosecutors Intensify Efforts to Harden Their Case against Milosevic," BCR No. 351, July 18, 2002 (available at <www.unmovikonline.org>).

62. Prosecutor v. Milosevic, Transcript 020725IT, July 25, 2002, 8726-27.

63. Mirko Klarin, "Milosevic Feels the Heat," Tribunal Update 275, July 15–20, 2002.

64. Witness "K32" quoted in ibid.

65. Mirko Klarin, "Judges Face Milosevic Dilemma," Tribunal Update 276, July 22–27, 2002.

66. Paddy Ashdown quoted in Mirko Klarin, "Milosevic Needs to Rethink Defence," Tribunal Update 258, March 11–15, 2002.

67. Prosecutor v. Milosevic, Transcript 020315ED, Mar. 15, 2002, 2466–67.

68. Ibid., 2473.

69. Zoran Lilic quoted in "Ex-Yugoslav Leader Refuses to Testify," BBC, July 22, 2002, <news.bbc.co.uk/1/hi/world/europe/2144234.stm>.

70. Del Ponte interview, Oct. 17, 2002.

71. Judith Armatta, interview with the author, The Hague, Oct. 16, 2002.

72. Prosecutor v. Milosevic, Transcript 020613ED, June 13, 2002, 6991.

73. Eugene O'Sullivan, co-counsel to Biljana Plavsic, press statement following plea hearing on Wednesday, Oct. 2, 2002.

74. Biljana Plavsic quoted in ibid.

75. Zeljko Cvijanovic, "Bosnia: Plavsic passe un marché avec le tribunal," Le Courrier des Balkans, Jan. 10, 2001.

76. Jelisic's case is IT-95-10 ("Brcko"), judgment rendered Jan. 21, 1999.

77. Richard Dicker quoted in Ambrose Evans-Pritchard, "Old Ally Poised to Testify against Milosevic," Daily Telegraph (London), Mar. 10, 2002.

78. Christophe Châtelot, "Le Procès Milosevic s'enfonce dans la routine," Le Monde (Paris), May 25, 2002.

79. Dragoslav Ognjanovic quoted in Mirko Klarin, "Milosevic Running Out of Steam," Tribunal Update 259, Mar. 18–23, 2002.

80. Del Ponte interview, Oct. 17, 2002.

81. Statistics provided by the Office of the Prosecutor.

82. Del Ponte interview, Oct. 17, 2002.

CHAPTER 9

1. Sakib Ahmic and Sinisa Avramovic quoted in Pierre Hazan, "En Bosnie, la guerre attend ses juges," Libération (Paris), July 30, 1999.

2. Article 9 of the ICTY statute states, "The International Tribunal and national courts shall have concurrent jurisdiction to prosecute persons for serious violations of international humanitarian law committed in the territory of the former Yugoslavia since 1 January 1991. The International Tribunal shall have primacy over national courts. At any stage of the procedure, the International Tribunal may formally request national courts to defer to the competence of the International Tribunal in accordance with the present Statute and the Rules of Procedure and Evidence of the International Tribunal."

3. Zarko Puhovski, interview with the author, Zagreb, Feb. 2, 2000.

4. Julie Mertus, "Only a War Crimes Tribunal: Triumph of 'The International Community,' Pain of the Survivors," in Belinda Cooper, ed., War Crimes: The Legacy of Nuremberg (New York: TV Books, 1998), 233.

5. Ahmic quoted in Hazan, "En Bosnie, la guerre attend ses juges."

6. Julia Bokeva, interview with the author, The Hague, June 15, 1999.

7. Puhovski interview, Feb. 2, 2000.

8. Bokeva interview, June 15, 1999.

9. Ibid.

10. Amended consolidated indictment, Prosecutor *v.* Momcilo Krajisnik and Biljana Plavsic, IT-00-39 and 40-PT, Jan. 31, 2002, and Plea Agreement, IT-00-39 and 40-PT, Sept. 30, 2002.

11. Carla Del Ponte herself was the object of an attempted assassination, according to the confession of an extremist. From an article in the October 17, 2002, issue of the Belgrade weekly *Nacional,* Del Ponte learned that she was to have been killed during her trip to Belgrade in autumn, 2001. The ultranationalist leader Sinisa Vucinica admits that with the aid of forty men from Herzegovina, he sought to kill her but that he was arrested on November 29 by special antiterrorist units and held in prison until the prosecutor's departure. In the article, Vucinica promises not to make a second attempt but warns that if anyone tries to arrest him for trial in The Hague, he will respond with gunfire (Del Ponte interview, Oct. 17, 2002).

12. Zoran Djindjic quoted in Milanka Saponja-Hadzic, "Morals Don't Earn Money," Tribunal Update 260, Apr. 1–6, 2002.

13. Carla Del Ponte, address by the prosecutor of the ICTY and ICTR to the U.N. Security Council, ICTY document jjj/PIS/709-e, Oct. 30, 2002. See also Claude Jorda, "President of the ICTY reports the noncooperation by the Federal Republic of Yugoslavia to the Security Council," ICTY press release JDH/PIS/706-e, Oct. 23, 2002.

14. See, e.g., "Ivanisevic Backs Croat Suspects," CNN, July 12, 2001, <www.cnn.com/ 2001/WORLD/europe/07/12/croatia.goran>.

15. President Stjepan Mesic of Croatia, address, Zagreb, Sept. 25, 2002 (available at <www.predsjednik.hr>).

16. Carla Del Ponte, address by the prosecutor of the ICTY and ICTR to the U.N. Security Council, ICTY press release jjj/PIS/709-e, Oct. 30, 2002.

17. Prosecutor *v.* Sefer Halilovic, IT-01-48 ("Grabovica-Uzdol"), Initial Indictment, Sept. 12, 2001.

18. "The Ex-Chief of the Muslim Bosnian Troops Surrenders to the ICTY," Agence-France Press, Oct. 24, 2001.

19. Muharem Murselovic quoted in Pierre Hazan, "En Bosnie, la guerre attend ses juges," *Libération* (Paris), June 30, 1999.

20. Dusko Tadic, Prosecutor *v.* Tadic, Transcript 961029IT, Oct. 29, 1996, 8028.

21. Quoted in Pierre Hazan, "A Srebrenica, il ne s'est rien passé en juillet 1995," *Libération* (Paris), July 10, 1999.

22. Initial Indictment of Radislav Krstic, IT-98-33, Nov. 2, 1998, para. 23.2.

23. Quoted in Hazan, "A Srebrenica, il ne s'est rien passé en juillet 1995."

24. Dragan Yevtic quoted in Hazan, "En Bosnie, la guerre attend ses juges."

25. Prosecutor *v.* Krstic, IT-98-33 (Srebrenica), Trial Chamber Judgement, Sept. 2, 2001.

26. Mertus, "Only a War Crimes Tribunal," 222.

27. Sulejma Pezer quoted in Hazan, "En Bosnie, la guerre attend ses juges."

28. Christian Chartier, interview with the author, The Hague, June 15, 1999.

29. "Harrija" and Develeta Omerovic quoted in Hazan, "A Srebrenica, il ne s'est rien passé en juillet 1995."

30. Hasan Nuhanovic quoted in ibid.

31. Milan Bogdanic quoted in Hazan, "En Bosnie, la guerre attend ses juges."

32. Zeljko Karan quoted in ibid.

33. Mladen Tadic quoted in ibid.

34. Sinisa Avramovic quoted in ibid.

35. "Srebrenica Mothers Name and Shame Senior UN Officials," Tribunal Update 162, Jan. 31–Feb. 5, 2000.

36. Francis Boyle quoted in "Mothers Demand Arrest of UN Officials," BBC, Apr. 2, 2000, <news.bbc.co.uk/1/hi/world/europe/631129.stm>.

37. Graham Blewitt quoted in "Bosnia: Srebrenica Accusations Dismissed," UN Wire (United Nations Foundation), Feb. 11, 2000, <www.unfoundation.org/unwire/archives/ UNWIRE000211.asp#14>.

38. Confidential interviews with the author.

39. Jacob Finci quoted in Hazan, "En Bosnie, la guerre attend ses juges."

40. Stuebner telephone interview, June 13, 2000.

41. Confidential interview with the author.

42. Quoted in Rony Brauman and Eyal Sivan, Éloge de la désobéissance (Paris: Éditions du Pommier, 1999), 41.

43. Claude Jorda, interview with the author, The Hague, June 17, 1999.

44. Ibid.

45. Christian Chartier, interview with the author, The Hague, Oct. 7, 1999.

46. Exactly eighteen indictments were withdrawn, which is considerable.

47. Claude Jorda, interview with the author, published in Pierre Hazan, "Claude Jorda, magistrat au tribunal de La Haye: 'Le TPI est menacé de paralysie,'" Libération (Paris), June 21, 1999.

48. "Drazen Erdemovic sentenced to 5 years of imprisonment," ICTY press release CC/PIO/299-E, Mar. 5, 1998.

49. Prosecutor v. Aleksovksi, IT-94-14/1, Appeals Chamber Judgment, Mar. 24, 2000, para. 183.

50. Arbour interview, Nov. 26, 1999.

51. Ibid.

52. Claude Jorda, president of the ICTY, address to the UN Security Council, U.N. doc. JDH/PIS/708e, Oct. 30, 2002.

53. Liam McDowell, telephone interview with the author, June 18, 1999.

54. Confidential interview with the author.

55. Richard Goldstone, interview with the author, Geneva, Nov. 16, 1999.

56. Olivier Russbach, interview with the author, published in "Crimes de guerre: 'utilisons les instruments que nous avons déjà à disposition,'" Le Temps (Geneva), Sept. 20, 1999.

57. Antoine Garapone, interview with the author, Geneva, Nov. 22, 1999.

58. Carla Del Ponte, interview with Isabelle Wesselingh and Stéphanie Van den Berg, Agence-France Presse, Sept. 23, 2002.

59. "Legal aid to accused Zoran Zigic withdrawn," ICTY press release CC/PIS/686-e, July 8, 2002. See also ICTY press release CC/PIS/631-f, Nov. 2, 2001.

60. Speech by His Excellency, Mr. Claude Jorda, ICTY press release, The Hague, SB/PIS/512-e, June 20, 2000.

61. The preparatory phase, before proper court hearings, is currently quite long: one year for Dusko Tadic, twenty-eight months for Vlatko Kupreskic, close to fifteen months for Tihomir Blaskic. The average trial then takes at least one year.

62. Claude Jorda, ICTY president, speech before the General Assembly of the United Nations, ICTY press release, JDH/SIP/707-e, Oct. 29, 2002.

63. Claude Jorda, ICTY president, speech to the Security Council of the United Nations, ICTY press release, JDH/SIP/708-e, Oct. 30, 2002.

CONCLUSION

1. Charles de Gaulle quoted in Brauman and Sivan, *Eloge de la désobéissance,* 53.

2. Valérie Rosou, "La Belgique et la diplomatie 'éthique': forces et limites d'une image," *Revue esprit,* December, 2001, 198.

3. In June, 2002, charges were lodged against Israeli prime minister Ariel Sharon at the Court of Appeal in Brussels for his alleged role in crimes against humanity committed in the massacres at the Sabra and Chatila refugee camps in Beirut in 1982. Charges were also filed in Brussels against the president of Ivory Coast, Laurent Gbagbo, for the murders of fifty-seven ethnic Dioluas. These charges were rejected by the Court of Appeal after it determined that the charged persons "were not found in Belgium at the moment of the lodging of the complaints" (quoted in "Affaires Sharon et Gbagbo; la compétence universelle: le législateur au pied dumur," press release, Human Rights Watch, June 26, 2002, <www.hrw.org/french/press/2002/justice0626.htm>).

4. Its raison d'être has never been a quantitative objective, but this being said, its productivity has been dramatically low. The Arusha tribunal had cost some $600 million, supplied by the international community, and pronounced fewer than a dozen judgments in the space of seven years. The U.N. inspectors concluded,

> According to the report, in the Tribunal's Registry not a single administrative area functioned effectively: finance had no accounting system and could not produce allotment reports, so that neither the Registry nor United Nations Headquarters had budget expenditure information; lines of authority were not clearly defined; internal controls were weak in all sections; personnel in key positions did not have the required qualifications; there was no property management system; procurement actions largely deviated from United Nations procedures; United Nations rules and regulations were widely disregarded; the Kigali office did not get the administrative support needed; and construction work for the second courtroom had not even started.

The Office of the Prosecutor in Kigali had administrative, leadership and operational problems. Functions were hampered by lack of experienced staff as well as lack of vehicles, computers and other office equipment and supplies. Lawyer posts were vacant and, of the almost 80 investigator posts, only 30 had been filled. Prosecution strategy deficiencies were noted. The witness-related programmes had not been fully developed. (Report of the Office of Internal Oversight Services on the ICTR, U.N. doc. A/51/789, 1997)

5. Babak Dehghanpisheh, John Barry, and Roy Gutman, "The Death Convoy of Afghanistan," *Newsweek*, Aug. 26, 2002.

6. Amnesty International, Appeal to All States to Ratify the Statute of the International Criminal Court as Soon as Possible, AI Index #IOR 40/007/1999, May 13, 1999.

7. President George W. Bush says the United States will not sign on to the International Criminal Court (ICC) because, as the nation works to build peace around the world, its diplomats and soldiers could be dragged "into this court and that's very troubling." President Bush, White House spokesman Ari Fleischer explained, "thinks the ICC is fundamentally flawed because it puts American servicemen and women at fundamental risk of being tried by an entity that is beyond America's reach, beyond America's laws, and can subject American civilian and military [*sic*] to arbitrary standards of justice" ("U.S. Will Not Sign on to International Criminal Court, Bush Says," <www.uspolicy.be/issues/icc>, July 2, 2002).

8. By December, 2002, the United States had concluded bilateral "Article 98" agreements with fifteen countries: Romania, Israel, Timor Leste (previously East Timor), the Marshall Islands, Tajikistan, Palau, Mauritania, the Dominican Republic, Uzbekistan, Honduras, Micronesia, Afghanistan, Gambia, Sri Lanka, and El Salvador.

9. On innumerable occasions, American officials have justified this policy. On May 6, 2002, Secretary of Defense Donald Rumsfeld was particularly limpid: "We want to make clear that the United States rejects the purported jurisdictional claims of the ICC—and the US will regard as illegitimate any attempt by the Court, or state parties to the Treaty to assert the ICC's jurisdiction over American citizens. The US has a series of serious objections to the ICC—among them, the lack of adequate checks and balances on powers of the ICC prosecutor and judges, the dilution of the UN Security Council's authority over international criminal prosecutions and the lack of any effective mechanism to prevent politicized prosecutions of American service members and officials" ("Rumsfeld, Bolton and Powell on ICC, the US mission to the European Union," U.S. Mission to the European Union, <www.useu.be>, May 6, 2002).

10. Robert Kagan, "The U.S.-Europe Divide," *Washington Post*, May 26, 2002, B7.

11. Antoine Garapon, *Des crimes qu'on ne peut ni punir, ni pardonner: pour une justice internationale* (Paris: Odile Jacob, 2002), 341.

12. For the Universal Declaration of Human Rights preamble, see <www.un.org/Overview/rights.html>.

SELECTED BIBLIOGRAPHY

A NOTE ON SOURCES

This book is a work of both history and journalism, and much of its source material is from original reporting written for and published in *Libération* (Paris) and *Le Temps* (Geneva) as well as the original French edition of the book, *La Justice face à la guerre: de Nuremberg à La Haye*. The source material includes personal interviews with several individuals central to the war crimes tribunal and efforts at resolving the war in the Balkans. To tell the story behind the scenes, this book employs several accepted conventions of journalism, including anonymous or confidential sources. These confidential or anonymous sources are noted to distinguish them from named interviews and other source material cited in the endnotes.

Much of the original reporting on the proceedings of International Criminal Tribunal for the Former Yugoslavia is still being conducted by Mirko Klarin and the Institute for War and Peace Reporting (IWPR). The invaluable Tribunal Updates, reported almost weekly for the past eight years, are repeatedly sourced here and can be found on the IWPR website, <www.iwpr.net>.

Source material of the United Nations, and in particular the tribunal, have been reverted to and cited in their official English versions. They include all U.N. reports, ICTY indictments, proceedings, and transcripts. Much of this material can be found on the ICTY's website, <www.un.org/icty>.

Fortunately, much of the original source material cited in the original French-language edition of the book—reports, transcripts, international materials, and so on—also exist in official or reputable English translations or sources. These English versions were substituted as much as possible given what is available in the public domain, to avoid producing what would be in effect a triple-hearsay translation.

Arendt, Hannah. *Eichmann in Jerusalem: A Report on the Banality of Evil.* New York: Penguin Books, 1977.

Bildt, Carl. *Peace Journey: The Struggle for Peace in Bosnia.* London: Weidenfeld and Nicolson, 1998.

Boutros-Ghali, Boutros. *Mes années à la maison de verre.* Paris: Fayard, 1991.

Brauman, Rony, and Eyal Sivan. *Éloge de la désobéissance.* Paris: Éditions du Pommier, 1999.

Cassese, Antonio. *Inhuman States: Imprisonment, Detention, and Torture in Europe Today.* Cambridge: Polity Press, 1996.

Delmas-Marty, Mireille. *Trois défis pour un droit mondial.* Paris: Seuil, 1998.

Dérens, Jean-Arnault. *Balkans: la crise.* Paris: Gallimard, Folio, 2000.

Dizdarevic, Zlatko, and Gigi Riva. *J'accuse l'ONU.* Paris: Calmann-Lévy, 1995.

Finkielkraut, Alain. *La Mémoire vaine.* Paris: Gallimard, 1989.

Garapon, Antoine. *Des crimes qu'on ne peut punir, ni pardonner: pour une justice internationale.* Paris: Odile Jacob, 2002.

Gilbert, G. M. *Nuremberg Diary.* New York: Da Capo Press, 1995.

Gutman, Roy. *Bosnie, témoin d'un génocide.* Paris: Desclée de Brouwer, 1994.

Hartmann, Florence. *Milosevic, la diagonale du fou.* Paris: Denoël, 1999.

Hesse, Carla, and Robert Post. *Human Rights in Political Transitions: Gettysburg to Bosnia.* New York: Zone Books, 1999.

Holbrooke, Richard. *To End a War.* New York: Random House, 1999.

Human Rights Watch. *Civilian Deaths in the NATO Air Campaign.* Report issued February 7, 2000.

Jaspers, Karl. *La Culpabilité allemande.* Paris: Éditions de Minuit, 1990.

Jankélévitch, Vladimir. *L'Imprescriptible: pardonner? dans l'honneur et la dignité.* Paris: Seuil, 1986.

Krulic, Joseph. *Histoire de la Yougoslavie, de 1945 à nos jours.* Brussels: Complexe, 1993.

Malcolm, Noel. *Bosnia: A Short History.* London: Macmillan, 1994.

Mertus, Julie. "Only a War Crimes Tribunal: 'Triumph of the International Community,' Pain of the Survivors." In *War Crimes: The Legacy of Nuremberg,* edited by Belinda Cooper. New York: TV Books, 1998.

Moore, Jonathan, ed. *Des choix difficiles: les dilemmes moraux de l'humanitaire.* Paris: Gallimard, 1999.

Morillon, Général Philippe. *Croire et oser: chroniques de Sarajevo.* Paris: Grasset, 1993.

Neier, Aryeh. *War Crimes: Brutality, Terror, and the Struggle for Justice.* New York: Times Books, 1998.

Le Nouvel Observateur and Reporters sans frontières. *Le Livre noir de l'ex Yougoslavie: purification ethnique et crimes de guerre.* Paris: Arléa, 1993.

Owen, David. *Balkan Odyssey.* London: Harcourt Brace, 1995.

Rohde, David. *A Safe Area—Srebrenica: Europe's Worst Massacre since the Second World War.* London: Pocket Books, 1997.

Scharf, Michael P. *Balkan Justice: The Story behind the First International War Crimes Trial since Nuremberg.* Durham, N.C.: Carolina Academic Press, 1997.

Stark, Hans. *Les Balkans: le retour de la guerre en Europe.* Paris: Dunod, 1993.

Taylor, Telford. *Procureur à Nuremberg.* Paris: Seuil, 1995.

Wieviorka, Annette. *L'Ère du témoin.* Paris: Plon, 1998.

———. *Les Procès de Nuremberg et de Tokyo.* Brussels: Complexe, 1996.

INDEX

Photos are indicated with *italic* type. The abbreviation ICTY is used for International Criminal Tribunal for the Former Yugoslavia.